HEIR TO THE
EMPIRE CITY

From left to right: Mayor William Jay Gaynor,
Theodore Roosevelt, and Cornelius Vanderbilt III on the
day of Roosevelt's New York homecoming, June 18, 1910.
(Courtesy of the Theodore Roosevelt Collection,
Harvard College Library)

HEIR TO THE EMPIRE CITY

NEW YORK *and the* MAKING *of*
THEODORE ROOSEVELT

EDWARD P. KOHN

BASIC BOOKS
A Member of the Perseus Books Group
New York

Published by Basic Books,
A Member of the Perseus Books Group

Books published by Basic Books are available at special discounts for bulk purchases in the United States by corporations, institutions, and other organizations. For more information, please contact the Special Markets Department at the Perseus Books Group, 2300 Chestnut Street, Suite 200, Philadelphia, PA 19103, or call (800) 810-4145, ext. 5000, or e-mail special .markets@perseusbooks.com.

Designed by Cynthia Young

Library of Congress Cataloging-in-Publication Data

Kohn, Edward P. (Edward Parliament), 1968–
    Heir to the Empire City : New York and the making of Theodore Roosevelt /
    Edward P. Kohn.
            pages cm
    Includes bibliographical references and index.
    ISBN 978-0-465-02429-2 (hardback)
    ISBN 978-0-465-06975-0 (e-book)
    1. Roosevelt, Theodore, 1858–1919.   2. Politicians—New York (State)—
Biography.   3. New York (N.Y.)—History—1865–1898.   4. New York
(N.Y.)—Biography.   5. Presidents—United State—Biography.   I. Title.
E757.K64 2013
973.91'1092--dc23
[B]
                                                          2013032232

10 9 8 7 6 5 4 3 2 1

For Pelin

Contents

Introduction
New York Knickerbocker

THEODORE ROOSEVELT'S path to the White House may have gone through the West, but it did not start there.

Biographers of Theodore Roosevelt have come to a consensus that he was really a westerner, or a man torn between East and West. The person most responsible for this image was Roosevelt himself. In his writings, including his 1913 *Autobiography*, he carefully painted a portrait of himself as a rancher, hunter, and cowboy. Before he ever charged up Cuba's San Juan Heights, Roosevelt had published several books reflecting his western experience, including his four-volume history *The Winning of the West*. Roosevelt's actions in Cuba in 1898 only underscored his western image, as did Frederic Remington's famous painting *Charge of the Rough Riders at San Juan Hill*, which portrayed him as a leader on horseback in a broad-brimmed hat, waving a six-shooter. After becoming president, Roosevelt published *Outdoor Pastimes of an American Hunter*, a 1905 work, and his 1913 memoirs seemed to leave little doubt to future historians of the impact of his Dakota days: "It was a fine, healthy life, too," he wrote. "It taught a man self-reliance, hardihood, and the value of instant decision." Without his time in the West, Roosevelt stated repeatedly during his life, he never would have been president.

Professional historians took up the theme almost immediately. Roosevelt's first biographer, Hermann Hagedorn, published *Roosevelt in the Bad Lands* in 1921, only two years after the former president's death. Since then, Roosevelt has appeared in books as a western phenomenon. His hunting and ranching have been credited not just with driving his later conservation efforts, but also with influencing his domestic and even his foreign policies as president.

But, however romantic, the western image of Roosevelt is incorrect, and it ignores the central facts of Roosevelt's life. Theodore Roosevelt was born in Manhattan, not the West. He was raised in the most thoroughly urban setting of late nineteenth-century America. Roosevelt's grandfather was one of New York City's richest men, and his father one of its leading philanthropists. Even his love of nature and animals began in an urban rather than a rural setting. In the city, Roosevelt collected mice and frogs and studied taxidermy. In the attic of his Gramercy Park home, he established the "Roosevelt Museum of Natural History," a precocious mirror to one of the institutions his father helped to found, the American Museum of Natural History, which opened its doors to its first exhibits in its temporary Central Park quarters when Roosevelt was just twelve years old. And late nineteenth-century New York was not completely urban. With backyards full of chicken coops and exotic animals kept as pets, the young Roosevelt did not have to go far to immerse himself in flora and fauna.

Theodore Roosevelt's early political career was also firmly rooted in New York City, not the Dakota Territory. He served for three years in the New York State Assembly representing his uptown brownstone district. In Albany, he sat on the Cities Committee that wrote laws for New York City, which did not then enjoy "home rule." He ran unsuccessfully for mayor of New York in 1886. Later, his first act as US civil service commissioner was to return to the city of his birth and attack corruption in the New York Custom House. He served as New York City police commissioner for two years. Then, as governor, he constantly dealt with the affairs of New York City and the Republican boss Thomas Collier Platt, who held court at Manhattan's Fifth Avenue Hotel. As president, Roosevelt continued to concern himself with the minutiae of New York politics and government, from mayoral elections to police promotions and from Republican politics to the war on vice. Even while occupying the White House, Theodore Roosevelt was still a New Yorker, and his politics reflected this. Roosevelt was no agrarian populist from west of the Mississippi. He was an urban progressive, concerned with such issues as civil service, municipal reform, and political machines.

In addition to writing about the West, Roosevelt also wrote about urban affairs. In 1891, he published a history of New York from the time of its discovery by Henry Hudson in 1609. Years before he wrote his famous 1894 essay "True Americanism" in *The Forum*, Roosevelt wrote in *New York* that "the most important lesson taught by the history of New York City is the lesson of Americanism—the lesson that he among us who wishes to win honor in our life, and to play his part honestly and manfully, must be indeed an American in spirit and purpose, in heart and thought and deed." In 1895, while he was police commissioner, Roosevelt penned the essay "The City in Modern Life," as well as another essay entitled "The Higher Life of American Cities." Throughout his career, he wrote essays on machine politics in New York, the New York police, and efforts at reform. In writing about the West, Roosevelt adroitly tapped into Americans' romantic obsession in order to sell books and promote an image of himself, whereas in writing about New York, he arguably wrote about the experiences and ideas closest to his heart.

Roosevelt's political career grew and developed in concert with the city. During his lifetime, the population of New York City grew from 800,000 to an astonishing 5.5 million, which made it the second largest city in the world. The expanding population strained basic city services, such as water and sanitation. Limited housing forced the working class into ever more densely packed tenements, which became visible and decrepit symbols of poverty, crime, and disease. Such areas became fertile ground for social reformers, and political reformers, such as Roosevelt, took aim at the city government. A growing city and its infrastructure meant that New York politicians oversaw increasingly large budgets. Inevitably much of this money found its way into the pockets of unscrupulous city officials and their allies. There was never enough revenue to finance the building of roads, bridges, parks, and courthouses, and so the city depended increasingly on raising money by issuing bonds. Such bloated debt caused one New York mayor to note in 1882 that the city owed to creditors the equivalent of about 10 percent of the total value of all Manhattan real estate. At the same time, it became harder to understand who was actually in charge in the city. A shadowy, unelected Board of Aldermen checked the policies and appointments of the mayor, who was elected to only a two-year term. In turn, the party bosses, especially from the city Democratic organization known as Tammany Hall, manipulated mayors, aldermen, and city officials. Throughout his career in the city and Albany, Roosevelt championed measures that increased the executive power of the mayor while seeking to undermine the influence of party bosses and their puppets on the Board of Aldermen.

Roosevelt entered city politics at a time when New York was renowned as the most corrupt of American cities. The city lived under the shadow of William Tweed, Tammany Hall's most notorious boss. Tweed had initially bought controlling interest in the companies that sold printing services and office supplies to the city at inflated prices. He soon had interest in or sat on the boards of half a dozen companies that did business with the city, including gas and light providers and railway lines. He protected his interests by exerting influence in Albany, where he was chair of the New York State Senate's Committee on Cities, helping to craft legislation governing New York City. From this position in 1870, he helped usher through the legislature a new charter for the city that established a new Board of Audit to oversee municipal spending. Tweed staffed the board with his own men, who came to be known as the Tweed Ring. The board authorized numerous bond issues from which Tweed and his ring stole millions.

As a result, from 1869 to 1871 the city's debt tripled and taxes rose. The most visible symbol of the ring's malfeasance came to be the Tweed Courthouse, construction of which was used as a pretext to steal millions from the city. In 1871, the *New York Times* ran a series of articles exposing the ring, which eventually led to Tweed's arrest and trial for hundreds of counts of fraud and embezzlement. Estimates of how much Tweed and his ring stole from the city range from $30 million to $200 million. Tweed's prison sentence and eventual death did not bring Tammany's corrupt practices to an end, however. Office seekers paid handsomely for city posts from which they would line their own pockets. To protect their interests with favorable legislation, the bosses spread the money around Albany as well. As a result, city Democrats wielded disproportionate influence in the legislature. Beginning in Albany, Roosevelt would witness this corruption firsthand.

New York City shaped Theodore Roosevelt, and Theodore Roosevelt helped to shape the city. He was sophisticated and cosmopolitan, as comfortable in a silk top hat and tails in his box at the opera as he was sitting atop a horse on his ranch. The city afforded Roosevelt a network of important Americans of the late nineteenth century, from old friends of his father's to top Republicans, reformers, and journal editors. It provided him with an in-depth and intimate education in the ills facing a growing America, including government corruption, police brutality, poor sanitation, poverty, and decrepit housing. Roosevelt became a champion of urban reform, with ideas that guided him throughout his nearly thirty years in public service. He consistently backed changes in civil service, housing laws, and labor relations, seeking to ameliorate the problems of the rapidly expanding city brought about by massive industrialization and immigration. Perhaps the most profound concept that Roosevelt would champion from the 1880s on was the radical notion of government responsibility for the welfare of individual Americans. He did not advocate a government that tried to create equality. Instead, he advocated government's responsibility in creating equality of opportunity, equality in the marketplace, and equality before the law. Roosevelt's contact with the laboring poor of New York, unique among presidents until that time, profoundly shaped his ideas, which in turn would resonate throughout American history. Governmental responsibility and equality of opportunity for the nation's most vulnerable citizens became hallmarks of Roosevelt's thought, and ultimately, of the Progressive Era that he promoted.

Roosevelt's rise also reflected the fluid and intricate world of late nineteenth-century American politics. Such a world resembled, to use one of Roosevelt's favorite metaphors, a kaleidoscope. Throughout his nearly thirty years in public office, Roosevelt constantly grappled with multiple party factions and interest groups at the city, state, and federal levels. New York's Republican political machine struggled to maintain strict party unity in the face of such divisions, as independent reformers—so-called Mugwumps—frequently bolted the party. Roosevelt constantly railed at these two irreconcilable factions of his party. The divisions often split the Republican ticket, allowing the election of Tammany governments in the city. At the same time, Roosevelt often served as a bridge between the two groups, gaining a valuable skill that would serve him well both as a candidate and later as governor and president. Roosevelt's experiences in New York politics prepared him, as President Roosevelt, to maneuver his progressive legislation through a skeptical and often hostile Congress. Despite his uneasy position between the two factions, Roosevelt was able to shape a remarkable agenda of reform. Of all his progressive ideas, the most important was that of civil service reform, the simple idea that government workers, from the policeman to the postal clerk, should receive posts and promotions based on merit. His career in public life reflected thirty years of continuous advocacy of civil service reform at the city, state, and federal levels. During those thirty years, the tide turned against political blackmail and graft, and Roosevelt played a vital role in that change. And all of this came about because Theodore Roosevelt was born between the East and Hudson Rivers in America's largest city.

Placing Roosevelt in his proper, urban context requires following him as he walked through nineteenth-century New York City. Such a tour would start at his birthplace on 20th Street near Gramercy Park, and range north to his second family home on 57th Street, wedged between the mansions on Fifth Avenue and the saloons on Sixth. The young Roosevelt can be spied taking sleigh rides through Central Park with his Harvard friends and future Boston Brahmin bride. Later, he can be seen entering the dingy Republican Party headquarters at Morton Hall, possibly dressed in top hat and tails en route to the opera or Patriarch's Ball. Even while an assemblyman in Albany, Roosevelt wrote laws for New York City and convened investigating committees in Manhattan. His brief detour to the West in the 1880s requires riding with Roosevelt on the numerous train rides he took back to New York every fall to ensure he kept a hand in Republican Party politics, which led to him eventually receiving his party's nomination for mayor in 1886. Even while occupying appointed positions in Washington, DC, Roosevelt interested himself in all things New York, from family to politics. It was in 1891 that he penned his history of New York City. And when war with Spain broke out in 1898, Roosevelt did not attract cowboys to the Rough Riders as much as he attracted wealthy, educated, upper-class New Yorkers like himself. These "Ritz Riders" helped to make Roosevelt a household name and made him palatable to the New York state bosses for the gubernatorial nomination.

From the governor's mansion in Albany, Roosevelt continued to insert himself into the life and politics of New York City, championing health and housing reform while backing fellow New York City reformers in Assembly elections. It was Governor Roosevelt's very strength in New York City that prompted Republican boss Thomas Platt to kick Roosevelt upstairs to the vice presidency, with unintended consequences. With William McKinley's assassination in 1901, President Roosevelt could apply to the nation progressive ideas learned on the streets of New York City. Moreover, from the White House Roosevelt reached into New York City politics in a way unprecedented for American presidents. In so doing, he contributed to the destruction of his old political nemesis, Boss Platt, and strengthened the executive power of the city's mayor. In his thirty years of public life, Roosevelt helped to make New York cleaner, safer, and less corrupt, while New York helped to make him one of America's greatest presidents.

Prologue: *June 18, 1910*
Homecoming

IT WAS ONE OF the greatest days in the history of New York City. It was one of the greatest days in the life of Theodore Roosevelt.

Shortly after seven in the morning, the SS *Kaiserin Auguste Victoria* broke through the mist of Ambrose Channel, steaming along the border between New York and New Jersey before turning north toward Manhattan. Following her was an escort of honor consisting of the new battleship *South Carolina* and five torpedo destroyers. Construction of all the ships had been authorized during the presidency of Theodore Roosevelt. The *South Carolina* was the first dreadnought ever to enter the Hudson River, and the first American dreadnought the former president ever laid eyes upon. From the top four decks of the *Kaiserin*, passengers waved handkerchiefs and cheered, while from a large porthole, Roosevelt leaned, waving his silk hat at the reporters on the approaching tugboat. At the sight of the former president, the captain of the tug blew three long blasts on his whistle, a salute taken up by scores of river craft, from the shores of Staten Island and New Jersey to the west across to Brooklyn to the east. At Fort Wadsworth, located at the narrows between Staten Island and Brooklyn, four companies of the US Army Coast Artillery Corps stood at attention as cannon sounded a twenty-one-gun salute.

Colonel and Mrs. Roosevelt gazed at the spectacle from the upper bridge, surrounded by their children Alice, Ethel, and Kermit. When the *Kaiserin* dropped anchor at quarantine, the health officer immediately boarded the ship, accompanied by Roosevelt's closest friend, Senator Henry Cabot Lodge; Alice's husband, Congressman Nicholas Longworth; President William Howard Taft's aide, Archibald Butt; and the secretary of agriculture, James Wilson, the longest-serving cabinet member of all time, who had also served in the administrations of McKinley and Roosevelt. Butt and Wilson, representing Taft, greeted Roosevelt, but the former president was more interested in the parade of ships just then passing to starboard—the massive gray battleship *South Carolina* followed by the five destroyers. Along all decks of the battleship her crew "dressed" her sides, while the members of the US Marine Band in their scarlet uniforms could easily be spied on the quarterdeck. Just as eight bells struck on all the ships, the band struck up "The Star Spangled Banner." The large national ensigns were hoisted at the stern, and along the entire lengths of all the ships red, white, and blue bunting was unrolled. It was an impressive sight.

While Roosevelt stood mesmerized by the ships, Edith's attention was drawn to the approaching *Manhattan*, a revenue cutter operated by the New York Custom House. Edith caught sight of her other three children on board the boat. Soon a gangplank connected the two vessels, and young Theodore, Quentin, and Archie climbed aboard to greet their parents. When the entire party disembarked onto the *Manhattan*, Roosevelt shook hands with all of the boat's crew, including the black cook in his white suit. Another transfer was made to the boat carrying the welcoming committee, including the architect of the day's festivities, Cornelius Vanderbilt III. When he saw Vanderbilt, Roosevelt exclaimed that he was happy to be home and "ready to put his shoulder to the wheel," as a *New York Times* reporter put it. Among the two hundred dignitaries welcoming Roosevelt was his old friend Jacob Riis. "Oh Jake! I'm glad to see you!" Roosevelt boomed down the line of men waiting to shake his hand.

Roosevelt seemed less happy to greet Republican Party State Chairman Timothy Woodruff. Roosevelt knew exactly what kind of man Woodruff was—merely a henchman to the new boss of the state Republicans, William Barnes Jr. The old boss and Roosevelt's nemesis, Thomas Platt, had gone to his grave only that March, and Barnes had been a self-serving doppelganger of the Easy Boss. Barnes and other state Republican leaders were conspicuously absent among this first welcoming party, leading the *New York Times* to observe in a headline: "Old Guard Didn't Appear Overjoyed." Woodruff had been dispatched in their place, and he found it an unhappy job that became increasingly difficult as the morning wore on. He had been late and almost missed the boat, which was already under way when Woodruff reached the quay, his having just missed the removal of the gangplank. A sailor threw a rope ladder over the side of the boat, and Woodruff was forced to leap across the water for it and clamber up the side. When he reached Roosevelt, the former antagonist of the state party machine gave Woodruff's hand the most cursory of shakes. A nearby reporter spoke aloud the words he wrote on his pad: "During the reception of Mr. Woodruff the ex-President exhibited remarkable power of self-control." Woodruff heard the remark and looked even more pained.

When the boat docked at Battery Park, Roosevelt stepped onto native soil for the first time in over a year. Fittingly, he stepped ashore onto Manhattan, the island of his birth. There, another crowd received him, including his sisters, Anna Cowles and Corinne Robinson; a distant cousin, Franklin, and a niece, Eleanor, who had married each other five years earlier; and Theodore Roosevelt Jr.'s fiancée, Eleanor Alexander. The Roosevelt-Alexander nuptials were planned for the very next day.

The New York dignitaries who welcomed the former president reflected his always-precarious political position in the state and the continued fractious politics of the Republican Party. State boss William Barnes was accompanied by none other than Louis Payn, the former state superintendent of insurance who had been removed by then-governor Roosevelt, but was still boss of Columbia and Duchess Counties. William Loeb, Roosevelt's personal secretary from his governorship right through his presidency, received a warm welcome from his old boss. Loeb had been nominated by President Taft as collector of the New York Custom House, the same position that had plagued both

Theodore Roosevelt and his father for decades. While Roosevelt was still in Africa big-game hunting, Lodge had written his friend of Loeb's great work in cleaning up the custom house. He had added, "The evils in the Institution are periodic and have to be dealt with about once in so often." Lodge did not need to remind Roosevelt of that particular institution's evils.

Aside from cabinet secretaries past and present, one former federal officer in particular received much attention from the former president. Gifford Pinchot had served under both Roosevelt and Taft as chief of the US Forest Service, which in 1905 had gained control of the national forest preserves. Pinchot had quickly come into conflict with Taft's new secretary of the interior, Richard Ballinger, who restored millions of acres of forest to private use amid accusations that he was colluding with mining companies. Pinchot sent a letter critical of Taft and Ballinger to a US senator, and when the senator read it into the *Congressional Record*, Taft had little choice but to fire Pinchot, angering many preservationists and progressives—such as Roosevelt. Pinchot had even visited Roosevelt while he was resting with his family on the Italian Riviera. In his fiery attacks against Taft and the administration, Pinchot symbolized the split among Republicans. Now here he was given a place of honor in the audience at Battery Park. Just as Roosevelt readied to speak, he caught sight of Pinchot and ostentatiously nodded his head and mimicked a handshake across the distance between them, to which Pinchot replied in kind. Although no words passed between them, for anyone watching it boded ill for the Republican Party for the upcoming midterm elections, and raised serious questions about Taft's presumed reelection bid in 1912.

In the end, the speeches of Roosevelt and of New York City Mayor William J. Gaynor in Battery Park that day were so short that they disappointed the 3,000 ticketholders listening in the roped-off area around the platform. But Roosevelt's cryptic remarks would prompt much speculation in the press over the following days. The ostensibly retired Roosevelt said to the throng, "I am ready and eager to do my part so far as I am able in helping solve problems which must be solved if we of this the greatest democratic Republic upon which the sun has ever shone are to see its destinies rise to the high level of our hopes and its opportunities." Somewhere within the overblown rhetoric, Roosevelt seemed to be saying something important. After the speeches, Roosevelt's family departed, while Roosevelt himself, with his friends and escorting dignitaries, boarded nineteen carriages for the five-mile parade up Broadway and Fifth Avenue.

New York had never seen such a display, certainly not for a private citizen. Estimates put the crowds at 1 million as New Yorkers welcomed home the only president ever born in their city. Every element of the festivities reflected Roosevelt's life and career in New York. The escort of Rough Riders included Charles Knoblauch, one of the members from New York City, who the following day would host a clambake for his former comrades. The parade route was lined by hundreds of New York's Finest, the city police, and from time to time, Roosevelt, the former police commissioner, recognized a face and called out greetings. "Well, I'm glad to see you," he called to Captain "Big Bill" Hodgins, reaching down to shake the officer's hand. Despite the large police presence, people—and objects—broke through the police line. Near City Hall, a woman tossed a red peony from the window of an office building. The flower grazed Roosevelt's head and landed in the bottom of his carriage, whereupon he picked it up and bowed to the woman. Joseph Youngwitz, a messenger boy, tried twice to break through before he succeeded in handing the former president a bouquet of flowers. "I wanted to give you these," Youngwitz panted. "I bought them myself because I admire you so." "I think I've seen you before," Roosevelt said to the astonished boy. Youngwitz later confirmed to reporters that he had shaken Roosevelt's hand about five years earlier when the president had visited New York.

As the parade reached Washington Square, the entire procession made a slow turn west onto Fourth Street to reach Fifth Avenue. The next few miles along the route reflected the political, ethnic, and religious flavor of the city. From 10th to 14th Streets, the Republican organizations had arrayed themselves, including the Twenty-First Assembly District and the Federal Club. Spectators took up precarious posts on the ledges of the Fifth Avenue and Flatiron Buildings, and the pedestal of the statue of Admiral David Glascow Farragut in Madison Square Park was covered by a multitude. Next came the Italian and Hungarian societies, while out-of-town delegations took position across from the Waldorf.

Most everyone in the crowd passed by 433 Fifth Avenue without a second look, but Colonel Roosevelt made a point of bowing to the family there, whose members were hanging from windows and standing on the sidewalk. This was the home of the Alexanders, the family of young Theodore's fiancée. Sixteen-year-old Quentin Roosevelt balanced on a board on the sidewalk to glimpse his father, while both Miss and Mrs. Alexander could be seen at the center window in the company of Theodore Roosevelt Jr. In the doorway stood Alice and her sister, Ethel. Once the procession had passed the house, the crowds became thinner. But the twenty-five remaining members of the Grand Army of the Republic, Peter Cooper Post—New York's last Civil War veterans—still stood in front of Temple Emanuel. The Dutch Reformed Church displayed both the German and American flags. The Hotel Buckingham flew the colors of the Rough Riders, a massive yellow flag with the American eagle. Even the nearby Democratic Club had hung a flag in Roosevelt's honor. The parade came to an end near the Plaza Hotel at 59th Street, just past the palatial home of Cornelius Vanderbilt, which was decorated with standards of small American flags. Roosevelt stepped into a waiting car, and just as the vehicle moved away, someone thrust a cluster of sweet peas into his hand.

THE PARADE HAD BARELY ENDED when the temperature began plummeting and the sky darkened. In only a few minutes the thermometer dropped twenty degrees, the rains came, and the winds rose. Although it was only afternoon, the electric lights on Broadway came on, as the wind became a gale. Clotheslines, flags, window frames, and newspapers flew through the air. Within an hour, the storm had passed, but in that short time, the subway flooded, the floating crane in the Brooklyn Navy Yard sank, and thirteen people lost their lives. Several men and women drowned in local rivers, while others were killed by falling objects: a pane of glass, a tree, a collapsed smokestack. One old-timer told a reporter the tempest exceeded in power and grandeur anything he could remember. He might have been speaking of Roosevelt.

What did Roosevelt mean when he returned to his city and spoke of dedicating himself to solving the problems facing the nation? The *New York Times* observed that a "political purpose" might have been behind the welcome he received. Politicians did not hold back their views. "Roosevelt can have the [presidential] nomination if he wants it," said former secretary of the navy Paul Morton. "He has not been associated with any faction, but belongs to the whole Republican Party and to the country." The Republican Club of upstate Oneida adopted a new slogan, "For Governor of New York, Theodore Roosevelt." Taft had recently tapped current governor Charles Evans Hughes for the US Supreme Court, and many Republicans looked to Roosevelt to continue Hughes's progressive policies in the face of machine opposition. Upstate party leader and customs collector at Plattsburg John O'Brien echoed the Oneida club in plainly stating, "We want a boss— that's what we want, and Colonel Roosevelt is the kind of boss we want and need. He can go in and unite the party in this State and get us in shape for the Gubernatorial campaign this Fall." In 1910, New York Republicans called on Roosevelt to serve the same role he had during much of his New York career, uniting opposing wings of the Republican Party.

With regard to Roosevelt's future, however, many looked beyond Albany, to Washington. In their letters to each other starting in 1909, Lodge and Roosevelt had openly spoken of Roosevelt running again in 1912. Throughout 1910, Roosevelt's unhappiness with Taft grew. His chosen successor allied himself with the Republican Old Guard and failed to carry out Roosevelt's policies. As President Roosevelt had convinced many skeptical Republicans in 1908 to support Taft, Roosevelt felt doubly betrayed. Even before he stepped ashore on Manhattan, Roosevelt had to admit that Taft "had gone wrong on certain points" and that, "deep down underneath," he "had all along known he was wrong." Perhaps Republicans could forgive Roosevelt for backing Taft, if indeed he had been deceived, but they would not forgive him if he allowed the deception to continue. All of this was spinning through Roosevelt's mind as he arrived home.

As battleships escorted him and cannon saluted, how could Roosevelt not be affected? As the Marine Band struck up the "Star

Spangled Banner" while Roosevelt laid eyes upon the Statue of Liberty for the first time in over a year, how could he not think of his duty to his nation? As political friend and foe waited to shake his hand, how could he not contemplate his own political future? And as his carriage moved slowly through the canyons of Lower Manhattan, past the cheering throngs, the New York policemen, the Rough Riders, the city's Republican organizations, and the out-of-town delegations from across the country, how could President Roosevelt—an honorific he was entitled to—not see it as a sign, as an indication, if not of divine will, then of overwhelming public sentiment? True, Roosevelt never seemed swayed by popular acclaim. It meant nothing, he said, "unless it can be turned to good tangible account, in the way of getting substantial advance along the lines of clean and wise government." This was the president who had said, "I want to accomplish things." That June 18, 1910, welcome to a private citizen and native son, unprecedented in American history, must have helped push Theodore Roosevelt toward once again entering the political fray, first in New York in 1910, and then nationally in 1912. The great New Yorker could not have done otherwise.

ONE

"*This Little Rocky Island*"
New York at Roosevelt's Birth

THE STORY OF NEW YORK in 1858 is a tale of two cities. Contrasts were everywhere. Great affluence rubbed shoulders with grinding poverty. On some streets pedestrians picked their way among piles of garbage, while on others the residents took regular street-cleaning and new cobblestones for granted. There was the city of the elite, and there was the city of the huddled masses, and the city a person lived in depended greatly upon that person's wealth or lack thereof. Segregation based on wealth began at birth and continued even after death. Rich New Yorkers were buried in Green-Wood Cemetery in Brooklyn. New York's poorest were buried in a Potter's Field on Wards Island in the East River.

There were other contradictions as well. Though it was an island bound on all sides by rivers, New York suffered chronic water shortages, even as the East River seeped into basement tenements. The New York police, organized to protect the citizens from crime, were often criminals themselves engaged in blackmail and bribe-taking. A hundred saloons, brothels, and burlesque houses easily outnumbered the city's two dozen churches. With more hospitals than any other American

9

city, New Yorkers still feared disease most of all, especially the periodic cholera epidemics that took thousands of lives. Another one was only eight years off, but who could blame the pathogens for taking up residence and multiplying? They were practically invited into the filthy city, a place where roaming pigs still did much of the street cleaning.

On October 27, 1858, the day that Theodore Roosevelt was born in a luxurious brownstone in the posh neighborhood near Gramercy Park, Michael and Catherine Hertel, a father and daughter, suffocated to death in their Lower East Side tenement. The cause was smoke from a fire in an adjacent brewery, set alight by a blaze in a neighboring cooperage. The Hertels were typical New Yorkers. Arriving in America from Germany, they had settled in New York's *Kleindeutschland*, Little Germany, along with tens of thousands of their compatriots. The Hertels lived in a brick tenement, a five-story building of small one- and two-bedroom apartments. Many of the rooms had no outside window, making for a dark and fetid existence. It would be another half-century before the housing laws began to catch up with the squalid life in the tenements. The dozens of residents living in this building with the Hertels shared a common latrine in the back lot. They toted water up the stairs from a common spigot in the same place. To dispose of the dirty water, they most often opened a window and dumped the contents of their buckets or washbasins out into the street. And at the time when the fire broke out next door, New York still had no law mandating any kind of fire escape. During a fire, the tenements became deathtraps for the working poor of Manhattan.

No zoning laws existed to separate commercial and residential properties, and, like a spreading inkblot, the booming industrial city seeped into whatever vacant land was available. Among their neighbors in Kleindeutschland, the Hertels counted shipyards, coal yards, and factories of all types, which were also common places of employment. With New York the meatpacking capital of the United States, the laborers of the city worked as well in the neighborhood slaughterhouses, operations that added blood and manure to the ever-pungent odors of the Lower East Side. Inevitably, from time to time an animal would escape from one of the slaughterhouses, and pedestrians would flatten themselves against the walls of buildings and watch as men in blood-spattered aprons chased a maddened cow down the street. The brewery next to the Hertels' tenement was also typical of the city, as was the adjacent coppersmith, conveniently located to make casks for the beer. By midcentury, there were more than 1,000 cooperages in the city making barrels for nearly every kind of industry, from sugar and flour to nails and coins. Barrel making was so ubiquitous in New York that two barrels were included on the city seal. The mostly immigrant workforce would often work late into the night by lantern or gaslight, making the barrels by hand. In the fire that killed the Hertels, which broke out at almost 9 p.m., wood shavings had probably been set alight by a careless worker.

In addition to the Hertels, twelve horses also perished in the fire. These were likely the enormous draft horses that New Yorkers were accustomed to seeing pulling brewery wagons. In any case, they were in the basement of the brewery when the fire broke out. Their deaths must have represented a considerable loss for the brewer. But stabling horses right inside a business was common, and at midcentury the city contained thousands of stables housing tens of thousands of horses. Horses represented the backbone of the city's transportation and delivery system. There were private saddle horses, carriage horses, and giant drays for pulling freight and the city's aboveground trolleys. By the 1850s, the city's street railways carried some 35 million passengers each year. And every day, New York's horses left on the streets tons of manure and thousands of gallons of urine, representing a formidable challenge to the city's street-cleaning forces. When a horse died in the harness, the owner simply unhooked his carriage or wagon and moved on, leaving the removal and disposal of the carcass to the city contractor. In summers, the air was ripe with the smell of steaming manure and rotting horse. By 1858, disease remained a constant concern for New Yorkers.

Next to a cholera epidemic, fire represented the city's greatest threat. Only a generation had passed since the Great Fire of 1835 had destroyed seven hundred buildings. And only three weeks before the fire that killed the Hertels blazed through their tenement building, the great Crystal Palace, the massive exhibition hall built in 1853, had burned to the ground—remarkably, without a single loss of life. When the fire broke out in the cooperage, several things occurred that illustrated some modest improvements that had been made in New York firefighting. The alarm was telegraphed to the Fifth District bell tower, which rang to alert the volunteer firemen. A horse-drawn pump arrived, possibly one of the steam-powered pumps introduced only that year. The firemen enjoyed a large supply of water thanks to the Croton Aqueduct, which had been completed in 1842. Still, the lack of a permanent, professional firefighting force meant a delayed response that night. This allowed the fire to spread from the cooperage to the brewery, the smoke then permeating the Hertels' tenement. Saving a few minutes might have saved their lives.

In New York at midcentury, the Hertels' miserable existence in their decrepit tenement coexisted with the affluence of others, such as the Roosevelt family. Growing up in postbellum New York, Theodore Roosevelt would be keenly aware of the growing disparity between great wealth and great poverty. He would note this years later when writing his history of New York City, contrasting the growth of "colossal fortunes" with the poverty of the tenement-house population. Roosevelt decried the conformity of the upper classes in Gilded Age New York. In the summers, the elite took the Grand Tour through Europe; in winter, they returned to their identical brownstone-front houses. Inside, the houses were all decorated with the same dark furniture, heavy drapes, gilded mirrors and picture frames, and ormolu *objets d'art*. Roosevelt might have been describing his own family and their home, as it was into such a brownstone-fronted, gilded house that he was born.

Martha Bulloch Roosevelt gave birth to her first son in a lavish home situated a short distance from Gramercy Park. A true southern belle whose family still owned slaves in Georgia at the time of Roosevelt's birth, "Mittie" was something of an alien living in New York. And when she arrived in the city after her wedding to Theodore Roosevelt Sr., New York must have appeared alien to her. For Mittie, one consolation was surely that she married into one of the most prominent New York families of the era. Since the first Roosevelt had come to New Amsterdam in the middle of the seventeenth century, every generation of the family had been born in Manhattan. By the mid-nineteenth century, the name "Roosevelt" conjured images of wealth and success in business. Manhattan boasted a Roosevelt Street, and, by 1871, a Roosevelt Hospital. The head of the New York City branch of the Roosevelt clan was Cornelius Van Schaack Roosevelt, Mittie's father-in-law, one of New York's wealthiest men, who presided over a business and real-estate empire from his grand Union Square mansion.

The earliest photo of Theodore Roosevelt dates from 1865; in it, he and his brother Elliott can be spied watching Abraham Lincoln's funeral procession from a window in their grandfather's house. The photograph gives a hint of the family's economic and social standing. C. V. S. Roosevelt had built his massive, four-story mansion after making money in banking, mining, Manhattan real estate, and imported glass. Years later, Theodore Roosevelt would describe his grandfather's house as one of New York's grand homes on Union Square, with a large central hall that rose all the way up to the roof. This cavernous central hallway, not to mention his grandfather's wealth and position, must have made a great impression upon the young Theodore, perhaps confirming the importance of C. V. S. as head of the family.

Although Union Square Park was open to the public, Gramercy Park, near Theodore's home, was not. The idea of a private park was not entirely new to New York. St. John's Park in Lower Manhattan had been deeded to the owners of the houses that surrounded it in 1827. The following year it was enclosed by a locked cast-iron fence, and, as Gramercy would be some years later, St. John's was designed with gravel paths and trees and shrubs. St. John's Park, though, only lasted until 1866, when Cornelius Vanderbilt bought it for $1 million. Still, the idea of a private park was certainly more English than American, and Gramercy Park would not have been out of place in London. Perhaps this was part of the appeal of the new development to the Roosevelt family and others. The 1850s were a time when the elite of New York—the "aristocracy" of old money—sought to separate themselves from the plebian class, not only in terms of where they lived, but also, increasingly, of where they socialized.

The Union Club was New York's oldest social club. It had been formed in 1836 as an exclusive men's club for the wealthy, the "old-stock" elite of the city. Just as the wealthy built their houses above

14th Street, so now, too, in 1855, they moved their club to a specially designed Florentine building at the corner of Fifth Avenue and 21st Street, barely two blocks from the Roosevelt home. Gramercy Park was a quaint and discreet enclave, but Fifth Avenue became the ostentatious address of choice for the very wealthiest New Yorkers. Beginning in the late 1840s, ornate mansions and townhouses began appearing on lower Fifth north of Washington Square and running up to the new Madison Square, which the city had built between 23rd and 25th Streets in 1847. William Astor and John Jacob Astor IV built neighboring mansions between 33rd and 34th Streets at the end of the 1850s, ensuring the cachet of the Avenue. Many of the new houses were built not with marble, limestone, or brick, but with Triassic sandstone, which, owing to the presence of iron ore, turned from pink to brown as it weathered. The term "brownstone" would now be used as an adjective indicating wealth and prestige.

To serve the new neighborhoods, all manner of institutions—not just the Union Club—moved north of 14th Street. Columbia College moved to a new campus at 49th and Madison in 1856, aiming to shape the minds of New York's elite, while new places of worship were built to save their souls. Grace Church on Broadway at 10th Street replaced Trinity in Lower Manhattan as the church of choice for upper-class New Yorkers, with pews selling for as much as $1,600 apiece, and other churches opened along Fifth Avenue. The Church of the Ascension opened its doors in 1851 just down the street from Grace on 10th, followed by First Presbyterian Church in 1846, Fifth Avenue Presbyterian in 1852, and eventually, St. Patrick's Cathedral at 50th Street in 1879. In 1845, James Renwick Jr., the architect who had designed Grace Church, was asked to draw up plans for Calvary Church on 21st Street, closer to the Roosevelts. To the original Early English Gothic building that had been moved from Fourth Avenue in 1842, Renwick added a Gothic Revival sanctuary with twin spires and a five-sided apse. The two styles clashed terribly. New York lawyer and diarist George Templeton Strong called the new church, just steps away from his own home, "a miracle of ugliness." The twin spires, although presaging Renwick's future masterpiece, St. Patrick's Cathedral, did not last at Calvary. They had not been built straight from the ground, but added directly atop the church's towers, and the unstable spires were removed in 1860. It was unlikely that Theodore Roosevelt would have remembered the spires, although growing up he could probably still glimpse, from the top floor of his own home, the remaining towers rising above the other houses.

With his father a partner in the family firm Roosevelt and Son, Theodore enjoyed a comfortable existence from the moment he was born. While the Roosevelts never ascended to the level of wealth enjoyed by such New York families as the Astors and the Vanderbilts, they were still considered one of the city's top families. Moreover, by having an interest in New York banking, commerce, and real estate, the Roosevelt family became directly linked to other families of the city with great fortunes to their names. Sometimes, such fortunes seemed tenuous, as the nation's economy, centered in New York, experienced periodic booms and busts. In fact, Theodore Roosevelt was a "bust baby," born into the mid-nineteenth century's worst economic slump.

In September 1857, about a year before Roosevelt's birth, a heavy storm hit the North Carolina coast. In Wilmington, heavy rain washed away bridges, and drifts of sand blocked railway traffic. Offshore, the storm battered a number of vessels, ripping away sails and rigging and overtaxing pumps. As of September 17, no deaths had been reported, although the steamship *Central America* was missing. Newspapers speculated that the ship had simply run out of coal or had some of her machinery damaged, which must have forced the ship to make way slowly under sail. The papers were wrong.

The next day brought news of the disaster. The *Central America* had sunk, losing more than five hundred of her passengers and crew. Although it was a terrible tragedy, New Yorkers immediately focused on the treasure of gold the ship had been carrying. "Loss of the *Central America* steamer," George Templeton Strong wrote in his diary, "the first of our treasure-ships that has perished. She foundered with several hundred passengers and a million and a half in California gold, sorely needed in Wall Street just now. The pressure there is cruel." The *Central America*'s anticipated arrival in New York, with its $1.6 million in gold, was supposed to have relieved the pressure caused by bank

depositors withdrawing massive amounts of gold, as a panic had hit
the financial sector at the end of August. Plummeting farm prices had
caused Midwestern businessmen to withdraw their funds from New
York banks, which then immediately called in their mature debts. The
New York branch of the giant Ohio Life Insurance and Trust Company
failed, and credit dried up overnight. The American economy came to
a standstill.

The great slump of 1857–1859 radiated outward from New York,
affecting every major American city and reaching across the Atlantic to
London and Paris. If New York prided itself as the "Empire State," surely
Manhattan was the "Empire City," the capital of American finance,
banking, commerce, shipping, and manufacturing. The recession that
was in progress at the time of Theodore Roosevelt's birth helped to transform the nation on the eve of the Civil War. Unemployment soared and
half of Wall Street's brokers went bankrupt. Homelessness surged, and
the recession forced New Yorkers into increasingly crowded and run-
down tenements. Banks collapsed, wages fell, and retailers cut prices to
unload their goods at almost any price. With grain shipments from the
American West stalled because of the credit crunch, food prices stayed
high and the normally busy shipping industry sat idle. Manhattan bristled like a porcupine with its usually bustling docks and piers at the end
of every street, but now agricultural exports and manufactured imports
dried up, and the once mighty shipbuilding industry, particularly for
freight-hauling clipper ships, died out. Out-of-work stevedores crowded
the waterfront saloons, waiting to unload ships that never arrived.

The business of Roosevelt and Son reflected the business of New
York. In addition to importing glass, the firm owned extensive real
estate in Manhattan and upstate New York. It also owned two piers
in Lower Manhattan, and through C. V. S., Roosevelt and Son held
stock in banking, mining, and insurance interests. Other records show
the Roosevelts shipping coal and bidding on $100,000 blocks of US
Treasury notes. The recession did not leave the Roosevelts untouched.
And yet, it afforded new opportunities as well for the rich. Cornelius
Vanderbilt, for example, gobbled up local railroad companies to form
the New York Central Railroad, a company in which the Roosevelt
firm was to own stock.

Vast amounts of Manhattan's wealth passed through the hands of men named Roosevelt. Yet Theodore Roosevelt Sr. seemed little motivated by wealth. Unusual for New York at the time, the senior Roosevelt instead dedicated himself more to charitable and cultural pursuits than to empire building. He helped found the Children's Aid Society, Newsboys' Lodging House, New York Orthopedic Dispensary and Hospital, the Metropolitan Museum of Art, and the American Museum of Natural History. He also helped found the Republican Reform Club, and by the 1870s had a reputation as a reform Republican. Such endeavors would have a profound impact on his son.

Although Theodore Roosevelt Sr. differed from other elite New Yorkers in his dedication to charity, art, education, and reform, he shared such values with the elite of another American city. Indeed, he might have been mistaken for a Boston Brahmin rather than a New York Knickerbocker. His son's life would early on reflect the importance of the New York–Boston axis of the late nineteenth century. From marriage to friendship to political alliances, Roosevelt would always have one foot firmly planted on the shores of Massachusetts Bay—a much more important Roosevelt touchstone than the American West.

THE CIVIL WAR was the single greatest defining event for Americans of the nineteenth century. American presidents such as General Ulysses S. Grant and Major William McKinley were defined by their service in the war. But so, too, were average Americans. Although Theodore Roosevelt was only two years old at the outbreak of the war in 1861, the legacy of the war helped define his world.

In 1863, Theodore Roosevelt Sr. paid a substitute in order to avoid the risk of being drafted under the new Conscription Act—a routine practice followed by tens of thousands of men during the war, with no stigma attached. At the same time, he and two other wealthy New Yorkers conceived of a plan allowing soldiers to send money home to their families, who often were left nearly destitute in the absence of the main breadwinner. Without such a plan, New York families often had to wait for a regimental chaplain to travel to the city from the battlefield, whereupon the chaplain would distribute the soldiers' pay. With congressional and presidential backing, the Allotment Commission came into existence. President Abraham Lincoln named Roosevelt one of New York State's three allotment commissioners. Thus began a long period of the elder Roosevelt being away from home, returning only for holidays, birthdays, and family vacations. The Roosevelts were enjoying such a vacation during the hot July of 1863, spending it in New Jersey, when the most important event of the Civil War affecting New York City occurred, the New York Draft Riots.

Theodore Roosevelt was only four and a half years old when the riots broke out—and was on the other side of the Hudson River—but the riots had a profound impact on every New Yorker of the time, even a boy only overhearing his parents' conversations. Moreover, given that much of the violence occurred in the Gramercy Park neighborhood, the young Roosevelt likely saw some of the damage the riots left behind when they returned home. Roosevelt's own account of the draft riots in his history of New York hints at their effect on his view of the city and its citizens. He placed most of the blame for the riots on "the low foreign element," especially the Irish. Many New York Republicans blamed Democrats for the Civil War in general, and Roosevelt saw the state and city Democrats as allies to the rioters. Neither the political bosses nor the Catholic authorities had acted as good shepherds to their flock, Roosevelt believed. Placing the blame for the draft riots squarely on Democrats and Irish Catholics was the norm among Roosevelt's class. The riots cast a dark shadow over the late nineteenth-century politics of the city and the relations among its ethnic and religious groups. In short, the draft riots instilled in the young Roosevelt some very distinctly New York prejudices.

One lasting effect was to underscore Roosevelt's ethnic identity. Growing up hearing Dutch spoken around his grandfather's dinner table made young "Teedie" acutely aware of his European origins— mainly Dutch, but also Welsh, English, Irish, and German. His mother's side was largely Scottish, and the Bullochs were true southern "cavaliers" who looked across the Atlantic for their romantic heritage. Such ethnic self-identification only underscored Roosevelt's elite background. But "Dutch" signified class more than any real connection with Holland. With increasing immigration from southern and eastern

Europe taking place by the end of the nineteenth century, Roosevelt understood that his family was "native," old-stock American. So, too, were the family friends of the Roosevelts in New York—the John Hays, the Joseph Choates, and the Elihu Roots. At an early age, Roosevelt understood where his family's ethnicity, religion, and class placed him among the teeming throng of the city.

IN APRIL 1868, Theodore Roosevelt Sr. and Mittie Roosevelt boarded a ship for the American South. Exactly three years had passed since the end of the Civil War. Docking in Savannah, they were met by Mittie's Georgia relatives, including a slew of Stewarts, Elliotts, and Bullochs. The Roosevelts then took a slow carriage ride northeast to Bulloch Hall, the family estate in Roswell, Georgia. In following this road from Savannah to Atlanta, they were traveling in reverse the path taken by Union Army General William Tecumseh Sherman in his notorious "March to the Sea" after the fall of Atlanta. Signs of the war and the utter destruction it had caused met the Roosevelts wherever they looked. Railroad tracks still lay by the roadside, rails torn from the ground and twisted over fires by Union troops—Sherman's "neckties." Blackened stone and brick chimneys peeked from behind the tops of trees, forlorn survivors of Sherman's fiery scourge.

The elder Roosevelts had taken seven-year-old Corinne with them, but left behind in New York twelve-year-old Anna, known as "Bamie"; nine-year-old Theodore, then called "Teedie"; and eight-year-old Elliott. Taking the very youngest of the children to war-ravaged territory seems an odd decision, but perhaps Corinne was least prepared to part from her parents. Ill health may also have contributed to the older children remaining in New York. Although Elliott was still regarded as the strongest of the children, having yet to suffer the seizures that would afflict him as a teenager, Bamie's and Teedie's health were matters of constant concern for the family. Pott's disease—actually a form of tuberculosis—had weakened the bones of Bamie's spine to such an extent as to leave her something of a hunchback for the rest of her life, while Teedie's bouts with asthma, stomachaches, and headaches often held the entire family hostage to his maladies. Still, the family managed to travel extensively despite such afflictions. During the Civil War, the elder Theodore Roosevelt had taken Bamie, always his favorite, to Washington, where she sat upon Abraham Lincoln's lap.

Anna, Theodore, and Elliott were left in the care of Mittie's sister, who dutifully made the children sit and write out laborious letters to their absent parents and sister. The young Theodore's letters illustrate his boyhood fascination with wars and battles, and a bit of insensitivity to his southern mother's feelings concerning the war. Aside from asking for battlefield trophies, Theodore also asked for the climbing vine known as a "supplejack," which, he said, "will figure greatly in my museum."

Young Theodore's natural history museum in the Roosevelt home included plants, birds, and mice. In this he was not copying his father, but taking the lead. Theodore Roosevelt Sr. would help found the American Museum of Natural History the following year, but for the present, no such institution existed in New York, a situation lamented by the *New York Times*. Banvard's Museum had opened on Broadway in 1867 with the promise of displaying scientific collections and natural wonders. So far, however, the only animals on display were trained birds, mice, and a cat, which were made to draw toy wagons, fire a cannon, and walk on tightropes. "This part of the entertainment must bring rare delight," the paper wryly noted, "to those who think these tiny prisoners ought to be made to earn their sustenance and endure their confinement too, as the culprits in our penitentiaries do—by hard labor." New York was behind Boston and most European cities in its lack of an institution dedicated to natural history. "Even at the present time," the *Times* concluded, "an enterprising man with capital could, in a single year, obtain material for a popular museum that would be a credit to New York, and a constant source of wonder, instruction, entertainment and study to young and old, wise and simple, citizens and stranger." The charter for the American Museum of Natural History would be signed in the Roosevelt parlor exactly one year later.

Teedie was not the only Roosevelt to keep animals at home. From their third-floor piazza at the back of the house the children could spy Aunt Lizzie Roosevelt's menagerie of guinea pigs, birds, and a monkey next door. Roosevelt later recalled that his interest in natural history was sparked by seeing a dead seal that had been fished out of New

York Harbor. That seal told volumes about the state of nature in New York City, even at the middle of the nineteenth century. Modern observers of New York's caverns of steel and concrete can barely imagine the wealth of species that once occupied Manhattan. When Henry Hudson stumbled across "Manhatta," home of the Lenape Algonquins for hundreds of generations, the island was a cornucopia of native plant, animal, and bird species. Wolves, black bears, mountain lions, beavers, mink, and river otters prowled the land while whales, porpoises, seals, and sea turtles swam the waters. The air was filled with millions of birds, the water with millions of fish. No wonder a small child might still encounter some of this profusion of nature even in the middle of America's largest city.

The Roosevelts supplemented their interest in nature with summers in New Jersey and, later, at their summer home at Oyster Bay, Long Island. The children rode horses, played in streams, and heard stories of bears and wild dogs in the woods. Teedie's asthma seemed to bother him less the more time he spent outdoors, but ill health always accounted for at least some of his introspection.

Such illness became a key element of the family's first Grand Tour to Europe. The Roosevelt family took two such tours, the first in 1869–1870 as Theodore turned eleven, the second in 1872–1873 when he turned fourteen. The first trip was troubled by Theodore's near-constant bouts of headaches, asthma, and homesickness. Later, in his memoirs, Roosevelt himself would note that this trip was colored by his immature "chauvinism and contempt" toward Europe, while the second trip reflected growing maturity, a sense of "discernment and appreciation," and a love of Germany that was cultivated during a long stay with a German family in Dresden. Roosevelt's direct boyhood contact with Europe was certainly important in the development of his ideas, both about America and the world. Much of the pride and prejudice Roosevelt would display resulted directly from his New York upbringing.

Despite the difference in Roosevelt's age at the time of the two trips, the same love-hate relationship to Europe is reflected in his journal entries for both trips. Roosevelt's self-described chauvinism was decidedly pro-American. He appreciated the art, history, and landscapes of England, France, Switzerland, Italy, and Germany, but he continually decried the poverty, decrepitude, and dishonesty of Europe, as well as of some very European things, such as the Pope and Roman Catholicism. Such attitudes, coming from any upper-class, native-stock young man from Manhattan, were not surprising.

For all of his appreciation of European art and scenery, Roosevelt had only disdain for the continent's poverty and filth. This was ironic, as New York's lower wards were notorious for their abject poverty and mountains of garbage. During his childhood in New York, aside from trips with his father to the Newsboys' Lodging House, located at the corner of Fulton and Nassau Streets, Roosevelt had been largely shielded from such sights. Taking place before Roosevelt had similar contact with New York's "other half" in the 1880s, the European trips probably afforded him his first close observations of real poverty. In the journal for his second trip, he noted the filthy streets of Bonn and the "queer inhabitants" of Italy, where "everybody combines to cheat you." His father was always there, acting like the perfect ugly American. In a particularly revolting scene, Theodore Roosevelt Sr., one of the great philanthropists of New York, taunts and abuses Italian beggars. While his children watched, the father bought small cakes and tossed them into the beggars' open mouths or at the feet of the poor women and children—"like chickens," as young Theodore observed. "For a 'Coup de Grace' we threw a lot of them in a place and a writhing heap of human beings," Roosevelt recounted. "We made the crowds that we gave the cakes to give three cheers for U.S.A. before we gave them cakes."

In the summer of 1873, Theodore and Elliott lived with the Minckwitz family of Dresden, where they were immersed in German language and culture. This is when Roosevelt began a love affair with all things German that would last until the Great War. The choice of Germany, and Dresden in particular, was no accident. In the nineteenth century, German was the language of literature, history, and science. In New York, the German people were considered sober, cultured, and industrious. With unification having taken place only two years before, the German Empire was an important European power. Finally, while Berlin was the political capital of the new country, Dresden was the German capital of art, music, science, and education.

A beautiful city often compared to Florence, Dresden boasted some of Europe's best galleries, museums, and libraries. In Dresden, Theodore Roosevelt Sr. had found a city that would provide his children with all the intellectual stimulation they could possibly need.

But, just as Roosevelt's trips through Italy confirmed previously formed prejudices about Catholics and Italians, his long stay in Dresden reinforced his ideas about Germans. By the time of his German sojourn, New York's Kleindeutschland comprised about four hundred blocks of the city, concentrated in the Tenth, Eleventh, Thirteenth, and Seventeenth Wards in Lower Manhattan. Germans made up over 64 percent of the population of these four wards, which contained approximately half of the city's Germans. Moreover, Roosevelt's own home was only a few blocks from the northern border of Kleindeutschland, making Germans a familiar sight for the young Dutch-descended Knickerbocker. By the 1870s, Germans were becoming ubiquitous in city life, business, and politics. Between 1860 and 1890, the German American population of the city rose from 15 percent of the total population to 28 percent. New York would soon become the third largest German-speaking city in the world after Berlin and Vienna.

As a boy growing up in mid-nineteenth-century New York, the young Theodore did not have to travel to Europe to develop profound ideas about that continent, its people, and its religions. The city had shaped Roosevelt's worldview even before he departed for Europe. Young Theodore returned from Europe more cosmopolitan and worldly, and more in tune with the immense demographic changes about to occur in his city. And just as Theodore took a ship west across the Atlantic back to New York City, millions of Europeans were getting ready to do the same.

Upon returning from Europe, fourteen-year-old Theodore began preparing for entrance into college. In Dresden, the Roosevelt boys had encountered one of the most accomplished European cities of the time in terms of art, science, and education. The same could not yet be said of New York. If Dresden appeared as a sort of European Athens, the only comparison in the United States was Boston. And Boston meant Harvard.

TWO

"It's Roosevelt from New York"
Roosevelt at Harvard

THEODORE ROOSEVELT WOULD recall his time at Harvard with little enthusiasm. "I thoroughly enjoyed Harvard," he later wrote in his memoirs, "and I am sure it did me good, but only in the general effect, for there was very little in my actual studies which helped me in after life." This less-than-enthusiastic assessment of Harvard's academic usefulness may have resulted from the fact that Roosevelt entered Harvard with the ambition of becoming a natural scientist. His courses were dominated by natural history and languages. Of his twenty-nine classes, Roosevelt took six in natural history and nine in languages, including German, Italian, French, Latin, and Greek. His classes did reflect the abiding interest in natural history that would lead to his contributions to the cause of conservation, but they give no insight into his future political career, other than one class on Anglo-American constitutional history and one on political economy. For Harvard's influence on the young Roosevelt, one must look beyond the classroom, not only to the university's boxing ring and social clubs, but also to the parlors of the Boston Brahmin merchant princes.

If there was one experience in Roosevelt's life that threatened to sever his New York roots, it was not his time in the West. Nor was it the long periods of his political career that he spent posted in Washington, DC. Instead, it was Roosevelt's four years as a Harvard undergraduate that gravely challenged his New York connections. While many Roosevelt biographers have closely examined Harvard as it existed under its reforming president Charles Eliot, few have looked at the way in which Harvard was inextricably entwined with a small group of leading Boston families. Theodore Roosevelt's four years at Harvard were also four years spent in Boston and its environs.

Harvard's close identification with Boston and its small, closed, interrelated upper class begs the question why Roosevelt's father decided to send his namesake there. The scions of New York's top families, if they attended college at all, usually went closer to home, to Columbia, Yale, or Princeton. Neither Theodore Roosevelt Sr. nor any of his brothers attended college. Yet, soon after the family's return from Europe, the decision was made. By the winter of 1873, when Roosevelt was still only fourteen, he began receiving tutoring from Harvard graduate Arthur Cutler with the single goal of passing the university admission exams. Certainly President Eliot's reputation as a reformer had spread to Manhattan. In early 1874, the *New York Times* was already commenting on the controversial system of "electives" instituted by Eliot, which allowed students to choose courses that simply interested them, such as botany and history. Probably Roosevelt's father agreed with the paper's conclusion "that in a period and country where material interests are all-powerful, those studies should be most encouraged by a university . . . which tend to the general elevation and refinement of and ennobling of the whole man." Botany and history might not seem to prepare America's top young men for careers in law, medicine, or business, but that was the point. The United States needed more than mere specialists. The country also needed men who could think.

The elective system emphasized educating the individual student, rather than imposing a one-size-fits-all curriculum. Eliot rejected the idea that schools should be merely factories of homogeneity. For the hidebound traditionalists on Harvard's Board of Overseers, such "liberal" thinking was hard to tolerate. Education, Eliot wrote in *Harper's*, should cultivate each student's special skills: "We Americans are so used to weighing multitudes and being ruled by majorities that we are apt to underrate the potential influence of individuals." This seemed to reflect Roosevelt Sr.'s attitude toward raising his own children by cultivating their individuality and responding to each child's unique needs. His eldest son's unique talent clearly lay with the natural sciences, and under Louis Agassiz, Harvard had become the leading university in the field.

Eliot also placed an emphasis on athletics. "There is an aristocracy to which the sons of Harvard have belonged," Eliot declared in his inaugural address, "and, let us hope, will ever aspire to belong—the aristocracy which excels in manly sports." Himself part of that aristocracy, Eliot took a gentleman's view of the proper place of athletics in campus life. Having rowed Harvard crew while a tutor at the college, the twenty-four-year-old Eliot wrote his fiancée that he cared little for winning. Rowing was neither his profession nor his love: "It is recreation, fun, and health." Later, as college president, Eliot urged students to make sports "one of the incidental pleasures" of their time at Harvard. While at Harvard, Roosevelt kept with him a letter his father wrote in which he warned him, "Take care of your morals first, your health next and finally your studies." The younger Roosevelt would always endeavor to follow this advice, and threw himself with vigor into wrestling and boxing.

Harvard was more than just the university and the town of Cambridge. In Gilded Age America, Harvard meant Boston. The city of Boston and its ruling class must have figured prominently in the Roosevelts' decision that Theodore should attend Harvard. One reason was probably Boston's reputation as the "Athens of America," as *North American Review* founder William Tudor put it. For its small size, Boston boasted an enormous array of authors, poets, historians, artists, and scientists. Roosevelt's father perhaps viewed Boston as he regarded Dresden in Germany, not as the political or financial capital of the country, but as the cultural capital. Just as the European Grand Tours were meant to broaden and enrich his children's view of the world, sending his son to Boston was meant to make Theodore a refined and cultured gentleman. Again, President Eliot: "The country suffers when the rich are ignorant and unrefined. Inherited wealth is an unmitigated curse when divorced from culture." No doubt the elder Theodore Roosevelt agreed.

Still, Harvard's close association with Boston and its ruling families made it an unusual choice for most New York families. Yet the very things that might have put off most New Yorkers probably attracted Theodore Roosevelt Sr. As the son of Cornelius Van Schaack Roosevelt and a partner in the Roosevelt and Son conglomerate, Theodore Sr.'s wealth placed him on the same financial and professional footing as Boston's merchant class. Unlike their New York counterparts, however, the Boston Brahmins had the reputation of being morally rigid, ever on guard against their accumulation of wealth leading to a decline in Christian values. Samuel Eliot, Charles Eliot's grandfather, cautioned his son to pursue only those paths in life "that will best conduce to the establishment of your character as a gentleman, a man of honour, the moralist, and the Christian." How similar to Roosevelt Sr.'s advice to his own son upon his departure for Harvard: "Take care of your morals first." For a Harvard undergraduate, this meant more than just abstaining from alcohol and sex. In an increasingly materialistic world, men such as Eliot and Roosevelt also feared losing their sons to avarice and excess. More than one Boston Brahmin family had watched its young men get sucked into the immoral maw of Gotham, never to return.

As President Eliot had noted, culture and refinement should accompany wealth. Indeed, culture served as a balm and buffer to a life spent pursuing wealth. The Boston Brahmin families reflected this notion, with many of their sons, like President Eliot, dedicating themselves to a life of letters. Culture also provided an avenue for Boston's elite to serve the community. Eliot's cousin Samuel, a professor of history and political science, in both age and philanthropic endeavors was almost a Boston equivalent of Theodore Roosevelt Sr. Samuel Eliot was active as a director and trustee for Boston's Museum of Fine Arts and the Boston Athenaeum, one of America's largest libraries. Ralph Waldo Emerson believed that by patronizing culture, the Boston Brahmins were building a city that would "lead the civilization of North America," much as Renaissance Florence did for Italy. Although Thomas Perkins began as a slave trader and opium smuggler, by midcentury, having invested in a host of New England companies, he was a leading Boston philanthropist who helped found Massachusetts General Hospital. "All history and all experience show," his eulogist proclaimed in 1854, "that literature, science, art, all that ennobles and refines humanity, are intimately connected with the prosperity of commerce." Allowing the wealthy to become patrons of the arts, commerce might serve culture, but the Boston Brahmins also believed that culture served commerce. In a continuous cycle, prosperity depended upon those things—literature, science, art—that wealth could foster.

Like Theodore Roosevelt Sr., the Boston Brahmins had a keen sense of noblesse oblige. Wealth and status, they believed, conferred upon them an obligation to help those less fortunate in their communities. For both Theodore Roosevelt Sr. and the Boston families, religion underpinned these notions of charity. To follow in Jesus's footsteps as portrayed in the Gospel of Luke, a man must serve his neighbor and tend to the poor and needy. In this sense, Boston far outpaced New York City. In Boston, charities had flourished in the first half of the nineteenth century. In 1830, the city had only 26 incorporated charities; only twenty years later, it boasted nearly 160. Brahmin money poured into the city's philanthropic societies. Between 1828 and 1852, Amos Lawrence, a prominent textile merchant, gave away an astonishing $639,000. Thomas Perkins gave his mansion to the Massachusetts Asylum for the Blind, which was then renamed the "Perkins School" in his honor (and still exists today). Charles Eliot's cousin Samuel was a director and trustee of the Massachusetts School for the Feeble-Minded. In all their good works, the parents of Roosevelt's friends and classmates—who included a Bacon and an Otis, a Cabot and a Choate, a Quincy and an Adams, a Saltonstall and a Weld, a Thorndike and a Peabody—would provide a continuing example of, and education in, the responsibilities of wealth and privilege.

As religion helped establish charity, so charity helped foster reform. Always at the intellectual forefront of Americans, Bostonians had long led the rest of the country in reform ideas. In antebellum America this meant finding in Boston the most rabid abolitionists. But the Civil War did not do away with the reforming spirit. With the rapid immigration, industrialization, and urbanization of the Gilded Age, Boston's reformers had plenty to do. Far from eschewing politics as a rough game, the Brahmins took the reins of city political power. Certainly as the biggest taxpayers and property owners they had the most to lose from corrupt city management, working-class violence, or inefficient police and fire departments. But, as with abolitionism, the Boston elite also sought reform at the highest levels of American government. By Theodore Roosevelt's time, Boston had become the capital of the good-government and civil-service reform movements. In an era when US senators and congressmen sat on corporate boards, earning thousands of dollars in "fees," and political machines ran cities and entire states, the Boston Brahmins would have none of it. By 1881, they had helped found the National Civil Service Reform League, backed by the quintessential Boston intellectual journal *The North American Review*. In New York, *Harper's* was Gotham's answer to the *Review*, and a belated one at that. *The North American Review* began publishing in 1815, whereas the first issue of *Harper's New Monthly Magazine* appeared only in 1850. Once again, Boston provided the young Theodore with examples of civic-mindedness that appealed to his father, who himself was about to be caught up in an ugly fight with New York machine politicians that helped usher in the civil-service reform movement.

Like the Boston elite, Theodore Roosevelt Sr. was a reformer. He had joined with other men, such as Joseph Choate and John Jay—top New York lawyers—and J. Pierpont Morgan—head of America's most powerful banking house—to form the Republican Reform Club, an early movement to press for good municipal government. In the summer of 1876, Roosevelt traveled to the Republican National Convention in Cincinnati to secure the nomination of reform candidates to the national ticket in lieu of the corrupt James G. Blaine of Maine. The eventual nomination of Rutherford B. Hayes marked something of a triumph for the reform forces, especially as the New York delegation initially supported the state party boss, US Senator Roscoe Conkling. After the election, President Hayes would take direct aim at Conkling's power in New York. The new president ordered an investigation of one of the richest plums in Conkling's basket, the New York Custom House, headed by Conkling lieutenant Chester A. Arthur, who held the official title "collector of customs." Loyal Republicans had long been rewarded with choice appointments in the custom house, which in turn became a powerful political base for the machine. As it was a federal institution, Hayes ordered all political activity at the custom house to cease.

The president was not finished. Against the New York boss's wishes, Hayes nominated Theodore Roosevelt Sr. to replace Chester Arthur. This was tantamount to a declaration of war by the president on the New York Republican machine. The elder Roosevelt was caught in the crossfire. Hayes's efforts were complicated by the fact that Roosevelt's appointment had to be approved by the Senate's Committee on Commerce—a committee chaired by Conkling. Roosevelt's rejection by the committee was inevitable. Conkling would score a victory against the president and strike a blow against the New York and Boston reformers.

For Theodore Roosevelt Sr., then, Harvard provided the perfect environment in which to educate his namesake. There he would rub elbows with the sons of the Boston elite and ingest their ideas on morality, culture, patronage, charity, and reform. This was far from evident in September 1876, however, as young Theodore departed for Cambridge. In New York he left behind not only his family, but also a serious love interest: Edith Kermit Carow, a childhood friend who had become something much more. Roosevelt would begin his four years at Harvard a homesick, awkward, and solitary youth, spending far too much time alone in pursuit of specimens for his natural science collection, and mooning over Edith back in New York. At first, he would not quite fit in among this different type of American elite, almost inbred in its exclusion of outsiders. This was the grim fate facing seventeen-year-old Theodore as he stepped off the night boat from New York.

To A NEW YORKER, Cambridge, Massachusetts, in 1876 appeared little more than a village. Three miles from Boston, Harvard Square was almost somnolent, the absolute quiet of the area disturbed only by the infrequent bells of the horse-drawn carriages. "Once in a while," a contemporary observer wrote, "its dust is stirred by some mortuary procession of cattle on their way to the abattoirs." The university and its buildings on their surrounding twenty-two acres dominated the town, just as the massive tower on the new Memorial Hall dominated the skyline. Residents and students were quick to point out to visitors the old wooden Wadsworth House, former home to university presidents, and to note, "George Washington slept here." When in 1866 British writer Sir Charles Dilke visited Cambridge, he commented on the town's hushed atmosphere. "Even the English Cambridge has a breathing street or two, and a weekly market-day," Dilke observed, "while Cambridge in New England is one great academic grove, buried in a philosophic calm which our universities can not rival." On Sundays, the streets were even more empty than usual, as most of the Harvard men went into Boston to spend the Sabbath with their families. Roosevelt would usually spend these days teaching a Sunday school class, writing to his family, and collecting specimens of birds and toads.

At Harvard he fell in with some of the Boston crowd, joining a dining club for meals rather than partaking of the "uneatable" food in the student commons. In addition to throwing himself into his studies—all required classes the freshman year, including Greek and Latin—he began boxing and wrestling. Although Roosevelt was frequently knocked down, he undertook these sports as a way to continue to "make" his body, as his father had once instructed his weak son. Outside the boxing ring, Roosevelt became close friends with Henry Davis Minot—"Harry" or "Hal"—who shared his passion for nature and had even published a small book at age seventeen on *The Land and Game Birds of New England*. Although busy, Roosevelt felt strongly the pull of friends and family in New York. He wrote letters home all the time and made sure to return for Thanksgiving and Christmas. During the first winter break at the end of 1876, he began a tradition of hosting some of his Boston chums in Manhattan. For Roosevelt, still something of an outsider in Boston, this must have proved a particularly enjoyable experience. Now Roosevelt could play guide in America's greatest city, showing Bostonians the towers of the Brooklyn Bridge and taking them sleighing in Central Park. He could introduce them to his father, one of the city's great citizens, and to his lovely southern belle mother. He could even show off his love interest in New York, introducing his classmates to Edith Carow. These New York holiday gatherings would grow ever larger and longer, and would eventually include his future Boston Brahmin bride.

Not only did Roosevelt frequently visit New York; New York frequently visited him. Shortly before his final exams in the spring of 1877, a large party of New Yorkers spent several days with him in Cambridge. Much to his delight, his entire family, minus his mother, made the trip. Cousin Maud Elliott, with whom he had spent much time in Dresden, also came along. While always very proud to show off his father and siblings to his Harvard friends, Roosevelt was probably most pleased with the visit of the only one who was not a family member. The very fact that Edith Carow made the trip showed that the two were very much an item. Surely, their families and friends back in New York expected them someday to marry. The party's return to New York three days later left Roosevelt depressed. Memories of "pretty Edith," however, seemed to buoy him. "I do'n't [*sic*] think I ever saw Edith looking prettier," Roosevelt wrote his younger sister, Corinne, after the visit. He made a point of concluding the letter, "When you write to Edith tell her I enjoyed *her* visit *very* much indeed." Clearly Edith had no cause for worry that a Boston belle would snatch Theodore away from her—just yet.

In fact, Roosevelt's first year at Harvard seemed to be an almost entirely male affair, without mention of a single other woman's name either in his letters or in his diary. Roosevelt had spent the year getting to know his Boston classmates and their families. Eventually, he would be invited into their homes as almost another son. Through them Roosevelt would meet a tantalizing array of young ladies from the very best New England families. By the summer of 1877, however, that was still in the future as Theodore and his friend Hal Minot departed for a birding trip to the Adirondacks.

Long before he went west, Roosevelt fed his love of nature as a young New York gentleman should, either out on Long Island or upstate in the Adirondacks. When he and Hal arrived at St. Regis Lake, they stayed in the fashionable Paul Smith's Hotel. This was hardly roughing it. Although the hotel intentionally maintained a primitive facility—including no indoor bathrooms—it was still a favorite of the members of the nineteenth-century elite coming from New York or

New England to have a "real" wilderness experience. Future presidents Grover Cleveland and Calvin Coolidge would also stay at the hotel before it burned to the ground in 1930. The hotel provided outdoor guides for its guests, and it would eventually boast a casino, a bowling alley, and a direct wire to the New York Stock Exchange. This was wilderness for the wealthy, and it foreshadowed the elegant resorts that would soon pop up all over the American West.

The young men stayed in the mountains for about three weeks, including a week camping out. On July 5, Roosevelt shot his first deer, "a buck." He and Hal emerged from the woods a few days later with only a bit of bread and tea left.

Roosevelt returned to Oyster Bay to spend the rest of the summer there before returning to Harvard in late September. That fall, things seemed to come more easily to Roosevelt, who turned nineteen on October 27. He had a set of friends with whom he socialized, and he spent an increasing amount of time staying in the homes of the Welds and Saltonstalls. He threw himself into boxing and wrestling. Roosevelt also began taking two elective courses in natural history, one in botany and one in zoology with William James. He was having a grand time. In the past year, the young man had made a comfortable world for himself in Cambridge and Boston. Events in New York were about to bring that safe and secure world to an end.

Although Roosevelt claimed never to have seen the reclusive Charles Eliot during his time at Harvard, he was probably aware that the college president was scheduled to talk at the opening of the American Museum of Natural History just before Christmas. After all, Roosevelt's father was one of the prime movers behind the museum's founding. The museum's charter had been approved in 1869 in the parlor of the brownstone where the younger Theodore was born. President Grant had laid the cornerstone in June 1874. Now, on December 22, 1877, President Hayes officially opened the museum, while the august audience listened to speeches by the museum president, Robert Stuart, and the Harvard president, Eliot. The dignitaries on the platform with the speakers included Joseph Choate, Congressman Abram Hewitt, and the presidents of Columbia and Yale. Eliot wowed the audience with a speech that began by asking, "In whose honor is this brilliant audience assembled? Whose palace is this? What divinity is worshiped here?" As eighty-six-year-old Peter Cooper—the great inventor and builder of America's first steam engine—put his hand to his ear to catch Eliot's words, Harvard's president answered, "The power is the beneficent power of Natural Science." No doubt Theodore Roosevelt Sr. would have enjoyed the speech and made a point of congratulating Eliot. But the elder Theodore Roosevelt was not there; he lay dying from a painful tumor of the bowel.

Roosevelt Sr.'s illness came hard on the heels of his failed nomination for the custom-house position. On December 3, Conkling had prevented Roosevelt's confirmation from coming to a vote in the Senate, and the issue died. Young Theodore was home for Thanksgiving at the time, and he returned to Cambridge the next day. A few days later, he wrote his father, "I am afraid that Conkling has won the day," his earliest reference to the Republican machine of New York. He added that he had read "quite a sensible editorial on it in the Times of yesterday." Perhaps this was the son trying to impress his father. Yet the *Times* editorial was a striking critique of President Hayes's mismanagement of the collectorship issue. While praising the elder Roosevelt and generally sympathetic with Hayes's efforts at reform, the paper took issue with the president's handling of the matter. By provoking a conflict with Senator Conkling and his Republican followers, the president had simply made the battle one of factions within his own party, rather than a movement for real reform. In order to win, Hayes would need support from Democrats who would eagerly seize the chance to divide and conquer. "He could have appeared before the Senate," the paper said, "not as dividing the Republican Party by Democratic aid, not as setting up one clique in the Republican Party against another, but as presenting the fruits of a candid and rational attempt at a reform of the system of civil service."

That sentence encapsulated ideas that would guide Roosevelt throughout much of his political career. He could see through the articles in the *Times* and the *New York Tribune* that civil service reform was becoming a prominent topic within the Republican Party, and that his father stood alongside some of the great men of New York in his advocacy of it. Though he would one day be an independent reformer within the Republican Party, until 1912 Roosevelt never sought to divide the party against itself—especially if doing so would mean a Democratic win. In the 1880s and 1890s, Roosevelt would always seek to work for—and within—a united Republican Party, casting aspersions on those Republican Mugwumps who would side with Democrats against their own party.

What Roosevelt did not know, as he penned his letters from Cambridge in that last month of 1877, was that for several weeks his father had suffered severe intestinal pains. As Christmas approached, Roosevelt expressed only mild concern. Not knowing of the cancer that was at that moment killing their forty-six-year-old father, he told his sister Anna he thought their father was merely overworked and suffering from exhaustion. Only on December 21 did the family consider Theodore Roosevelt Sr.'s health enough of a concern to summon his son back from Harvard. The older Roosevelt's health improved over the holidays, though, allowing Theodore to step out and see friends in New York. On New Year's Day, he made about twenty calls, taking particular note of the young ladies he visited, including Edith Carow.

With his father seemingly better, Roosevelt returned to Cambridge a couple of days later. Unlike the previous year, now his diary entries chronicled his attendance of dance classes, parties, and evenings at the theater. Roosevelt took note of the ladies with whom he spent time, as well as the high scores he received on midyear exams. As February began, he was having a swell time. Then, on February 9, Theodore Roosevelt Sr. died.

The son plunged into a deep depression that would not lift for months. Until then, Roosevelt's diary entries had been short and perfunctory: "Party in the evening. Went with the Hoopers." Now he poured his grief into the diary, penning long, emotional entries. From the time he started observing ants, mice, and birds as a small child, Roosevelt had always had the gift of vivid description. His diary entries regarding his deceased father reflect this. They are at once rich and bitter, full of adjectives and similes describing his most intimate feelings. "He has just been buried," Roosevelt began a long entry on February 12. "I should never forget these terrible three days; the hideous suspense of the ride on; the dull, inert sorrow during which I felt as if I had been stunned, or as if part of my life had been taken away; and the two moments of sharp, bitter agony, when I kissed the dear, dead face and realized he would never again on this earth speak to me or greet me with his loving smile, and then when I heard the sound of the first clod dropping on the coffin holding the one I loved dearest on earth." Roosevelt's account of his grief is so descriptive and detailed—"dull, inert sorrow"—it almost reads like literature. "He looked so calm and sweet," Roosevelt continued, in an entry that filled several pages of the diary. "I feel that if it were not the certainty, that as he himself has so often said, 'he is not dead, but gone before,' I should almost perish. With the help of my God I will try to lead such a life as he would have wished."

Upon the elder Theodore Roosevelt's death, church bells pealed throughout New York City, and the Union League Club lowered its flag to half-mast. Special meetings of the plate-glass importers and the trustees of the American Museum of Natural History passed resolutions in honor of Roosevelt: businessman, patron, and philanthropist. As visitors paid their respects to the family at No. 6 West 57th Street— where the family had moved after their second European tour—all praised the late Roosevelt effusively. This may have led his son to quote in his diary a passage from Job: "Truly 'he was eyes to the blind, feet to the lame, and a father to the poor.'" Published eulogies referred to Roosevelt as "the upright merchant, the honorable gentleman, and the faithful friend," and noted his enormous charitable contributions. Indeed, the loss of Theodore Roosevelt Sr. made some in the city wonder why New York possessed so few men like him. Why, for instance, did Boston boast so many more patrons of the arts, sciences, and charities than New York? About a week after Roosevelt's death, the *Times* posed this question to its readers in an editorial. "It is well known," the paper observed, "that the number of gentlemen of prominence on whom any important enterprise of charity, philanthropy, art, or science, in this City, can depend is extremely small. Not more than twenty men head most of the really useful public efforts in New York." Referring to Roosevelt's recent death, the *Times* continued, "It is for this reason that the fall of one makes such a gap in the ranks and is so widely felt."

In what might have been a sentence written for the younger Theodore Roosevelt, the *Times* placed the blame upon the scions of

New York's elite. The sons of the wealthy were not inculcated with a sense of responsibility and obligation. In England, in contrast, a young man of rank and fortune must endeavor to preserve the honor of the family name and discharge the duties of his rank. Boston had followed this English pattern. "A similar class in this country have surrounded Harvard College with the fruits of their wealth and intelligent generosity," the editorial observed, "and crowded Boston with institutions of mercy."

As the grieving young Theodore Roosevelt scoured the papers for praise of his late father, he likely read the *Times* editorial and interpreted it as damning the sons of New York's wealthy for their lack of civic responsibility. No doubt the elder Roosevelt would have agreed, as he had attempted to invest in his children that very sense of obligation. He had taken his children with him to the Newsboys' Lodging House and the Orthopedic Hospital to impress upon them the responsibility of their favored position. In the days that followed his father's death, Theodore Roosevelt now noted that those who had received such largesse from the elder Roosevelt paid their respects to the family. "He was wise and good in public as in private life," Roosevelt wrote in his diary. "He was a great personal worker among the poor." His father's enormous legacy was pressed upon Roosevelt time and time again in the weeks and months that followed.

In calling for the members of New York's elite to devote themselves to civic duty, the *Times* editorial did not stop at the arts and sciences, or even the charities. By the 1870s, "civic responsibility" increasingly meant taking an interest in government. "The practical exclusion in this City of the rich from politics," the paper noted, "no doubt tends to separate them from the public enterprises. Such men as Mr. Roosevelt and his dozen or more compeers, ought to, and in most other communities would, have been our political administrators and leaders." Here was the *Times*, in the wake of the Tweed Ring scandal that stole millions from city coffers, and even Theodore Roosevelt Sr.'s own failed bid for the collectorship, taking the idea of noblesse oblige a step further to include politics and government. When his son commented on the elder Roosevelt's good work in public life, he possibly meant more than just as a patron of charities and museums: the senior Roosevelt had been involved in Republican matters, too, not only in the Reform Club, but also as commissioner of the State Board of Charities. His father's work with the party seemed to cause Roosevelt to agonize over his preferred vocation as a natural scientist. "Looking back at his life," Roosevelt wrote a month after his father died, "it seems as if mine must be such a weak useless one in comparison. I should like to be a scientist: oh, how I shall miss his sweet, sympathetic advice!" His father's premature death had not only unsettled Roosevelt's life, but also made him worry for the future.

Theodore Roosevelt Sr. had been the dominant person in Roosevelt's life until his death during his son's sophomore year at Harvard. Even after leaving home, Roosevelt followed his father's advice and his example, and longed for time in his presence. Now his father's death and legacy underscored the influence he had always had on Roosevelt's life, as the young man ached with grief and looked to the future. The collectorship episode had given Roosevelt a crash course in New York politics and in the reform and machine factions within the Republican Party. His father's death had highlighted the great man's stature in the city, as all New Yorkers praised his many civic and charitable contributions. Roosevelt read in the New York papers how Boston led other American cities in practicing noblesse oblige, a fact Roosevelt was in an ideal position to witness firsthand. And he was now, for the first time, forced to contemplate his future as the head of the family and as his father's namesake. Even after his death, Theodore Roosevelt Sr. loomed large in his son's life.

ROOSEVELT RETURNED TO Cambridge at the end of February to see to his midyear exams. His loss had given him another way to measure his friends, and he was touched by the thoughtfulness of Hal Minot, Harry Shaw, and his professors. He began spending more time with Dick Saltonstall out at his home in Chestnut Hill, and there he met Saltonstall's cousin, the central figure of the next six years of his life: Alice Hathaway Lee. Despite his awkward start at Harvard, Roosevelt eventually was welcomed almost as another son into the homes of the top Boston Brahmin families. He cemented friendships that would prove key to his political career and presidency. And he would marry, if only briefly, into one of the most prominent Boston banking families, the Lees.

So began a relationship with Boston and its ruling class that would provide friendships and political alliances to Roosevelt for the rest of his life. Although he might have comfortably stayed in Boston, New York drew him back home, as it would so many times in his life. Arguably, his wife was not the most important thing he brought back with him. By absorbing the Boston Brahmin sense of noblesse oblige, the idea that privilege conferred duty and civic service, Roosevelt brought to New York the moral and intellectual underpinnings of his life and career in the city. Such notions not only helped shape Roosevelt. They helped transform New York.

THREE

"The Dirtiest City in the Universe"
1881: A Year in New York

HENRY ADAMS, the great-grandson of President John Adams, taught briefly at Harvard just before Roosevelt enrolled in 1876. Adams considered his time there a failure. The only part he thought a success were the students. "He found them excellent company," Adams wrote in his memoirs, written in the third person. "They were quick to respond; plastic to mould; and incapable of fatigue."

Certainly Roosevelt seemed incapable of fatigue, as his diary noted an increasing number of activities, clubs, and social commitments in his last two years at Harvard. Just before his twenty-first birthday, observing that he had his "hands altogether too full" of social and academic obligations, he listed his club offices, including librarian of the Porcellian Club, secretary of the Hasty Pudding Club, vice president of the Natural History Society, and editor of the *Harvard Advocate*. By the time he turned twenty-one, he was also contemplating the future. "I am thinking pretty seriously as to what I shall do when I leave College," he wrote as the summer of 1879 came to a close and he readied to begin his final year at Harvard. "I shall probably either pursue a scientific course, or else study law, preparatory to going into public life." Here was the

41

first indication that Roosevelt envisioned for himself a career in politics and government. Such a career could not be pursued in Boston. As Roosevelt envisioned life after college, he saw himself in New York.

Roosevelt did not plan on living that life alone. By the time he began his final year at Harvard, he had already asked Alice Lee to marry him. Being only seventeen at the time, she turned him down. Roosevelt did not seem heartbroken. Although frequent mentions of "pretty Alice" dominated his diary, other young women also caught his eye and his fancy. For a time he courted Nana Rotch, whom he found as sweet and pretty as Alice. He spent one afternoon at her house teaching her the five-step waltz, a midcentury dance requiring much handholding and touching. By the spring of 1879, he was calling on Elizabeth "Bessie" Whitney: "We are *very* intimate now," he wrote. Returning to Oyster Bay that summer, he called frequently on nearby Emily Swan, whom he found attractive and charming. He even saw Edith Carow when he was in New York, calling her "the most cultivated, best read girl." And when he threw a party at the Porc for Bamie and Corinne visiting from New York, he seated Bessie Hooper, sister of classmate William, in the place of honor on his right, with Alice Lee relegated to the second spot on his left. By Thanksgiving of his senior year, then, his choice of mate still seemed unclear.

Christmas in New York may have settled things for Roosevelt. Before the holiday, he was already noting that his friends were becoming engaged to girls who were part of their Boston circle. The day after Christmas, he dedicated only an abrupt entry to his old New York flame: "Took lunch with Edith." Gone were the flattering descriptions of Edith, or any acknowledgment that she was still one of his special *Freundinnen*. That same evening, a party from Boston arrived to spend the holiday week with the Roosevelts. For Theodore, Alice was the star of the show. They went for long walks and buggy rides. On New Year's Eve, as Roosevelt recounted, "We had a small party, and danced the old year out—and drank the new year in." With pretty Alice always at his side, champagne was not the only thing making Roosevelt light-headed.

Just as Edith's trip to Cambridge to visit Roosevelt had earlier indicated the strength of their romantic connection, now Alice's trip to spend a week with the Roosevelts in New York pointed toward a single outcome. Back at Harvard on January 24, Roosevelt indulged in "a little spree" at the Porcellian, and this liquid courage made him determined to get a clear answer from his prevaricating paramour. "After much pleading my own sweet, pretty darling consented to be my wife," Roosevelt wrote in his diary. "Oh, how bewitchingly pretty she looked!" Roosevelt headed to New York to tell the family and buy a diamond engagement ring. With the end of college on the horizon, he readied to make a man's life for himself, complete with wife and career. "I shall study law next year," he wrote, "and work hard for my own little wife." After four years at Harvard and Boston, New York beckoned.

During his final semester at Harvard, Roosevelt spent as much time as he could with Alice out in Chestnut Hill. Having fulfilled most of his required classes by the end of his junior year, Roosevelt took only five classes his senior year, four of them electives. He received honor grades in four of the classes, enough for Phi Beta Kappa, but not enough to make him a candidate for honors upon graduation. It is unlikely Roosevelt cared. In many diary entries the soon-to-be-alumnus indicated his complete satisfaction with his four years at Harvard. He had spent money lavishly on travel, gifts for his girlfriends, socializing, and keeping his own horse and cart in Cambridge. He had belonged to a number of the most prominent clubs, where he had made a number of close friends. Finally, as he noted, "above everything else put together—I have won the sweetest of girls for my wife. No man ever had so pleasant a college course." After graduating on June 30, 1880, Roosevelt returned to Oyster Bay with Alice for a short stay with the family. This was followed by a trip to Bar Harbor, Maine, and a hunting trip out west with his brother Elliott—a true "stag" party for the bachelors.

There is little evidence that Roosevelt was very enamored of the West during this first visit. True, he was sick during much of it and longed daily for his sweet Alice. Moreover, the trip was marred by an almost-comical succession of misadventures. He broke both of his guns, was bitten by a snake, and was thrown from a wagon, landing on his head. Mostly, Roosevelt loved the hunting and the time spent with his brother. His journals of his trips to Europe and the

Adirondacks are full of vivid, detailed descriptions of the landscape, something almost completely lacking in the entries about this month-long trip out west. Apparently the West had yet to infect him the way it would only a couple of years later. Returning to New York, Roosevelt entered Columbia Law School on October 6. He also noted in his diary the windfall his love of Alice had brought New York jewelers: Roosevelt purchased a diamond crescent, a ruby bracelet, and a sapphire ring valued at an astonishing $2,500. After four years away from the city, Roosevelt slowly settled back into his family, work, and social life. He attended law classes, saw the New York cousins and uncles, and, two weeks before the wedding, dined with Edith. It was as if he had never left.

On October 27, 1880, Roosevelt's twenty-second birthday, he married Alice Hathaway Lee. For now the newlyweds would have to settle for a two-week "honeymoon" alone at Oyster Bay, full of long walks, carriage rides, tennis matches, and chilly trips in the rowboat. On Sunday, November 14, Roosevelt noted the continuing effort at building a life together in New York, a life that seemed to follow his father's model. Alice planned to join the Presbyterian Church. Roosevelt visited the Newsboys' Lodging House, and, as his father used to, delivered a feast to the boys on Thanksgiving. The couple decided to live with Mittie Roosevelt in the house on West 57th Street.

By returning to New York, Roosevelt was actively taking up his father's mantle, an effort that soon included public affairs. On November 18, he attended a meeting of the St. Andrews Society, where he had a long conversation with Whitelaw Reid, owner of the *Tribune*, and perhaps more importantly, a leading New York Republican. Theodore and Alice also threw themselves into the city's social season beginning that December. They attended every party and ball, and Roosevelt noted his particular fondness for Mrs. Astor, wife of William Waldorf Astor—the very wealthy only child of John Jacob Astor III and a member of the New York State Senate. Sweet, pretty, charming, gray-eyed, nineteen-year-old Alice Lee Roosevelt of the Boston Brahmin Lees was bred for such a life—and perhaps not much more. "I am not very fond of going out," Roosevelt said after a huge Saturday night reception at the Roosevelt home. "However, Alice is universally and greatly admired; and she seems to grow more beautiful day by day." She was the perfect wife for New York society.

After a Christmas trip to Chestnut Hill, the couple returned to New York on New Year's Day 1881, one of the coldest days on record. At eight o'clock in the morning, the thermometer had dipped down to six below zero. A fine sheen of ice made walking treacherous, and everywhere horses slipped and struggled for traction. On Manhattan's East Side and across in Brooklyn, people stopped to gape as big chunks of ice floated along the East River. The ice filled the ferry slips, causing the greatest delays for the Williamsburg Ferry that departed from Roosevelt Street on the New York side. Hard, granular snow pelted pedestrians like a sandstorm, and New York hospitals filled with cases of frostbitten ears and fingers. The cold sabotaged the elevated railway lines, freezing tracks and engines, so commuters wanting to get to work on time abandoned the city's modern transportation marvel for horse-drawn trolleys. By the time Alice and Theodore arrived at Grand Central Depot, however, the weather had warmed, and New Yorkers were out enjoying the New Year's holiday. Twenty-five thousand skaters took to the skating ponds in Central Park, while countless thousands more were kept home by New Year's Day social obligations.

After four years of shuttling between Oyster Bay and somnolent Cambridge, Theodore Roosevelt faced the many challenges of living in America's largest city. While he and Alice lived just off fashionable Fifth Avenue, the saloons of Sixth Avenue were only a block away. And although the newlyweds lived on 57th Street, near the southern border of Central Park, Roosevelt actually spent much of the day walking the length of Manhattan to get down to his law school classes on Great Jones Street. When in later years Roosevelt wrote about the contrast between the rich and poor in Gilded Age New York, he may have been envisioning this very walk. He would likely have started by heading south on Fifth Avenue, passing the grand chateaux still being built for New York's wealthiest. He would have been able to follow the progress on construction of William Vanderbilt's enormous mansion at 52nd Street before continuing past the newly built St. Patrick's Cathedral, railroad developer and robber baron Jay Gould's house, and the Waldorf-Astoria. After checking the time on the clock in front of the

Fifth Avenue Hotel at Madison Square, Roosevelt would likely have turned onto Broadway, which would have allowed him to cut southeast toward Union Square. This route would have brought him within only half a block of his old home on 20th Street, and past the city's principal dry-goods and department stores. His law classes were held just around the corner from his favorite store for men's clothes, Brooks Brothers.

Despite such a fashionable route, Roosevelt still walked past tenements and street vendors, recently arrived immigrants, and some of the city's 10,000 homeless children. He walked directly through the 18th Ward, with its 1,300 tenements housing more than 40,000 residents. He skirted the Bowery, which was already being transformed into one of the city's seediest neighborhoods. Third Avenue—earlier known for the cheap entertainment of nickel museums featuring mermaids and dwarfs—and its pedestrians were now showered with oil and hot coals from the new elevated line. Soon there would be little left along the street but saloons and brothels. Roosevelt must have also seen the mountains of garbage that plagued some neighborhoods. Trash barrels overflowed, and horse manure remained on the streets so long that it became crammed into the cracks between cobblestones. Simply walking the city streets was a chore. No doubt more than once, Roosevelt had to pick his way over a pile of trash, a dead horse, or a drunk sleeping it off. He might have even come across one of his own newsboys from the Lodging House hawking the daily paper. Living in New York meant facing the constant threats of fire, crime, and disease—such as the typhoid fever that would kill Mittie Roosevelt in only a few years. As typhoid is contracted by ingesting food or water tainted by the feces of an infected person, having access to clean water and food was a constant concern. Even for New York's wealthiest, the city was like one of the hot-blooded thoroughbred horses that elite New Yorkers loved: one day it afforded a display of luxury and wealth beyond compare, and the next day, it could turn on you.

For the Roosevelts, the New Year brought more balls and parties, but it also brought a subtle shift in Theodore's activities. "Political meeting," Roosevelt noted in his diary on February 14. Roosevelt began attending meetings of the Twenty-First District Republican Association, held in Morton Hall on 59th Street, not far from the Roosevelt home.

As in that same February 14 diary entry Roosevelt also wrote, "then Patriarch's Ball," it seems likely that he attended the meeting in tuxedo and tails. For New York in the 1880s, this was an unusual sight. Here was the twenty-two-year-old Roosevelt, fresh out of Harvard and scion to one of Manhattan's top families, rubbing elbows with machine politicians and ward "heelers" in a grimy club room that reeked of cigar smoke and was decorated with spittoons. As the *Times* had mentioned during the fight between Hayes and Conkling over the collectorship, the sons of New York's finest families as a rule steered clear of city politics. Roosevelt himself seemed conscious that he was doing something out of the ordinary. True, his father had been identified with reform Republicanism in the city. Yet, for the most part, his involvement had followed the model typical of upper-class advocacy of good government: forming an association and trying to pressure the Republican Party from the outside, with "moral force." Uncle Robert Roosevelt had been a prominent anti-Tammany Democratic congressman, but that had been during Theodore's youth. As Roosevelt became an adult, his uncle seemed to have little influence on him, even though Theodore undertook a kind of informal apprenticeship at his law office. Roosevelt appeared to have more contact with his other uncles, especially Uncle Jimmie, a prominent banker and trustee of Theodore Roosevelt Sr.'s estate. Even out on Long Island, Uncle Robert's home was well removed from those of the other Roosevelts.

Though his father and uncles hardly modeled the importance of taking an active role in New York politics, a social acquaintance may have offered some encouragement. In 1877, while Roosevelt was a sophomore at Harvard, William Waldorf Astor ran as a Republican for the New York State Assembly from the Eleventh District. With the backing of the party machine and its boss, Roscoe Conkling, Astor won easily in the "safe" district. By the time Roosevelt returned to New York in the fall of 1880, Astor had been elevated to the State Senate and was running for a seat in the US Congress. The Republican machine backed Astor, with boss Conkling and even former president Ulysses S. Grant addressing his campaign meetings. Astor's managers lavishly spread around the candidate's money, and they urged him to campaign among the hundreds of slum properties that his family owned. When Astor refused, the newspapers labeled him simply a millionaire playing at politics. Astor lost the election by only 165 votes out of over 23,000 cast.

Astor and Roosevelt's paths crossed often during the New York social season. Astor's Aunt Caroline presided over New York society and the Patriarch's Ball. Astor and Roosevelt both belonged to the Union Club. They sat in adjacent boxes at the opera. Both had studied law at Columbia. The Astors and Roosevelts had both supported the Metropolitan Museum of Art and such charities as the Children's Aid Society. After the Roosevelts hosted a large dinner party in December, Roosevelt noted his fondness for Astor in his diary. And there were even familial ties. The Astors, Delanos, and Roosevelts had all intermarried, and that very February of 1881, when Roosevelt began attending his meetings at Morton Hall, his sister Corinne accepted the proposal of Douglas Robinson, trustee to John Jacob Astor IV. Moreover, Morton Hall was also utilized by other Assembly and congressional district associations. Astor and Roosevelt very likely bumped into each other at Republican meetings there, perhaps both en route to the Patriarch's Ball and wearing matching black eveningwear and silk top hats. Astor proved to the younger Roosevelt that the wealthy son of a top New York family could enter city politics and work with the machine. He might also have shown Roosevelt the political pitfalls of avoiding contact with the city's working poor.

National politics may have played a role in Roosevelt's decision to enter New York politics as well. In 1880, independent Republican reformers, refusing to be bound to party leaders, had thrown their party's presidential nomination to dark-horse candidate James Garfield. However, they lamented the fact that New York machine man Chester Arthur had been nominated for vice president just to entice boss Roscoe Conkling into supporting the ticket. *Harper's Weekly* wryly observed that Arthur was selected "in accordance with the principle which governs the practice of nominating conventions—to placate the minority." One of Charles Eliot's cousins, Harvard professor Charles Eliot Norton, called Arthur's nomination "a miserable farce." Treasury Secretary and presidential hopeful John Sherman of Ohio had been responsible for firing Arthur from the custom-house collectorship. Now, watching Arthur's nomination for the second-highest office in the land, Sherman could not help but call the scene "a ridiculous burlesque." In *The Nation*, editor E. L. Godkin noted that Arthur was certainly undistinguished, but so was the office of the vice president. "General Garfield, if elected, may die in office," Godkin reassured his readers, "but that is too unlikely a contingency to be worth making extraordinary provisions for."

After a close election, Garfield's brief tenure in office continued to reflect the divisions within the Republican Party. In states such as New York, where the Democrats were gaining strength, Republican bosses fought to maintain party unity and to preserve party strength through patronage. By 1880, they had begun to look to former president Ulysses S. Grant to restore the old ways of party patronage, adamantly backing the former president for a third term. These so-called Stalwarts were led by the Republican boss of New York State, Roscoe Conkling. The Stalwarts were opposed by an anti-Grant alliance whose members were derisively called Half-Breeds, a slur that indicated they were not pure Republicans. The most prominent contender for the Half-Breed nomination in 1880 was US Senator James G. Blaine of Maine, a very popular former Speaker of the House. But Blaine was dogged by accusations that while Speaker he had backed legislation favorable to a railroad company in return for a hefty bribe. Reformers succeeded in blocking his nomination in favor of Garfield. But while Hayes had named reformer Carl Schurz to a cabinet post, Garfield selected Blaine to be secretary of state. To both the independent reformers and Conkling's Stalwarts, this move indicated very strongly that President Garfield would rely heavily on the Half-Breeds.

Other cabinet appointments only confirmed Garfield's turn to the Half-Breeds, but Garfield had not finished sticking it to Conkling. Repeating Hayes's action of four years earlier, Garfield cleaned out the New York Custom House and appointed new officers without consulting the Republican boss of New York. Absolutely incensed, in 1881 Conkling and his lieutenant, Thomas C. Platt, resigned their seats in the US Senate, fully confident that the New York State Legislature would reelect them and show Conkling's continued strength as party boss. When the legislature refused, Conkling's career was finished.

New York, however, would still have a Republican boss. Thomas Platt emerged as the "Easy Boss" of the party, controlling the machine for the next twenty years. His ascension to power in the state corresponded exactly with the entry into politics of the young reformer Theodore Roosevelt.

Roosevelt would have ample opportunity to look back on those early days in Morton Hall and his reception by the machine politicians and "ward heelers." "Some of them sneered at my black coat and a tall hat," he recalled. "But I made them understand I should come dressed as I chose." For Roosevelt, these meetings soon became weekly affairs, and he apparently first addressed a meeting about a month later on the new city charter. Which of the many aspects of the charter Roosevelt discussed is unknown, but only a few days later, a mass meeting at the Cooper Institute called for the city to establish a separate department responsible for street cleaning. Prominent New Yorkers such as Abram Hewitt and Joseph Choate attended, and the chief justice of New York's Court of Common Pleas, Charles Patrick Daly, addressed the meeting in his capacity as chairman. "This is the dirtiest city in the universe," Daly charged, "and has been for the last half century or more." Choate lampooned the police commissioners, who were responsible for cleaning the streets under the present system. "If it is not possible for the Police Commissioners to clean out the streets," Choate proclaimed to great cheering, "it is possible for the people to clean out the Police Commissioners!" Choate noted that the police board itself was engineered to be ineffective, composed as it was of two Democrats and two Republicans. Such men were simply beholden to their respective parties, not to the good of the city. This would be the exact same deadlocked situation that Roosevelt would face when he became president of that very same Board of Police Commissioners fourteen years later.

Roosevelt did not remark on the Cooper Institute meeting in his diary, so he probably did not attend. But his long walks through the streets of Manhattan made him sensitive to the issue of sanitation and the absolute need of a separate department of street cleaning. It was this typical urban issue that drew him into ever more active participation in the Morton Hall meetings. With New York City essentially governed by the New York State Legislature, cleaning the city streets meant changing the laws in Albany. When in 1881 the sitting Assembly member for the Twenty-First District voted against a bill that would have established a separate department of street cleaning in the city, Roosevelt set out to secure the man's defeat. "Am going to try to kill our last years [*sic*] legislator," he noted in his diary, using unusually violent language. Had Roosevelt written this when he first started attending meetings, such words would have seemed like the hubris of a wealthy dilettante. By October 1881, though, Roosevelt had been attending the association meetings for nearly eight months and was working to actively shape the politics of his party.

While at Harvard, Roosevelt had considered a public career. Now he undertook a course of action that even his father had not. Perhaps the senior Roosevelt had balked at being beholden to the machine, or rubbing elbows with the coarsest of city politicians. His son did not share such reservations. In fact, he openly disdained them. Writing later of his experiences in the state legislature, Roosevelt lamented the "lack of the robuster virtues" among his educated peers, "which makes them shrink from the struggle and the inevitable contact with rough politicians." He repeated this observation, using similarly weighted words about virility and masculinity, on at least one other occasion. Writing an article in 1886 about "Machine Politics in New York City," Roosevelt concluded that "many cultured men neglect their political duties simply because they are too delicate to have the element of 'strike back' in their natures, and because they have an unmanly fear of being forced to stand up when threatened with abuse or insult." Roosevelt, then, saw something manly in his willingness to enter the political fray, a full contact sport equal to the boxing and wrestling matches of his undergraduate years. While so many Roosevelt biographers have claimed that he drew his confident masculinity from his time in the West, in reality it was while standing on the tobacco-stained planks above a 59th Street shop in New York City that he became christened in the manly virtues.

THE SECOND WEEK of April 1881 was typical for New York. The immigrant reception center at Castle Garden welcomed 11,459 people arriving on ships from European ports such as Liverpool and Rotterdam.

The Bureau of Vital Statistics recorded in the city 789 deaths, 387 births, and 125 marriages. Of those nearly 800 deaths in that spring-time week, about 100 were caused by consumption and another 100 by pneumonia. Typhus and typhoid accounted for another 30. Twelve people died of smallpox, while 26 new cases were reported, and as that disease had an overall mortality rate of about 30 percent, health officials were watching carefully for new outbreaks. Only cholera, with its rapid spread and a mortality rate double that of smallpox, scared New Yorkers more. Fortunately, no cases of cholera were reported that week.

The number of deaths by contagious disease only underscored the city's sanitation problem, which was also front and center that week. The police commissioners were still receiving abuse on a daily basis for their handling of the city's garbage. The Board of Aldermen had passed a resolution ordering the commissioners to remove piles of filth dumped by the street-cleaning bureau on an empty lot at South and Roosevelt Streets. The commissioners responded by bristling at being ordered to do anything by the aldermen; they rejected the notion that the site in question was really that dirty. Commissioner Sidney P. Nichols pointed out that the accumulation in that space had been caused by the dumping of snow and ice removed from Broadway and other streets the previous winter. The dirt was unsightly, he admitted, but not odorous or offensive. Noting that the alderman who introduced the resolution was a butcher, Nichols suggested that he swept more foul dirt into the city gutters everyday than was held in the empty lot in question. Commissioner Joel W. Mason cared little about the actual soiled lot discussed, instead taking umbrage that the Board of Aldermen would try to give orders to the police commission. Did the aldermen even have any jurisdiction over the matter? The commission's clerk replied that the aldermen had no more jurisdiction over the matter "than the Rector of Trinity Church." This answer appeared to offer the commissioners some satisfaction. The commissioners' meeting provided New Yorkers with a surreal sight: the men responsible for overseeing New York's Finest dickering over garbage.

In addition to disease, fire, and filth, New Yorkers daily faced another threat: crime. During the second week of April, the police arrested 1,321 people. One of these was William Johnson, who had attempted the "gold brick swindle" on businessman Colonel C. Ellis. Johnson tried to sell Ellis a long, heavily gilt piece of lead, plated with real gold at the end and at the center. Johnson assured Ellis that the brick was worth $9,000, and offered it to him at only $7,500, indicating he had eighteen other bricks he wished to dispose of. Police arrested Johnson, but let slip his accomplice and the only real piece of evidence against him: the imitation gold brick.

That same week, a swindler tried his luck with another wealthy-looking New Yorker, Theodore Roosevelt. Although few details survive of what transpired, Roosevelt was taking the train back from Boston to New York at the time, and it is possible the swindler cozied up to him on the train. Upon arrival in New York, Roosevelt, struggling to keep the man in his custody, called for the police. Within a week, Roosevelt had testified before the grand jury, which indicted the swindler, who, a week later, was sentenced to six months in the state penitentiary. Battling crime in New York was a hallmark of urban reformers such as Roosevelt. In a few years, when he became an assemblyman battling graft, newspaper cartoons would depict Roosevelt as a policeman ridding the city of corrupt politicians. Years later Roosevelt would serve as president of the same Board of Police Commissioners that debated about the foulness of a pile of garbage. But in April 1881, the young Roosevelt faced New York crime head-on at street level, and, more importantly, took satisfaction in the fact that he had fought crime and won. Future struggles to enforce New York law would not be half so easy.

By the spring of 1881, Roosevelt was juggling a full slate of responsibilities. He was married, studying law, and attending political meetings; escorting Alice to the opera, balls, and dinner parties; acting as trustee for the Orthopedic Dispensary and the New York Infant Asylum; and working on his naval history of the War of 1812. For a twenty-two-year-old not long out of college, Roosevelt had quickly acquired all the trappings of full adulthood. Not surprisingly, there was still something of the adolescent about him. Some part of Roosevelt longed to be free of the obligations of work, society, and family. According to their mother, Mittie, when his brother Elliott wrote from India about his big-game hunting adventures, Roosevelt longed to be with him "and walks up and down the room like a Caged Lynx." Worried that she was giving Elliott the wrong idea about the state of Roosevelt's marriage to Alice, Mittie added that Theodore "feels he is perfectly happy with her but sometimes he must go off with his gun instead of pouring [*sic*] over Brown versus Jenkins, etc." As Mittie lived with the newlyweds, that phrase—"he is perfectly happy with her but . . ."—appears loaded with meaning. Gone were the days of calling on any number of girls in Boston, Chestnut Hill, Manhattan, and Oyster Bay. After a long chase, Roosevelt had won his fair maiden. As in hunting, perhaps Roosevelt enjoyed the chase more than the kill.

As Roosevelt made plans for their European honeymoon, Alice left to visit her family in Chestnut Hill for two weeks. Roosevelt was primed to make full use of the absence of "Darling Wifie." With Alice away, Roosevelt stepped up his own social activities. Within a week of her departure, Roosevelt gave a whist party for some of his male friends, invited old Harvard chum George Minot—Hal Minot's cousin and Forest Hills neighbor—to stay with him in the city, and took a couple of women out for drives—including his old flame Edith Carow. When he attended a dinner party stag, he spent the evening talking to several young ladies. Of this dinner party he attended without his wife, Roosevelt noted: "Pleasantest one I have been to this winter." Very quickly this second bachelorhood came to an end. Roosevelt retrieved Alice from Chestnut Hill, and the following month the couple departed for Europe.

WHEN VISITORS CALLED on the Roosevelts at their West 57th Street home, and saw Mittie and Alice sitting side-by-side, did they see similarities? There were differences, to be sure. Where Mittie was petite, Alice was five feet seven inches tall. Mittie's black, lustrous hair contrasted with Alice's blond curls. Both had fair, almost porcelain skin. Both were exceedingly prim, well-bred, cultured, and refined. Both were very feminine, and, especially for a young Roosevelt, must have served as almost textbook examples of what it meant to be "a lady" in late nineteenth-century America. Roosevelt called Mittie and Alice by very similar nicknames, "Muffie" and "Wifie." Living in such close quarters together in New York, Roosevelt probably made the common mistake of switching their names, as a person sometimes does with children. In February 1884, Mittie and Alice would share similar tragic fates, as different illnesses took their lives on the same day. In a foreshadowing of their dual deaths, Mittie and Alice shared another trait: they were frequently ill.

In their letters to Mittie, the two Theodore Roosevelts—husband and son—often struck similar chords. Theodore Roosevelt Sr. had worried incessantly about his wife's health, and Theodore Roosevelt Jr. often had to write to his mother lines such as, "I do hope my sweet one is getting better. *Do* take care of yourself Muffie darling, and avoid every kind of exposure." Theodore Roosevelt Sr. once teased his wife, "I have always been accustomed to think of you as one of my little babies." Years later, his son would tease Alice by calling her "my baby wife." During their first year of marriage, Alice grew frustrated with her husband's constant distractions by the law, writing, and politics. During evenings in their home while Roosevelt tried to write, Alice would constantly poke him to draw his attention. Roosevelt was irritated with such behavior and the couple's constant social obligations. The delayed honeymoon to Europe promised a long escape in each other's company. But the trip had an inauspicious beginning.

Alice spent the entire crossing aboard the *Celtic* violently seasick. During his childhood trips to Europe, Roosevelt had greatly enjoyed the sea voyages, playing with his siblings and striking up friendships with other passengers. For such a sickly little boy, the sea seemed to agree with him. On this trip with his wife, instead of enjoying the royal trappings of first-class sea travel, Roosevelt spent every moment tending to Alice. He grew impatient. "Confound a European trip, say I!" he fumed in his diary. "Alice is exceedingly sick; I haven't been at all sick but tired out by taking care of her." After ten days at sea they reached Ireland, and Alice improved. In his letters home, Roosevelt could not resist making fun of her. "We had a beautiful passage," Roosevelt wrote to Alice's sister Rose, "very nearly as gay as a funeral." He then gave a long description of poor Alice's travails and his own ministrations. The note to his sister-in-law contained some small cruelties. After each stomach convulsion, Roosevelt recounted, "Alice would conclude she was going to die, and we would have a mental circus for a few minutes;

finally after I had implored, prayed and sworn with equal fervency she would again compose herself for a few minutes." Roosevelt's letter about his wife's seasickness reflected poorly on them both.

This was Roosevelt's first trip to Europe since he was a boy, and the couple followed much of the same path Roosevelt and his family had taken years before. Theodore and Alice went to London, Paris, Venice, Milan, and Lake Como, spending some time up near the border between Italy and Switzerland. During their stay there, Roosevelt heard the news that President James Garfield had been shot on July 2 by a Stalwart office-seeker, Charles Guiteau. "Just heard of Garfield's assassination," he wrote, at first assuming the president had died. "Frightful calamity for America." The next day Roosevelt wrote, "Later news say Garfield's not dead. This means work in the future for all men who wish their country well." It is an interesting statement by Roosevelt, both grandiose and melodramatic, but it reflected the fact that Garfield's assassination was one of the most important events of the Gilded Age. Roosevelt just happened to be out of the country to miss the violent act that would have enormous ramifications for American politics, the Republican Party, and Roosevelt's own career. When Guiteau shot Garfield, he exclaimed that he had done it to elevate Arthur to the presidency. The resulting pall of suspicion over Arthur's presidency made a convention fight in 1884 almost inevitable. Roosevelt would be there.

As the Roosevelts made their way back across Europe to London, readying to sail on the *Britannic*, President Garfield finally succumbed to his mortal wound. Roosevelt, then, missed a rare event—a president taking the oath of office in New York City. Only George Washington had ever before been sworn into the presidency in New York, during his first inauguration in 1789. Now, on September 20, 1881, Chester Arthur privately took the oath at his home at 123 Lexington Avenue. Despite calls from outside to appear in public, Arthur stayed indoors surrounded by a few intimates, including old Roosevelt friend Elihu Root. Garfield's death was immediately capitalized upon by reformers. In July, as Garfield still lay on his deathbed, they had created the National Civil Service Reform League. When the president died, independents claimed Garfield as a martyr in the cause of civil service reform. In Congress, Ohio Senator George Pendleton took the lead, drafting a bill that would create a three-man civil service commission to oversee a system of competitive examinations for federal office-seekers. The bill only applied to jobs in federal offices with more than fifty employees, which covered a mere 15 percent of the roughly 100,000 federal employees. Still, this included such notoriously corrupt offices as the New York Custom House, and reformers rejoiced when both the House and the Senate easily passed the bill. President Arthur had risen to power as a result of exactly the sort of patronage abuse that the Pendleton Civil Service Reform Act sought to abolish. Without a hint of irony, Arthur signed the bill into law.

These events would have broad consequences for Theodore Roosevelt. The lines of battle within the Republican Party had long been drawn by the time he entered the political fray. By the early 1880s, the reformers could claim a number of victories. They had deprived Grant and Blaine of their party's nomination for the presidency twice, in 1876 and 1880. Roosevelt would join forces with them when they battled again in 1884. Moreover, the first national civil service reform law had been passed, then quickly followed by many more at the state level. Not only would the cause of civil service reform dominate Roosevelt's political career in the coming decades, but he would also eventually serve for six years on the Civil Service Commission established by the Pendleton Act. By championing the cause of civil service reform, Roosevelt would be tapping into a well-organized and powerful faction inside the Republican Party. The National Civil Service Reform League would provide Roosevelt with important political contacts throughout the United States. In the end, though, those contacts in Boston and New York would prove most important. In New York, Roosevelt would become acquainted with Carl Schurz, George William Curtis, and E. L. Godkin. Not only were these men important within the Republican Party, they were also editors of influential organs such as the *New York Evening Post*, *Harper's Monthly Magazine*, and *The Nation*. In Boston, through his Harvard contacts and his marriage, Roosevelt had already tapped into the reformers among the Boston Brahmin elite. He would soon make the acquaintance of the man who would prove his most

important friend and political ally until Roosevelt's death in 1919—
Henry Cabot Lodge.

ROOSEVELT AND ALICE returned to New York from Europe on
October 2. Their lives were about to take an unexpected turn.

On October 14, Alice departed for Chestnut Hill, leaving Roosevelt
at home alone in their large house on West 57th Street with only the
elderly Dora, the housekeeper, for company. He had no trouble keeping
himself occupied. "Am working fairly at my law," he wrote in his diary
on October 17, "hard at politics, and hardest of all at my book ('Naval
History')." On October 25, he and Uncle Jimmie attended the unveil-
ing of a new seven-foot "drinking fountain" in Union Square. During
the Roosevelt family's trip to Germany several years before, the elder
Theodore Roosevelt and the donor D. Willis James had conceived of
the plan to give the fountain to the city, but Roosevelt's death had prevented the execution of the plan until that time. The younger Theodore
Roosevelt made no note of his reaction to the new fountain—a depiction of a mother accompanied by two children and holding a pitcher
of water. Nor did he make an entry on October 27, his twenty-third
birthday. Politics must have been on his mind, though, because an
ugly fight was already underway over the Republican nomination in
Roosevelt's Twenty-First Assembly District.

Roosevelt himself had spoken in favor of censuring the current legislator, William Trimble, after Trimble had voted against the street-
cleaning bill back in April. That October, independent Republicans of
the district had been sending out a circular announcing a meeting to
nominate an anti-machine candidate for the Assembly. There was also
a fight brewing between the current boss of the district, Jake Hess, and
another local leader, Joe Murray. As Roosevelt himself recounted years
later, Murray thought the best way "to make a drive at Jake Hess" was
in the fight over the Assembly nomination. Murray asked Roosevelt to
stand for the nomination, and they beat Hess and Trimble by a vote of
16 to 9—"Much to my surprise," Roosevelt said. Immediately the independent Republicans gave up their search for an alternate candidate,
"the character of the candidate," the *Times* reported, "being regarded as
admirable, and the only cause for hesitation in supporting him [being]

the fear that he may be trammeled by pledges to the 'machine' men." Roosevelt made sure all knew of his independence. When the district committee visited Roosevelt at his home to officially offer the nomination, Roosevelt said he would not be subservient to local bosses. He also said he would vote with the Republican Party in national politics, but in local affairs he would keep his own counsel. Thus Roosevelt began the difficult balancing act between his independence and his loyalty to the Republican Party that would mark the next thirty years of his political career.

With only a week between Roosevelt's nomination and the election, the campaign was necessarily brief. Roosevelt's district included the grand homes along Fifth Avenue, but it also included a number of saloons along Sixth Avenue. Although Uncle Jim was "bitterly opposed" to Roosevelt's candidacy, Fifth Avenue was probably safe for Roosevelt. Jake Hess and Joe Murray joined forces to get their candidate elected, and they proposed a tour of the Sixth Avenue saloons. Perhaps sensitive to the barbs being hurled against William Waldorf Astor in the press for ignoring the tenement districts in his quest for Congress, Roosevelt agreed. According to Roosevelt, the canvass did not last beyond the first saloon. The candidate bristled as the saloonkeeper took on the tone "of one who is dealing with a suppliant for favor." When the saloonkeeper complained that the prices for liquor-selling licenses were too high, Roosevelt replied that they were not high enough, and he would endeavor to make them higher. When the conversation became "stormy," Hess and Murray hustled their candidate quickly outside. On the sidewalk they decided that Roosevelt would concentrate on campaigning on Fifth Avenue, while Hess and Murray looked after Sixth Avenue. It was an effective division of labor between a twenty-three-year-old "silk-stocking" reform candidate and the local party bosses.

On November 8, the voters of the Twenty-First District elected Theodore Roosevelt to the New York Assembly by a healthy majority of more than 1,500 votes. In this first campaign, Roosevelt was aided by several factors. The Twenty-First was a relatively safe Republican district even in an election that saw only five other Republicans elected to the Assembly, and saw Astor defeated by Roswell Flower, the future Democratic governor of New York. In the press, Roosevelt was always described as the son of Theodore Roosevelt Sr., a name above reproach in New York and associated with honesty and philanthropy. Roosevelt was also aided by family friends and prominent city Republicans, such as Elihu Root and Joseph Choate. These men would be associated with Roosevelt's career through his presidency. Finally, Roosevelt was aided by an astoundingly poor Democratic opponent, the Dickensian-named William Strew. Two years before, Dr. Strew had been removed from his position as medical superintendent of the New York City Lunatic Asylum on Blackwell's Island. Accused of gross mismanagement and a lack of executive abilities, Strew, when asked to voluntarily resign, had refused to do so. He then sent a petulant letter to the commissioners of public charities that was reprinted in the newspapers. Replying publicly to the letter, the commissioners underscored Strew's inability to carry out the duties of his office and said he was "lacking in executive capacity." These were hardly sterling qualities for a candidate to the New York State Legislature to possess.

Roosevelt had little time to revel in his victory. He and Alice traveled to Boston to spend Thanksgiving with Alice's mother, and Roosevelt finished his book on the naval history of the War of 1812, delivering the manuscript to his publisher, G. P. Putnam's Sons, in early December. The year ended the way it had begun, with an endless series of dinners and balls. Still, the newly elected assemblyman took time to start researching a bill to build a new aqueduct to supply the city with adequate amounts of water. At this point, Roosevelt was not yet certain he would be named to his committee of first choice, the Assembly's Cities Committee, which was responsible for drafting bills pertaining to New York. The choice of an aqueduct bill reflected a progressive approach to America's rapid urbanization and fit well into the plans of reformers such as Roosevelt, as they were looking for ways to make city living safer and healthier. A dedicated supply of clean water would prevent the outbreak of disease and limit the destructive power of fires. The choice reflected Roosevelt's sensitivity to the issues of the day.

During the summer of 1881, some city districts had received an insufficient supply of water, and the legislature had passed a bill authorizing the city to construct a new aqueduct. Republican governor Alonzo Cornell vetoed the bill. There followed a terribly dry summer and autumn that reduced the city's daily supply of water to one-tenth its usual level. Everyone was discussing the current water shortage, and the *Times* even published an editorial on the matter just days before the election. The paper noted that although the city needed a new aqueduct, the governor had been justified in objecting to the vast expense required to build one and the vast power given to the city's commissioner of public works, Hubert O. Thompson. In his veto, Cornell noted that the legislature's bill would have given Thompson sole authority to require the city to issue bonds to build the aqueduct, which would add to the city's debt burden. Cornell objected to such "immense and arbitrary powers" for an unelected city official. The governor's veto foreshadowed Roosevelt's time in the New York Assembly. He would battle graft and corruption in city departments and seek ways to strip unelected city officials of their immense and arbitrary powers for the next three years.

THE YEAR 1881 had been an exceptionally eventful one for Roosevelt and his new wife. As they returned to New York the previous January 1, they could not have foreseen how their lives would be changed within a single year. On the surface, little seemed very new, as the couple again dove into the city's social season presided over by Caroline Astor. They celebrated Thanksgiving and Christmas with family, and they continued to live with Mittie Roosevelt at the 57th Street house. No children were on the immediate horizon, despite their months-long European honeymoon in romantic environs such as Paris and Lake Como. The year had begun with Roosevelt studying law and writing his history book. Now the book was finished and the law forgotten. Instead, Roosevelt had taken the unusual step of entering politics.

He had indicated his interest in public life while still an undergraduate, but that had been before he married Alice and took up so many of his late father's charitable responsibilities. The opposition of his Uncle James reflected the standard opinion of the Roosevelt-Astor class of New York. As the newspapers had ruefully noted upon Theodore Roosevelt Sr.'s death, the sons of New York's wealthy class did not make a habit of running for office. Far from being a dilettante, Roosevelt had earned his seat in the barn-like room of Morton Hall, attending meetings regularly for nine months before his nomination, and speaking out against the current assemblyman from the Twenty-First. And, once elected, Roosevelt threw himself with vigor into the task, working on an aqueduct bill even before he took his seat in the Assembly or knew his committee assignment.

Roosevelt had been drawn into New York City politics by dirty streets, and he began his career by advocating clean water and clean government. Truly, these were the marks of a budding urban progressive, and from his seat in the Assembly, Roosevelt would confirm his reformist inclinations and hone his political skills.

FOUR

"A Revolting State of Affairs"
Roosevelt's Work in the
New York Assembly

As TWENTY-THREE-YEAR-OLD Theodore Roosevelt boarded the train for Albany on January 2, 1882, he could not have imagined that he was embarking on a forty-year career in politics. For the next three years in the New York Assembly representing his New York City district, Roosevelt would receive an education in the intricacies of state and local politics. He would lock horns not only with Democrats, but also with his own Republican leaders. He would take on the Tammany boss of New York, and he would publicly interrogate the city's mayor. Roosevelt chaired investigations, gave speeches, and wrote legislation. He also learned the power of the press, befriending the Albany correspondent of the *New York Times* and becoming the focus of headlines and favorable editorials. Through it all, Roosevelt would grapple with the challenges of how to make America's largest city more livable.

As his train moved slowly along the Hudson River, Roosevelt also followed an uncertain path. William Waldorf Astor had lost his bid for Congress. Could the silk-stocking Roosevelt really make headway among the hacks and lobbyists in Albany? Could he really make a difference in the Republican Party, even as he claimed his independence? The next three years would prove crucial in shaping the savvy Republican politician Roosevelt would become.

FOR ANYONE PAYING attention, that second day of the year—and the coldest day of winter so far—held a lesson in city and state politics. Following cues from their boss, "Honest" John Kelly, and in a snub to their party's choice for Senate president, Tammany Democrats in the legislature refused to caucus. In New York City, Kelly scored a victory by getting his man William Sauer elected president of the Board of Aldermen, a body that had great control over departmental appropriations and mayoral appointments. In his message to the board, Mayor William Grace lamented the fact that the city had over $135 million in debt, the largest municipal indebtedness in the United States. Grace blamed past "extravagance and misgovernment" by the "plunderers of our City." Sauer's election as president was a blow to the mayor, whom Sauer had repeatedly denounced as a liar. The president of the Board of Aldermen also served on the Board of Estimate and Apportionment, which would advise the mayor on all departmental appropriations for the coming year. Since the Board of Aldermen also had the power to confirm or reject the mayor's appointments, Sauer and Tammany Hall would thus have control over much of New York City's government. It was understood that candidates for city jobs regularly paid Tammany Hall for its support and then pocketed city money once they received their appointments. No wonder New York City had a debt equivalent to about 10 percent of the total evaluation of all Manhattan real estate.

While Democrats in Albany wrestled with Tammany obstructionism, Republicans continued to split along the lines of the factions that plagued the party nationwide. With Garfield's assassination and Arthur's ascension to the presidency in September of the previous year, Stalwarts seemed to have scored a victory. But the many-sided divisions within the party—Stalwarts, Half-Breeds, and independent reformers—meant that no single faction could gain the balance of power. These party divisions had played themselves out in city and state elections across the country as Republican factions battled each other. The results would be reflected in the midterm congressional elections of 1882—a Democratic rout of Republicans. Closer to home, New York had seen the drama of Republican factionalism played out in a battle between the state's two US senators and President Garfield, when Roscoe Conkling and his lieutenant, Thomas Platt, had resigned their Senate seats to protest Garfield's appointment of a Conkling foe, William Robertson, to the post of collector of the New York Custom House. Robertson had led the Blaine forces of New York during the 1880 convention, and Blaine had worked to prevent Conkling's reelection, ending the flamboyant boss's career and influence. Platt's seat was taken by a new leader in New York politics, Warner Miller, a Blaine man who would soon cross swords with a young maverick assemblyman named Theodore Roosevelt.

These Republican factional divisions could be found even at the state party caucus. The divisions resulted from the 1880 Republican National Convention, when the Stalwarts had backed former President Grant for a third term, while the Half-Breeds had advocated the nomination of James Blaine. When gathering to choose a candidate for Speaker of the Assembly in January 1882, the Stalwarts preferred George H. Sharpe of Ulster County, while the Half-Breeds backed Thomas G. Alvord of Onondaga County. Alvord, known as "Old Salt," was over seventy years old and had a political career reaching back before the Civil War. He had served as Speaker several times, the first being in 1858, and had even been lieutenant governor. Sharpe's career seemed to have crossed paths with every prominent American since the Civil War. During the war he had served on the staffs of Union generals Joseph Hooker, George Meade, and Ulysses S. Grant. As assistant provost marshal at the end of the war, Sharpe was responsible for paroling 28,000 Confederate soldiers, including Robert E. Lee. In 1867, Sharpe traveled to Europe at the request of Secretary of State William Seward to track down and return to the United States John Surratt, son of Mary Surratt, who had been hanged as one of the conspirators in Lincoln's assassination. By 1877, Sharpe was serving under Chester Arthur in the New York Custom House. As surveyor, Sharpe was one of the officials whom President Hayes had tried to remove as he took on Conkling and the Republican machine by appointing Theodore Roosevelt Sr. to replace Arthur. Hayes was unsuccessful, and Sharpe continued to serve under Collector Arthur, and alongside naval officer Alonzo Cornell, who was now governor. That episode, only a few years prior, had been an excellent primer on New York politics for Harvard undergraduate Theodore Roosevelt Jr.

In the contest between Alvord and Sharpe, one Stalwart and one Half-Breed, the recently elected Roosevelt found himself among those independent Republicans who didn't like either one. This reflected exactly the position of many New York and New England Republicans in the years between 1880 and 1884. In his diary, Roosevelt called Sharpe "a man of ability and shrewd enough to recognize the advantage of being considered respectable, but unless I am mistaken decidedly tricky and unquestionably a machine man pure and simple." Roosevelt was absolutely right, as Sharpe was a key lieutenant in the state Republican machine. But, just as many independents had rejected the candidacy of corrupt Half-Breed James Blaine in 1880, Roosevelt could hardly stomach Alvord: "a bad old fellow." Roosevelt lamented the "choice of evils" he faced. In the end, he chose Sharpe. The party chose Alvord. This would be the first of many times Roosevelt bucked the trend of his party and defied the wishes of party leaders such as Warner Miller and Thomas Platt.

With Republicans in the minority in the Assembly that year, their choosing Alvord appeared to be little more than pro forma. Democrats held the majority and would name the Speaker. But as the Tammany snub of the Democratic caucus on the same day indicated, John Kelly was not happy. In 1880, Kelly had helped elect William Grace as the first Irish American, Catholic mayor of New York, only to have Grace turn against Tammany. Now Tammany and anti-Tammany Democrats fought their battle in Albany. Only seven Tammany men from the city had seats in the Assembly, but that was enough. With Democrats holding 67 of the 128 Assembly seats, and Republicans holding 61, those seven Tammany seats held the balance of power. It was the power to obstruct. Roosevelt's first month in the Assembly was spent watching the Tammany men cast votes for their own candidate for Speaker—if they showed up at all—preventing a majority vote and stopping all work. This empty time allowed Roosevelt to observe his fellow members and draw conclusions he would hold for the rest of his career. He had few compliments for the Republican leaders, but he truly despised those Democrats whom he called "the City Irish." Roosevelt labeled them "vicious, stupid looking scoundrels with apparently not a redeeming trait, beyond the capacity for making exceeding ludicrous bulls." Roosevelt's reference to "bulls," papal decrees, reflected the typical anti-Catholic sentiment of his class.

Day after day, the absurd deadlock in the Assembly perpetrated by the Tammany Democrats continued. Roosevelt described one of the Tammany men, named Bogan, as "a little celtic liquor seller, about five feet high, with an enormous stomach, and a face like a bull frog." Roosevelt then related an exchange between Bogan and the clerk. "I rise to a pint of ardther (order) under the rules!" Roosevelt recounted in his diary, mimicking the man's Irish accent. "There are no rules," the clerk replied. "Then I object to them!" "There are no rules to object to," the clerk repeated. "Indade! That's quare, now; (brightening up, as he sees a way out of the difficulty) Very will! Thin I move that they be amended till there ar-r-r!" Despite his anti-Irish overtones, Roosevelt certainly had a knack for description, whether it was a cowbird in the Adirondacks or a Celt in the Assembly he was portraying. And Roosevelt's mimicry of the Irish brogue foreshadowed the farcical writings of Chicago journalist Finley Peter Dunne and his character Mr. Dooley. Years later, when "Mr. Dooley" wrote a mocking review of Roosevelt's *The Rough Riders*, he concluded, "If I was him I'd call th' book, 'Alone in Cubia.'" Roosevelt loved it, and Dunne became a frequent guest at the White House.

Roosevelt's harangue against assemblymen of Irish descent confirmed not only his own class and ethnic prejudices, but also his political prejudices. "The average catholic Irishman of the first generation as represented in this Assembly, is a low, venal, corrupt and unintelligent brute," Roosevelt wrote in his diary. He perceived a great contrast between the Republican and Democratic lawmakers. The Democrats were represented by the rougher urban classes and included liquor sellers and a pawnbroker. The Republicans, in contrast, were mostly lawyers or farmers.

Within a few weeks, Roosevelt was able to widen his understanding of his fellow legislators and see them in a broader context. Namely, he caught sight of the strings that manipulated the Tammany men, strings that stretched back all the way to Manhattan. "Of course such a hopelessly ignorant set of men as these Tammany members are can not do their own thinking," he observed. "They are managed entirely by the commands of some of John Kelly's lieutenants who are always in the Assembly chamber." County Democrats were little better, and were whipped into line by a New Yorker whom Roosevelt would soon target in his Assembly investigating committee. Roosevelt observed that Commissioner of Public Works Hubert O. Thompson, although filling a key post in the New York City government, spent most of his time in Albany. "He is a gross, enormously fleshy man, with a full face and thick sensual lips," Roosevelt wrote with characteristic descriptive flair. Thompson, he continued, "wears a diamond shirt pin and an enormous seal ring on his little finger." Thompson also kept several hotel parlors stocked with champagne and free food for assemblymen, lobbyists, officeholders, and party bosses. The question must have come to Roosevelt's mind: Where did Thompson get so much money for such a vulgar and ostentatious display of wealth? As the city department head responsible for building and maintaining New York's entire infrastructure, Thompson managed an enormous budget of millions of dollars. It would become Roosevelt's quest to root out corruption in Thompson's department, targeting the "wire-puller," or political operator, directly.

As the Tammany deadlock wore on, some Republicans became impatient and proposed throwing in their lot with the regular Democrats. In a crucial moment of insight, Roosevelt opposed such a move, understanding that a split Democratic Party could only aid Republicans. Perhaps he remembered the criticism of President Hayes for splitting the Republicans during the custom-house battle in 1877. Roosevelt wrote, "I consider it no part of ours to interfere in a family quarrel, it being a very pretty fight as it stands." Just as Roosevelt early on delighted in seeing the Democrats hopelessly split, for the rest of his career he would despair watching Republicans split along factional lines and go down to defeat at the hands of the Democrats. Still, some Republicans wanted an end to the deadlock for the sake of getting on with the job of passing legislation. Roosevelt thought this absurd and rose to say so in his first speech to the legislature. As the *Times* recounted in an article on the Assembly's fourth week of "unorganized existence," Roosevelt said in his speech that while the stalemate among Democrats might be a hindrance to legislation, "he has talked with a number of representative manufacturers and business men, and he was satisfied that they could get along quite nicely on their present allowance of legislation. [Laughter.]" It was a clever and pithy first effort, which, as Roosevelt noted in his diary, "was very well received."

Finally, on February 14, Valentine's Day, and a date that would come to haunt Roosevelt, the Democrats reconciled and elected a Speaker. Significantly, Roosevelt was assigned to the Cities Committee—"just where I wished to be," he wrote. As cities in New York State did not enjoy home rule, the Cities Committee was the most important organ for making laws affecting New York City. After Roosevelt's appointment, he quickly introduced four bills. The topics of these bills ranged from the city's finances to its drinking water, showing the range of challenges facing American cities in the late nineteenth century. The bills also included one to reform the organization of the Board of Aldermen, an unelected and shadowy body that sat in the pockets of the city bosses and was able to curb mayoral power. At that very moment in New York, Mayor Grace was battling with the board and its new president, Sauer, who took his orders from Tammany boss Honest John Kelly. Roosevelt hoped the bill would do away with such "dickering." This was putting it mildly, as Roosevelt would soon find out. More than just dickering, aldermanic control over budgeting and mayoral appointments represented a critical nexus of corruption in New York City's government. Until the day he stepped down from his Assembly seat three years later, Roosevelt would continue to view reforming or abolishing the Board of Aldermen as key to cleaning up New York's corrupt city government.

DURING THAT SAME first, one-year term in the Assembly, Roosevelt championed the impeachment of New York Supreme Court Judge Theodore Westbrook. Westbrook had been publicly accused of helping depress the value of Manhattan Elevated Railway Company stock to allow its acquisition by the notorious financier Jay Gould. Roosevelt took keen note of the fact that three months after the accusations had been made in the press, Westbrook still had not professed his innocence. Roosevelt called for a bill empowering the Assembly's Judiciary Committee to investigate Westbrook, thus taking on powerful interests while still only a freshman legislator. In the end, little came of the investigation, which did not involve Roosevelt's Cities Committee, and the majority report largely absolved Westbrook. Yet in defeat Roosevelt had achieved much, and perhaps learned even more. Roosevelt had made a name for himself throughout the state as a bold reformer, thus earning the loyalty of many other young, reform-minded men at Albany. He had given rousing speeches in the Assembly, including chastising his fellow legislators for letting Westbrook off the hook. "You cannot cleanse the leper," Roosevelt admonished. "Beware lest you taint yourselves with this leprosy." Finally, he had learned the power of the legislative investigating committee to uncover lurid backroom deals, the details of which could fill the press and inflame the public.

Roosevelt won reelection in 1882 in the face of, as he noted, a "Democratic Deluge" that elected Democrat Grover Cleveland governor of New York and further reduced the Republican minority in the legislature. With Democrats firmly in power, Republicans had little hope of passing significant legislation. In a nice nod to Roosevelt, fellow Republicans nominated him for Speaker, the de facto minority leader. Not everyone approved. The Stalwarts bitterly fought Roosevelt's selection, while independents backed him. Roosevelt noted that he got along well with the country Republicans, mostly farmers and storekeepers, "shrewd, kindly, honest men" who also happened to be "native Americans" rather than Irish. Roosevelt continued his differentiation between "native" Americans and those assemblymen who were immigrants or sons of immigrants. Moreover, from this point in his career onward, Roosevelt's strength would often be found among upstate Republicans. As an independent reformer from the city, Roosevelt frequently battled with city Republicans who viewed his frequent crusades with skepticism if not downright hostility.

During his second year, Roosevelt continued his education as an urban reformer. He helped usher through the Assembly a bill forbidding the rolling of cigars by residents of New York tenements, a filthy job that exacerbated the already horrific conditions inside the tenements. When the bill came before Roosevelt's Cities Committee, he was named one of three members tasked to investigate the problem. He was then approached by the local union representative, Samuel Gompers. When Gompers described the conditions in the tenements, the brown-stone-born Roosevelt did not believe the labor leader. Only after Roosevelt took three tours of the tenements did he come away shocked at what he saw. Writing in his *Autobiography* nearly three decades later, he could still vividly evoke the harsh conditions in which New York's working poor lived. "The work of manufacturing the tobacco by men, women, and children went on day and night," Roosevelt observed, "in the eating, living, and sleeping rooms—sometimes in one room." In one tenement he visited, two families occupied one room. They had even taken in a male boarder, who slept on whatever patch of ground was available. Tobacco could be seen everywhere, stored alongside the stained bedding and in a corner where bits of food had fallen. Roosevelt was revolted. When the bill reached Governor Cleveland's desk, Gompers asked Roosevelt to champion the bill to the skeptical governor. Roosevelt did so, acting not only as spokesperson for the labor leader and unions, but, as Roosevelt saw it, also for the exploited immigrants and tenement dwellers. Cleveland signed the bill.

A photo taken of Roosevelt in Albany that year shows the twenty-four-year-old surrounded by some of his closest colleagues in legislative work, including Walter Howe, Isaac Hunt, and William O'Neil. In his diary, Roosevelt noted that the four of them always sat together —"a pleasant quartette." Significantly, seated at the center of the photo is the legislative correspondent for the *New York Times*, George Spinney. Roosevelt's Albany experience began a long career in which he cultivated good relations with the press. As equally Republican and reform-minded as Roosevelt, the *New York Times* was usually a dependable ally and supporter of his efforts. In March 1883, the *Times* praised Roosevelt's "rugged independence": "Whatever boldness the minority has exhibited in the Assembly is due to his influence, and whatever weakness and cowardice it has displayed is attributable to its unwillingness to follow where he led." Roosevelt was making important allies as a reformer. The question was: Could Roosevelt also champion causes that would win him friends among the party's leadership? The year 1884 would provide key answers.

Before his successful bid for reelection in November 1883, Roosevelt made a life-changing trip west to hunt buffalo. He had already dipped his toe in the Dakota Territory on that pre-wedding trip west with Elliott in the fall of 1881. When he returned two years later, in autumn 1883, he traveled further west, to the Little Missouri River and the border of Montana. But for Roosevelt, with this first glimpse of the Badlands, more than just the geography had changed. By the early 1880s, books, articles, and even government reports were calling Montana and Dakota ready for a cattle boom, with beef barons claiming returns in excess of 50 percent. Roosevelt had even invested $10,000 in the Teschmaker and Debillier Cattle Company, which ran a herd north of Cheyenne. In 1883, Roosevelt indicated in his accounts an income of $500 from that investment, a return of 5 percent. At the same time, Roosevelt had made large investments back east. He put $20,000 in his publisher, G. P. Putnam's Sons, and had bought ninety-five acres of land on Oyster Bay, where he would soon start constructing a home for himself, Alice, and their expected brood of children. He had even contemplated buying a farm in the Adirondacks, scene of his youthful birding trips. By the fall of 1883, Roosevelt was on the lookout for several things: an investment that would provide him with a healthy and regular annual return; a nice piece of working agricultural land that would also afford him the enjoyment of outdoor life and opportunities for hunting; and an active, healthy, part-time occupation that would balance his more sedentary pursuits of politics and writing. No wonder that on that first trip to western Dakota, Roosevelt was primed to make a snap decision, one that would have large personal and financial ramifications for him. With a handshake and a personal check, Roosevelt returned to New York and his seat in the Assembly having invested one-third of his net worth in two cattle ranches.

ROOSEVELT'S FINAL SESSION in the Assembly in 1884 promised to be his greatest. It began badly. Republicans had regained a majority in the Assembly, and Roosevelt was up for the position of Speaker. Beginning in the fall of 1883, Roosevelt had written to fellow Assembly members soliciting their support. When Jonas Duzer of Chemung County inquired as to which faction, Half-Breed or Stalwart, Roosevelt belonged, Roosevelt replied, "I am a Republican, pure and simple, neither a 'half breed' nor a 'stalwart'; and certainly no man, nor yet any ring or clique, can do my thinking for me." This was classic Roosevelt, but it was an attitude that would hardly endear him to party leaders. Moreover, 1884 was a presidential election year. There was simply no way the Republican bosses could have allowed the independent Roosevelt into such a prominent position. Roosevelt lost the race for Speaker when the Republican machine, led by Senator Warner Miller, engineered his defeat. Instead, Roosevelt had to be content with the chairmanship of his Cities Committee and of a special committee to investigate corruption in New York City, namely, in Hubert Thompson's Department of Public Works.

At the opening of the new Assembly in January 1884, Roosevelt introduced three bills that indicated how reform of New York's municipal administration might be achieved. The first bill—called the "Aldermanic" or "Roosevelt" bill—would give the mayor complete power, without reference to the unelected aldermen, to appoint department heads. The model for Roosevelt and the other reformers in framing the bill was Brooklyn, where a similar law had invested Mayor Seth Low with sole appointing power. The result seemed to be better department heads and more public interest in municipal politics, with a visible and more powerful mayor. Indeed, in Brooklyn, more people voted for mayor than voted for governor. Roosevelt's second bill called for limiting municipal indebtedness. New York City's debt had increased more than tenfold over the previous quarter century, fueled by massive public works projects that also made many politicians rich. His third bill, finally, sought to break the Tammany Hall–saloon axis by establishing a high license fee to sell liquor in the city. The first two bills would eventually be passed, with the bill concerning the mayor's power of appointment labeled by the press the "Roosevelt Bill." The license bill failed, but it presaged the time when Roosevelt, as president of New York's Board of Police Commissioners, would again go after the corrupt alliance between politicians and saloon owners.

Roosevelt achieved more immediate success when the Assembly voted to establish a special committee to investigate New York City government. Roosevelt was named chairman of what came to be known as the "Roosevelt Committee." His associates on the committee were two Republicans, including his good friend William O'Neil, and two Democrats who were largely sympathetic to Roosevelt. The resolution specifically targeted the Department of Public Works under Commissioner Hubert O. Thompson, under whose management its annual expenditure had risen 65 percent, or almost $5 million, from only the year before. Taxes in the city had meanwhile risen by only about $3.5 million. The resolution also noted that the Union League Club and the city press had charged Thompson with fraud and that, in general, the public demanded an investigation of a city government notorious for corruption. Here was Roosevelt championing the reform elements of New York's press and Republican Party. And by targeting the Democratic city government, Roosevelt also pleased machine Republicans. When Roosevelt could figure out how to please both kinds of Republicans simultaneously, he achieved his greatest successes.

The committee met for the first time in the Metropolitan Hotel in New York City on January 19, only four days after the Assembly passed the resolution. Roosevelt and his fellow committee members would gather in the city three days a week, on Fridays, Saturdays, and Mondays, which allowed them to return to Albany for the rest of the week. This was a very busy time for Roosevelt. He was chairing his Cities Committee in Albany, writing and championing bills in the Assembly, and commuting to Manhattan for his committee hearings as well as attending to his very pregnant wife. The hearings themselves displayed Roosevelt's growing political acumen at only age twenty-five. As chairman, Roosevelt had to deal with hostile witnesses and their counsel, obdurate members of his own party, the mayor of New York, and even the Tammany boss, John Kelly. All the while, Roosevelt ensured a constant stream of sensationalist testimony to the press and public.

Although Roosevelt had been successful in calling for an independent Assembly investigating committee, the New York Senate had convened its own investigating committee, which was holding hearings simultaneously in the mayor's private office in City Hall. The Senate, too, was very interested in hearing from Commissioner Thompson, and had left a subpoena for him in his office at the Public Works Department. Perhaps foreseeing a conflict with the Senate, Roosevelt had personally gone to see Thompson and secured a promise from him to appear before the Assembly committee. Thompson fulfilled his promise to Roosevelt, ignoring the Senate subpoena. The questioning of Thompson had barely begun when a messenger interrupted the proceedings and handed Thompson a telegram from his counsel demanding his appearance before the Senate committee. Laughing, Thompson read the telegram to Roosevelt and his colleagues, and then he loudly told the messenger, seemingly for the benefit of his audience, "Tell them I will leave here in five minutes," a dismissive comment that drew laughter from those assembled. Roosevelt must have been displeased to be outmaneuvered by the chief target of the investigating committees. It was an inauspicious beginning.

The comedy of errors and evasions continued. The register, John O'Reilly, whose office was responsible for recording all property transactions in the city, had only been in office for three weeks and could offer little information, and his predecessor had gone to Cuba "on the advice of his physician." Cuba was a favorite of New York politicos fleeing investigations and prosecution, as witnessed by William Tweed's flight there in 1875. Next, the committee called the county clerk, Patrick Keenan. Keenan was the exact sort of politician that Roosevelt and other reformers wanted to target: Keenan was a former alderman, a former liquor dealer, and, of course, a Tammany man. Keenan readily admitted to the committee that he had paid $7,500 to Tammany Hall for his nomination, and had kept about $14,000 in fees paid to his office. Yet, apparently, Keenan knew very little about what his office actually did. He spent little time there, instead leaving the office in the care of his deputy. As he explained to the committee, "a man in the city of New York who is considered a local politician—they have a great many things to attend to sometimes and they can't attend to the business at all times." This led Roosevelt to ask, "Do I understand you to mean that your duties as a local politician occasionally override your duties as clerk?" Keenan was typical of machine appointees: they paid for their posts and pocketed departmental fees and expenses, simply padding their income from their normal business, frequently a saloon. For municipal reformers such as Roosevelt, Keenan perfectly reflected the corruption that made Tammany men rich while beggaring the city.

The committee then turned its attention to the Ludlow Street City Jail and its boss, the sheriff. One of the first things that Sheriff Alexander Davidson disclosed about the running of the jail was that he personally owned the van and team of horses used to transport prisoners. The fact that he had bought the team from his predecessor indicated that this was a moneymaking scheme handed from one sheriff to the next. When asked about the cost of the van and horses, Davidson replied, "Is that not a matter of private affair?" Roosevelt replied, "It is not a matter of private affair; we want to find out if the fees of this office are or are not excessive; therefore, we want to find out what the cost of your plant is." When the sheriff continued to claim it was a private affair, Roosevelt showed a flash of anger. "You say you consider that a private question," Roosevelt began. "The committee radically disagrees with you; you are a public servant, you are not a private individual; we have a right to know what the expense of your plant is; we don't ask for the expense of your private carriage that you use for your own conveyance; we ask you what you, a public servant, pay for a van employed in the service of the public; we have a right to know; it is a perfectly proper question." Davidson noted that his office also hired private carriages, or "hacks," to convey prisoners, including convicted murderers. When asked about the cost of hiring a carriage, the sheriff replied, "It depends entirely upon the generosity of the person who owns the hack. . . . When a deputy sheriff is handcuffed to a criminal, he is not apt to stand long for a dollar or two dollars."

Even the execution of prisoners seemed to be a moneymaker for the sheriff and his deputies, twenty of whom were paid to oversee a single execution. When asked about the necessity of having twenty deputies attend an execution, the sheriff replied that he was authorized to keep the peace. But, it was pointed out, the executions took place inside the presumably secure prison: "Why is it necessary to have twenty persons inside of the prison, twenty deputies to attend an execution?" The records also indicated a large fee of over $390 paid to Michael McGloin and Pascal Majone. Asked about this expense, Sheriff Davidson replied, "It is a contract that I make between the party that cuts the rope [for the hanging] and myself." The counsel for the committee, Charles Miller, began to ask the name of the person who cut the rope, but Roosevelt, seeing the real point of attack, cut him off. "You need not ask that," he said, then turned back to Davidson: "You pay $396 to the party that cuts the rope?" When both the sheriff and his counsel defended the expense, Roosevelt lectured them: "Mr. Sheriff, it is perfectly true that there is no occasion for squeamishness in answering a question like this; the occasion for squeamishness would be in taking advantage of your position for charging too much for things like this about which you think no inquiry would be made."

The investigation into the jail continued, with the sheriff's clerk, Jacob Wertheimer, and the undersheriff, Joel Stevens, called to testify about topics that included the practice of overcharging the city for a prisoner's stay in the jail and the cost of transporting prisoners. At the end of testimony on February 1, Wertheimer was arrested on the charge of collecting in the name of the sheriff, in 1883, at least $5,000 to which the sheriff was not entitled. The *New York Times*, which reported the committee hearings with great interest and sympathy for Roosevelt, noted almost in passing how Tammany had come to the rescue of one of its own. When Wertheimer appeared in Police Court, he was represented by a state senator; his $10,000 bail was posted by one Peter McGinnis, an East Side liquor dealer; and later that night a group of Tammany men went to the judge's home to secure Wertheimer's release. In New York City it paid to have friends in high places.

All the while that Roosevelt's investigating committee met, his Aldermanic bill was making its way through the Assembly. The blatant example of corruption offered by the committee's probe into the sheriff's department, and the subsequent arrest of the undersheriff on February 1, provided an ideal backdrop for Roosevelt's championing of the bill, which came up for a second reading in the Assembly on February 5. In what the *Times* referred to as an "excellent speech," Roosevelt defended the bill by citing the low character of the aldermen and accusing them of being merely tools of the political machine. Moreover, aldermen were largely unknown and unelected, while any mayor, though perhaps equally as dishonest or corrupt, was at least a highly public figure and subject to being kicked out of office at the next election. Despite opposition from Democrats, the Roosevelt bill was ordered to a third reading and thus probable passage by the lower house. With a sense of triumph, Roosevelt wrote to his wife, Alice, of his victory in the Assembly, saying he had "made a nice strike in my speech on the aldermanic bill."

The Roosevelt Committee hearings then took a dramatic turn when it was revealed that Mayor Franklin Edson and John Kelly had met before the election to discuss mayoral appointments. The city now enjoyed the spectacle of seeing both the mayor and the Tammany boss called before the Roosevelt Committee on February 9. In front of a packed parlor in the Metropolitan Hotel, Mayor Edson denied that any deals had been made—"No pledge or promise was made or suggested in regard to my appointments"—yet admitted to meeting at Kelly's house with the men who would later receive appointments as fire commissioner and police commissioner. The committee then called John Kelly, who did a fair job of not answering the questions put to him. When asked if he had any objection to telling the committee about the meeting at his house, he replied, "I have an objection, and I don't propose to tell it. The meeting was a private one, and this committee has no right to ask about it." Yet he freely admitted meeting with the mayor and future department heads, as well as with aldermen, to discuss the mayor's appointments. With no proof of any deals made other than the testimony of a disgruntled foe of the mayor, little came of Edson's and Kelly's testimony. For Roosevelt, though, the calling of Edson and Kelly had served its purpose: not to make their dealings the focus of his committee, but to expose them to the public as a way to garner support for his Aldermanic bill.

Despite Alice's advanced pregnancy, Roosevelt returned to Albany on Tuesday, February 12, prepared to speak on behalf of his Aldermanic bill the following day. On Wednesday, he recorded out of the Cities Committee fourteen bills, and received a telegram reporting the birth of a baby girl. With the third reading of his bill imminent, Roosevelt requested a leave of absence from the Assembly as he received the congratulations of his fellow members. Before any debate on the bill could begin, Roosevelt received a second telegram from New York City. Both his wife and mother lay dying. The Aldermanic bill was laid aside and Roosevelt caught the next train for the city. The next day his mother, Mittie Bulloch Roosevelt, died of typhoid fever, and his wife, Alice, died of Bright's disease, an inflammation of the kidneys that had been masked by the pregnancy. "On Feb. 12th 1884 her baby was born," Roosevelt found the strength to write in his diary, "and on Feb. 14th she died in my arms, my mother had died in the same house, on the same day, but a few hours previously." Their double funeral was held at the Fifth Avenue Presbyterian Church two days later. The next day, Roosevelt christened the baby Alice Lee. He took no joy in it, or in his newborn little girl—"her baby," as he wrote. "For joy and for sorrow my life has now been lived out," he lamented. He could not bear to call his daughter Alice, and instead referred to her as Baby Lee.

Four days after the funeral, Roosevelt was back in his seat in the Assembly, speaking on behalf of the Aldermanic bill. Roosevelt condemned "the aristocracy of the bad," the men who fattened themselves in public office on money wrung from the workingman and the taxpayer. Despite vigorous politicking by Tammany representatives on the floor of the Assembly, the bill passed by a vote of 70 to 51, with 12 Democrats supporting the measure and 8 Republicans voting against it. Seven Assemblymen were absent that day, reported the *Times*, "afraid to vote against the bill because of the political pressure put upon them," but also "afraid to take the opposite course because of the criticism which would follow them." The bill now went to the Senate's own Cities Committee.

Roosevelt's investigating committee would reconvene only on February 23, and its record of hearings indicated nothing about Roosevelt's tragedy. There was no call for a moment of silence or testimonials offered, as occurred in the Assembly in Albany. And while ink on a page does not easily reflect emotion, still, there appeared to be no change in Roosevelt's tone or in the proceedings in general. One of Roosevelt's favorite sayings was: "Black care rarely sits behind a rider whose pace is fast enough." Roosevelt tried to turn his back on his grief, throwing himself into his work.

Returning its attention to the sheriff and the Ludlow Street Prison, the committee heard from James Bowe, the warden and brother of the previous sheriff. The committee noted that the warden charged the city 75 cents a day for each prisoner's food, even though a large number of prisoners fed themselves. The warden was also asked about a bill for over $600 that the city paid, apparently to a furniture dealer for Brussels carpets ($175), a parlor suite ($150), a walnut table, and other items. The committee counsel asked, "Where did that furniture and bedding go?" "That is in my rooms," the warden replied. New York's taxpayers had outfitted Bowe's rooms in a style befitting an Astor.

The testimony of a former deputy warden at the jail, Philip Kiernan, former keepers, and former prisoners attracted the attention of the committee and the press. Kiernan and others testified that a bar was operated out of one of the jail cells; the proceeds from the sale of beer and tobacco went to the sheriff. In fact, it was a common sight to see jail keepers drunk, and once on a Sunday the chaplain complained about the noise and profanity coming from the bar. The committee also heard testimony that rooms were rented to prisoners for the purpose of entertaining women. The prison was overcrowded, with three or even four prisoners in some cells, and the prisoners were covered with lice. There also seemed to be a custom of asking prisoners for a sort of exit tax of $1.50 when they were discharged. Kiernan testified about the bad food and putrid meat served to prisoners, and the bad language and violence directed at prisoners. Female visitors, it was noted, were not searched when they came into the jail, and thus could carry in contraband, and the tin buckets used to transport food to the prisoners were also used for cleaning the floors.

It was perhaps this testimony, and the attention it received in the press, that led to the committee taking the dramatic step of holding further hearings inside the jail itself. Legally this was required, as the committee had no authority to call prisoners before it to testify. The committee first heard from Augustine Ralph McDonald, the jail librarian, who had been a prisoner for five years. McDonald testified that there was a systematic effort to extort money from prisoners for better conditions. When McDonald was unable to pay this money, he had been sent to a cell with no warm water and next to a toilet, so that foul air would come through a hole in the wall. He had been told it was "all a question of money" whether he could get out of that cell, and the deputy warden had asked him for $250. McDonald explained the system of extortion and described the near-constant drunkenness of the keepers. He also testified about the bad food, with leftover meat trimmings bought from butchers to make soup. And he said that the warden had offered to carpet his cell if he did not testify—perhaps with a $175 Brussels carpet.

The prisoner's litany of abuses continued. Some keepers continued to draw pay from the jail even after they had been discharged. The keepers supplied whiskey to, and borrowed money from, prisoners. Prisoners were allowed out of their cells as long as they had money to spend at the bar, and the revelry would continue late into the night. The sheriff, warden, and keepers would confiscate property and not return it. McDonald testified that when three keepers were discharged the previous May, they had three closets filled with furniture and other items taken from the prisoners' cells. Prisoners were not given changes of clothing for months, and those responsible for serving food would be so filthy that the vermin on them would drop onto the food. When asked if he knew anything about women being brought in for the prisoners, McDonald replied, "Well, the place goes by the name of the sheriff's whore-house." Once when he heard there were "strumpets" in the cells alongside his, McDonald got very indignant and complained: "I was willing to be imprisoned anywhere, but not in a house of ill-fame, and that the State of New York had no authority to do that." Nothing made headlines in New York like prostitutes serving prisoners.

Further testimony by other prisoners simply confirmed the stories the committee had already heard about drunkenness, extortion, theft, prostitution, bad language, filthy cells, and putrid food. Once again a city department had become the personal estate of a corrupt official, a situation allowed by Tammany's control over the aldermen and by the aldermen's power of confirmation of mayoral appointments. Once again the press covered the lurid tales of waste and corruption ("Abuses in Ludlow Street Jail Brought to Light," one headline proclaimed). And once again the Roosevelt committee hearings paralleled the progress of the Roosevelt bill through the state legislature. The Senate passed the Aldermanic bill on March 5. It was "an important triumph for the cause of municipal reform in this city," a *Times* editorial declared. All that was left now was for New York governor Grover Cleveland to sign the bill into law. The conclusion of the hearings of the investigating committee and its final report provided a perfect backdrop for the bill becoming law.

The committee adjourned only days before its final report was due on March 14. The report began with a sweeping statement that called the entire New York City government "absolutely appalling." In the report, Roosevelt again took aim at the Board of Aldermen and the nefarious powers behind it: "Under the present system the men who nominally hold the offices are not the ones who really exercise the power, . . . [and such men] are generally outside the political parties, [and] cannot be held responsible to the people for their deeds and misdeeds." The report then went through each department investigated and noted its findings. The clerk of the city of New York drew a salary of $3,000, but the current clerk had kept $13,700 in fees; his predecessor had kept $36,000. The register did not draw a salary and had only held his office since January 1, "but," the report claimed, "it appears clearly from the evidence that if subsequent months pay him as well as the month of January did his net income for the year will amount to between $30,000 and $40,000." The sheriff was being paid massive compensation for services that cost him very little, such as for transportation, food, and even hangings. But it was the committee's investigation of the Ludlow Street Jail that uncovered, in the report's words, "a most revolting and almost incredible state of affairs," where drunken and brutal keepers operated a system of extortion and blackmail. The sheriff, one of the city's top law enforcement officials, was in reality the ringleader of a massive scam involving the deputies and keepers at the jail.

Roosevelt followed submission of the report with the introduction of nine bills mainly having to do with reforming the system of fee collection in the various offices, which he claimed could save the city $200,000 a year. But the bills also included one to change the office of controller from an appointed to an elective office, and a bill to elect a president of the Board of Aldermen to preside over all aldermanic meetings. Most of these bills were eventually made into law, but none was as important as Roosevelt's Aldermanic bill, which Governor Cleveland signed into law on March 17, only a few days after the investigating committee submitted its report. Through his bill, Roosevelt sought to make the office of mayor more powerful by creating a strong executive who was directly responsible to the people. Whether for city mayor, state governor, or president of the United States, enhancement of executive power would be a hallmark of Roosevelt's political thought.

ROOSEVELT'S ALDERMANIC BILL and his investigative committee altered the way America's largest city was governed. For years to come, Roosevelt would refer to his intimate knowledge of New York politics. In 1886, for *Century* magazine, Roosevelt wrote an article on "Machine Politics in New York City," in which he recounted some of the committee's findings, including the large amounts of money that found their way through the city department heads to the political organizations. "The enormous emoluments of such officers are, of course, most effective in debauching politics," he wrote. "They bear no relation whatever to the trifling quantity of work done, and the chosen candidate readily recognizes what is the exact truth—namely, that the benefit of his service is expected to enure [hand over] to his party allies, and not to the citizens at large." In his 1891 history of New York, Roosevelt referred to machine politicians as "a solid, well-disciplined army of evil." And the value of the committee hearings to Roosevelt's career cannot be underestimated. In facing Senate opposition, press skepticism, and Tammany obstructionism, Roosevelt had faced down dogged opponents. He had secured an education in the intricacies of city government, from the clerk's office to the city prison. Roosevelt had also been exposed to a hierarchy of heelers and hacks, from men like Hubert Thompson, whom Roosevelt had first espied wearing his diamond stickpin in Albany, all the way to the mayor's office. Roosevelt had learned the power of the press in pursuing his legislative agenda, and how to pursue reform within the framework of the party. He had even worked with Democrats, securing their votes in the Assembly and securing Governor Cleveland's signature. Roosevelt had also affected real change in the way America's largest city was governed by enhancing the executive power of the mayor.

Roosevelt had proven himself a skilled and tough politician at age twenty-five. But with his double tragedy, any future political career was left very much in doubt. He would soon flee the city for his Dakota ranch, which he had purchased only the year before. Yet family, friends, and politics would constantly work to draw Roosevelt back home.

FIVE

"Hero Land"
Roosevelt's Trips West

Roosevelt's trips to the American West reflected the deep fascination that many in the East had with the nation's wild places—and wild people. Not only did easterners like Roosevelt go west; the West came east. By the 1880s, Delaware Indians had returned to Manhattan. Chiefs in feathered bonnets and war paint stalked down Broadway. From nearby buildings came the sound of gunshots, followed by blood-curdling, savage screams. Ten years after Custer's 1876 death by the Little Bighorn River, the country was mad with Western fever. New Yorkers flocked to theaters to experience the "blood curdling yells of the savages" and the "crack of the trusty rifle." "During Act II," one show promised, "Mr. Jack Dalton will present his great bowie knife act, in which 'Baby Bessie, the Pet of the Gulch,' will be pinned to a board by bowie knives." Those men expecting Baby Bessie to be a thinly clad beauty were disappointed. One writer called her "exceedingly hard to look at." When Dalton flung his knife at Bessie and the blade buried itself harmlessly next to her, one patron shouted disgustedly, "By Jove, he missed her!" When Frank Fayne tried to do the same with a "halo of real bullets," he killed his target, and the show was closed.

Alongside white men in stage makeup often stood real American natives imported from west of the Mississippi. In the lobby of the theater they were pressed into service selling audience members "traditional Indian remedies," such as "Pawnee Herb Tea" and "Rattle Snake Oil." A theatergoer remembered one such "long haired medico, in a sombrero, a dirty white shirt, embellished by a glass stud, and with finger nails showing no evidence of a recent acquaintance with soap." Such an appearance probably heightened his authenticity with most New Yorkers.

Many wealthy easterners attempted to slake their thirst for all things western by undertaking expensive and lavish expeditions. Raymond Tours began operating in 1879 and offered luxury winter trips to California for $750. The fabled Pullman "Palace" railroad cars—featuring carpeting, stained-glass windows, and elaborately frescoed ceilings—carried a constant stream of New Yorkers and New Englanders across the continent. Visiting America in 1883, Lord Charles Russell of Britain reveled in the lavishness of this elite mode of transportation. "It enabled the rich," he said, "to create the clearest possible inequality in the conditions of even ordinary travel." Travelers with means could rent entire private cars, as Ralph Waldo Emerson did in 1871 when he headed west. One wealthy family hired its own four-car train, which allowed them to travel with an entourage that included a maid, cooks, children's nurses, and a Pinkerton bodyguard. Raymond Tours' clients, the company noted in its advertising, were of only the "refined and cultured class."

Upon his arrival in the West, even greater opulence greeted the wealthy eastern traveler. Most of the grand western resorts tried to recreate the comforts of home for its demanding clientele. Although Theodore Roosevelt may have loved roughing it in the Badlands, most of his Gramercy Park or Fifth Avenue neighbors would have shuddered at the very idea. Western hotels and spas boasted shops, gardens, post offices, and nightly entertainment. For their stay at the Hotel de Paris in Georgetown, Colorado, tourists packed as if they were really going to Paris. One English visitor commented on the ladies' gowns, which were fit for a fancy ball. Their husbands sported fox-hunting coats. "The ladies breakfast toilets are good enough for the dinner table," British visitor Daniel Pidgeon observed in an 1883 book about his travels in

America, *An Engineer's Holiday*, "while for dinner they dress as we do for the opera." For Roosevelt, the West was about physical exertion and endurance. Not so for most other eastern tourists. "American ladies never walk," Pidgeon continued, "but they go out 'buggy-riding' in dancing shoes and ball dresses, or amble about on ponies in highly ornamental riding habits. All this seems very odd among the mountains." For their part, men shot clay pigeons and played polo. Instead of hunting foxes, they hunted coyotes. Studying the habits of most easterners on such holidays reveals little about the West, but much about eastern norms of etiquette and entertainment. "The guests . . . who rode out to the hunt at the sound of the horn," Pidgeon concluded, "probably had moved west only geographically." This could not be said of Theodore Roosevelt, who in the summer of 1884 appeared ready to settle down on his Dakota ranch.

WITHOUT A DOUBT, Theodore Roosevelt's time in the West affected him profoundly. Roosevelt himself continually repeated this, even going as far as saying his western sojourn helped put him in the White House. The West allowed Roosevelt to transcend his wealthy, urban, eastern origins. It allowed him to prove his masculinity. It allowed him an escape from grief. Finally, it allowed him a refuge from recent political defeats. The West helped transform Roosevelt into the man and politician he would become.

At the same time, Roosevelt himself had a keen interest in amplifying his short time in the West, for the very personal and political reasons stated above. And the amplification seemed to increase over time. The vast pressures of family and political life would enhance Roosevelt's nostalgia for a simpler, more solitary, and more romantic time of his life. That his amplification, even exaggeration, has been almost completely accepted by later biographers is a bit curious. Certainly, the romantic image of Roosevelt on horseback—herding cattle, hunting game, and sleeping by a campfire under the stars—is very attractive to both writers and readers of Roosevelt's life. But it seems absurd to suggest, as biographers from William Henry Harbaugh to Joshua David Hawley have, that Roosevelt truly became one of the cowboys, or that he ever seriously considered giving up his life in the East.

In evaluating the influence of the West on Roosevelt, few writers have searched for evidence beyond Roosevelt's own words. What did those closest to Roosevelt think of his stay in the Dakota Territory? The answer seems to be—not much. When shortly after Roosevelt's death his closest friend, Lodge, eulogized him before a rare joint session of Congress, Lodge summarized Roosvelt's entire life and career without speaking a word about the West. When the recollections of 150 people who knew Roosevelt were collected in a single volume, called *Roosevelt as We Knew Him*, in 1927, none of them mentioned his Dakota ranch. His cousin Nicholas Roosevelt related nothing about Theodore's time in the West in his book *Theodore Roosevelt: The Man as I Knew Him*. Old family friend and Roosevelt's secretary of state John Hay felt the West had mainly a maturing effect on Roosevelt, saying that there he "grew to full stature." Fellow urban reformer Jacob Riis said something similar, that Roosevelt "rested" and "grew" there before "hearing the trumpet call to another life." And the Reverend Ferdinand Iglehart, a friend of Roosevelt's after the mid-1890s, called Roosevelt's two years in the West a "post-graduate course," implying they rounded out the education he received in his four years at Harvard and three years in the New York State Assembly. None of these friends or family members placed very great importance on Roosevelt's western sojourn.

One of the most interesting accounts of Roosevelt as a western figure came from his sister Corinne. In 1890, Corinne traveled to the Badlands to visit her brother's two North Dakota spreads, Elkhorn Ranch and Maltese Cross Ranch. (He would sell both in 1898, although his last visit occurred in 1892.) Corinne, by then in her late twenties, was accompanied by her husband; her sister Anna, then thirty-five; and the Lodges' sixteen-year-old son, George. Staying for three weeks, Corinne gave a more sober and less embellished assessment of her brother in his western setting. She referred to his ranching endeavor as mainly a "business enterprise." Far from believing her "city-bred" brother had become one his cowboys, Corinne noted that the ranch hands referred to their boss as "Mr. Roosevelt" and held a "reverential attitude" toward him. No doubt Corinne saw firsthand what many in the East failed to appreciate in their romantic image of cowboys. Cowboys were a rough and poorly schooled bunch. Some of them were illiterate. Far from being the self-contained men on horse-back, traveling with their kits across lonesome plains, that western novels popularized, most cowboys were little more than itinerant workers, so poor they owned neither the horses they rode upon nor the gear they used when they found a job. And far from being excellent shots with a revolver, most could not afford the ammunition with which to practice, and were probably as good a shot as their near-sighted "Mr. Roosevelt." No wonder Corinne hesitated to identify her beloved brother too closely with this motley lot.

Corinne's party followed its stay at Elkhorn with a trip to Yellowstone. Significantly, in seeing her brother in both places, Corinne saw for herself his love of "wild places and wild companions, hard tramps and thrilling adventure." These, then, were all part of Roosevelt's ranching experience and his stay in, to use his own words, "hero land." His love for the outdoors, for camping and hunting, were part of a larger, lifelong love affair he had with the wild places of the earth. From boyhood until his death, Roosevelt sought adventure. This quest took many forms, from being a soldier to exploring the Amazon. It also explained his later safari to Africa, an experience that can be likened to his time in the West. In Africa, Roosevelt hunted game much bigger and fiercer than the antelope of the American West, and there he camped beneath the stars for weeks at a time with other men. Roosevelt spent a total of ten months in Africa—but no one has ever suggested that Roosevelt "became African." When Corinne sought to evaluate the effect the time in the West had on her brother, she echoed the sentiment of John Hay and others about Roosevelt's growing maturity. Roosevelt's time on his ranch, she said, mainly aided "the mental growth of the young man."

Roosevelt returned to New York matured, but he also helped in the maturing eastern view of the West. Whereas the West had once been seen as a shadowy, savage wilderness, a sort of anti-Eden, by the end of the nineteenth century easterners were looking west for an alternative—even a panacea—for the increasingly urbanized and industrialized East. And it was easterners who helped establish this image of the West, interpreting their western experience for an eastern audience. Frederic Remington, a onetime Yale art student, became the great artist, sculptor, and illustrator of the West. Owen Wister, who, like Roosevelt, was a Harvard man, would write a novel, *The Virginian*, that set the standard for the cowboy genre. Wister dedicated his 1902 book to his friend Theodore Roosevelt. Finally, through his voluminous writings, Roosevelt himself contributed enormously to America's image of the West. In his articles and books on western life—namely, *Hunting Trips of a Ranchman*, *Ranch Life and the Hunt-Trail*, and *The Wilderness Hunter*—Roosevelt sketched for his largely eastern audience vivid firsthand accounts of a rugged, manly outdoors existence. For those back east who were exhausted by modern urban life—the noise, the smell, the jostling crowds—Roosevelt's writings acted as a tonic. The reader was allowed to share a small sliver of a life spent riding, ranching, and hunting.

Roosevelt's glowing description of his ranch was beguiling. "My home-ranch stands on the river brink," he began. "From the low, long veranda, shaded by leafy cottonwoods, one looks across sand-bars and shallows to a strip of meadowland, behind which rises a line of sheer cliffs and grassy plateaus. This veranda is a pleasant place in the summer evenings when a cool breeze stirs along the river and blows in the faces of the tired men, who loll back in their rocking-chairs . . . gazing sleepily out at the weird-looking buttes opposite, until their sharp lines grow indistinct and purple in the afterglow of the sunset." Roosevelt contrasted the well-earned ease of the rancher at dusk with the masculine activity of the day. He also wrote of the freedom such a life afforded. Certainly Roosevelt had gone west seeking a sort of freedom from the responsibilities of politics and parenthood. Yet he also sought his manhood, a common quest for the Victorian male. Eastern, urban life could be an emasculating one, a life completely void of physical exertion or work with the hands, yet full of opera, fancy balls, and white-tie dinners. Roosevelt was far from being the only young man in late nineteenth-century America who had inherited his name, wealth, and social status, while earning little on his own. Harvard, Yale, and Columbia were chock-full of tennis-playing dandies with cushy jobs in their fathers' businesses awaiting them upon graduation. A previous generation of men had proven their worth and manhood in the Civil War. Roosevelt's generation had no such outlet for its masculine anxieties. Absent war, ranching and hunting in the Badlands allowed

Roosevelt, and through him, by proxy, thousands of other Victorian men, to savor the cult of true manhood. No one reading Theodore Roosevelt's name as the author of these works mistook him for a cowboy. Indeed, the value in Roosevelt's writing was that he was an easterner, he was *one of them*, and could help translate the very language of the West for his distant audience.

In addition to his accounts of western life, between 1889 and 1896 Roosevelt also authored the four-volume *The Winning of the West*. Much has been said about this work, particularly the claim that years before Frederick Jackson Turner stated his "frontier thesis" of American history, Roosevelt had already underscored the frontier as the unique characteristic of the American story. Yet Roosevelt's works go beyond merely a retelling of western expansion. Through the volumes, Roosevelt addressed key themes meant to resonate with an eastern, urban audience. As the United States filled with southern and eastern European immigrants who changed the face and the politics of American cities, Roosevelt underscored the success of the "English-speaking" peoples in conquering the continent. These hunters and settlers had done the real work of America, and had been a hardy bunch, in contrast increasingly to the urban, immigrant, industrial worker and the effete professional class. These early Americans had had no leaders, and so were truly democratic in their endeavors. Roosevelt underscored their "independent" nature—perhaps because they were free of the machinery of industrial America and even the political machinery of the American city. No leaders meant no bosses.

In Roosevelt's depiction of the Wild West, the continent became a kind of antagonist, with Roosevelt telling the story of its defeat. His heroes were not the Indians, but the men who subjugated them. Conquering the continent meant filling it up, and this had been done by English-speaking peoples. The message Roosevelt sent east about Anglo-Saxon superiority was aptly timed for an audience that was watching the newest shipload of immigrants stepping onto the dock. It also touched the nerve of those who were contemplating America's future. The United States was already an economic power and a continental power. Looking south to Cuba and west to Hawaii in the 1880s, the next obvious step was for the United States to become an imperial power. Roosevelt's writing expressed the vast latent power of a continental nation, one that was, by the 1880s—much like Roosevelt himself—reaching maturity.

In interpreting the West for an eastern, urban audience, Roosevelt also sent back messages that made an impression on late nineteenth-century Americans. Almost sixty years ago, one historian of the American West, Earl Pomeroy, called Theodore Roosevelt "the best-known exponent of the wild West after Buffalo Bill Cody" and his Wild West Show. Roosevelt and Cody's western stories were complementary. Not only was one highbrow, and the other decidedly low; their depictions also staked out different areas. Cody, a former cavalry scout, depicted exciting battles between Indians and American soldiers. Roosevelt described a life of hunting and ranching, punctuated by poetic descriptions of the scenery. Together, Roosevelt and Cody told the story of the western movement of American civilization at the expense of Native Americans. Although the heroes varied, from rancher and settler to scout and trooper, in the hands of their champions, they all became the romantic ideal of the manly, dynamic, and brave American. These were enduring images, and Roosevelt played a key role in creating the myth of the American West. The West did not "make" Theodore Roosevelt, but Theodore Roosevelt surely helped to make the West.

ALTHOUGH BIOGRAPHERS speak of Roosevelt's two years in the West, in reality his stay there was a series of trips. With no stay on his ranch longer than seven months, Roosevelt really spent only about a year and a half out west. And his time there was continually punctuated by long stays back in New York. This included a lengthy five-month period in late 1885 and early 1886 during which he became secretly engaged to his onetime adolescent love interest, Edith Carow. Moreover, there was a distinct pattern to Roosevelt's arrivals back in New York City: he made sure he was in Manhattan in October 1884, October 1885, and October 1886. October was not simply campaign time in New York City; it was nomination time. Throughout his western sojourn, Roosevelt made sure he was back in his hometown when Republican conventions picked their nominees for state and local office. Far from indicating that Roosevelt meant to give up his life in New York for a life on a ranch, this pattern indicated that Roosevelt meant to keep a hand in New York City politics. Making sure to be back in Manhattan at nomination time also suggested that Roosevelt was looking for a job.

Yet politics was not the only thing Roosevelt left behind him in New York. Upon returning to the city in the fall of 1884 Roosevelt made straight for sister Bamie's house on Madison Avenue. There, he was reunited with his infant daughter, Alice Lee, now almost eight months old. Roosevelt seemed to suffer little pain in leaving behind his own child during his trips to his ranch. Possibly Roosevelt could not bear to be reminded of his departed wife, Alice. In fact, he appeared to try to put her out of his mind almost completely. In letters to his sisters, he rarely asked after Alice Lee. After returning to Elkhorn in the fall of 1884, his first letter to Anna asked her to "give many kisses to wee baby." A month later, it was simply, "Best love to Baby Lee." After that, all the while recounting his escapades among cowboys, cattle ranchers, and hunters, Roosevelt did not even ask after his daughter for a time.

In the spring of 1886, Roosevelt told Anna that he missed "darling Baby Lee dreadfully," and that he was "hungry" to see her. Immediately, however, he qualified his feelings for his two-year-old daughter, who was growing up without either of her parents. He was thoroughly enjoying his life ranching, hunting, and writing. His affection for his little girl, it seemed, paled in comparison to his adventure in hero land. Significantly, Roosevelt only assumed the job of little Alice's father after he remarried in 1886. When Roosevelt remarried, took up his parental duties, and reentered the social and political life of New York City, it marked his final attainment of maturity, as those who were closest to him recognized.

Roosevelt's distant relationship with Alice Lee indicated strongly that his trips home to New York were more for political than for personal reasons. Even though his hat was not in the ring, Roosevelt still took a hand in the 1884 campaigns. Such work was not without controversy. In June, Roosevelt had attended the Republican National Convention in Chicago as a New York State delegate. He joined forces with rising Massachusetts politician and fellow Harvard alumnus Henry Cabot Lodge to oppose James Blaine as the favored presidential nominee of party leaders. Lodge had played this role before, helping to nominate dark-horse candidate James Garfield in 1880. When Blaine handily won the 1884 nomination, it was a bitter defeat for Roosevelt and Lodge. Still, both men eventually decided to back the party's nominee, rather than bolting the party, as so many independent Republicans chose to do that fall. When Roosevelt returned to New York in October, he found himself in a difficult position. He had been very publicly identified as one of the leaders of the reformers' rebellion in Chicago, yet he planned to campaign for Republicans. Roosevelt tried to use his time back home to mend fences with regular Republicans and show himself a loyal party man. This was not an easy thing to do, and he achieved only mixed results.

Roosevelt spoke to a number of Republican audiences that October, but wherever he turned—New York, Brooklyn, Boston—his independent revolt in Chicago dogged him. He became involved in a nasty public dispute with Mugwump Horace White, who related the story of an angry postconvention Roosevelt readying to bolt the party and support the Democratic candidate, New York governor Grover Cleveland. Roosevelt fervently denied it, but after Chicago, the story had the ring of truth about it. In Boston, he and Lodge were attacked by Josiah Quincy and the Massachusetts Reform Club, which opposed Lodge's election to Congress. In his own Twenty-First District, Roosevelt failed to elect a ticket of reform delegates to the various state and local conventions, losing to the Republican boss of his district, Jake Hess. Even when Roosevelt tried to mend fences with party leaders by publicly backing Blaine, he could only bring himself to assure listeners that President Blaine would be "the servant of the people." This was damning with faint praise indeed.

It did not help Roosevelt's cause that come Election Day, Blaine narrowly lost to Cleveland. The vote in New York State was so close that if only six hundred independent Republicans had stayed loyal to Blaine rather than voting for Cleveland, Blaine would have ascended to the presidency, and likely held the White House for Republicans for the next eight years. In New York, Republican leaders blamed Roosevelt. In Massachusetts, Lodge lost his bid for a seat in Congress. But Lodge remained deeply enmeshed in the apparatus of the state Republican Party. Roosevelt instead simply headed west.

Roosevelt returned just in time to experience the severest winter conditions. With the days shortening and the weather turning increasingly foul, Roosevelt spent more time indoors than usual, brooding over the past and contemplating the future. With the anniversary of his wife's and mother's death looming, this may have been the bleakest time of Roosevelt's life. Activity on the ranch came to a standstill, leaving Roosevelt with too much time to think. He spent much of his time occupying himself in writing *Hunting Trips of a Ranchman*, which he would deliver to the publisher that spring.

His chapter entitled "Winter Weather" captured his depressed frame of mind. Roosevelt referred to winter in the Badlands as "an irksome period of enforced rest and gloomy foreboding." His description of the barren landscape mirrored his own feelings of loss, isolation, and anxiety. During the winter, Roosevelt wrote, the landscape was absolutely desolate, raked by blinding storms of snow mixed with dust. Then the wind would stop, and the stillness held its own horror. Nights were the worst. Roosevelt referred to the "lifeless silence" and the "dead and endless wastes." With his constant references to death, Roosevelt probably contemplated the deaths not only of his wife and mother, but also of his beloved father, at the age of only forty-seven. With his own twenty-sixth birthday just past, no doubt Roosevelt speculated as to how much more time he had on the earth. Such gloomy thoughts were exactly why Roosevelt had fled to his ranch, seeing in the West a chance for escape and succor. Now, with the long winter stretching before him, perhaps it was at this moment that New York, rather than the West, beckoned him with the greater promise of comfort and support. Those he truly loved—his sisters, his baby, the Lodges—were all back east. The East held much greater opportunities for work and action. After the brutal winter of 1884–1885, Roosevelt began actively seeking to reinsert himself into life back in New York.

LODGE ALWAYS REMAINED a reliable conduit of political information from Washington and the East. In the spring, Roosevelt wrote his friend about newly inaugurated President Grover Cleveland's cabinet. While calling most of the new secretaries "respectable," Roosevelt took particular offense at the appointment of Daniel Manning, former head of the New York State Democratic Committee, as secretary of the treasury. Roosevelt went so far as to refer to the "Cleveland-Manning machine." Then, turning to New York City politics, Roosevelt noted with dissatisfaction that the new Democratic governor, David Hill, had refused to oust from the Ludlow Street Jail Roosevelt's old nemesis from the investigating committee, the utterly corrupt Sheriff Davidson. With the worst of Tammany's men receiving plum positions in Washington, Roosevelt wondered whether the equally corrupt former commissioner of public works, Hubert O. Thompson, might "get anything." By March 1885, Roosevelt had been in the Badlands for a few months, but his head was still in New York.

In that same letter to Lodge, Roosevelt spoke of American politics having reached a stage that he called "the Apotheosis of the Unknown." Roosevelt might have been speaking about himself and the uncertain point he had reached in his life. The past six months indicated that Roosevelt meant to split his time between his ranch and New York, and to keep a hand in New York politics. Yet he had no position in New York, or even the prospect of one. True, he had written a book on his time in the West, and might write more, but was this his new calling? With a year having passed since his wife's death, the official mourning period came to an end, and the grim black border on his stationery fell away. Moreover, his daughter, Alice Lee, was no longer a red-faced, shrieking, alien creature in her infancy. At a year old, a real person had begun to emerge, walking and babbling. Roosevelt must have seen at least something of his dead wife in the girl—a curl of hair, the shape of the eyes, her smile. And perhaps after a year Roosevelt realized that contemplating his daughter and the related grief did not hurt quite so much anymore.

All of this might have made Roosevelt yearn for a return to New York. But in the spring of 1885, his prospects were dim. Entering into any of the Roosevelt-affiliated businesses did not seem even to cross his mind. Since college, only politics had ever really interested him as a career. As long as he and district boss Jake Hess continued their feud at Morton Hall, a career path via the Twenty-First Assembly District was closed. A Democratic governor meant no appointment to a state position. Receiving a post from the current New York mayor, William

Grace, remained a possibility, as he was a reform-minded independent much like Roosevelt himself. With memories of Roosevelt and
Lodge's rebellion of the previous June, Republican Party regulars remained wary of Roosevelt as prone to independent action, while the
Mugwumps, led by editor E. L. Godkin at *The Nation*, and later the
New York Evening Post, kept up their screed against those who had remained loyal to the party and supported Blaine. In terms of New York
politics, Roosevelt was a man without a country.

Still, city, state, and federal politics remained very much on
Roosevelt's mind. Soon after returning for Christmas in 1884,
Roosevelt's article "Phases of State Legislation" appeared in the January
1885 issue of *The Century*. In the article, Roosevelt dissected state politics as conducted in Albany, including relating scenes from his three-
year career. He gave a very mixed picture of the quality of politicians
and the politics they practiced, pointing out the dishonesty and outright bribery he had witnessed. As an answer, Roosevelt called for
greater participation of the better classes, just as newspapers had after
the death of his father. So far, however, aside from loudly denouncing
corruption and demanding reform, New York's elite had done little.
Roosevelt took aim directly at members of his own class, painting a
ridiculous picture of such "swallowtails." "A number of them will get
together in a large hall," Roosevelt wrote, drawing a vivid picture of
countless Cooper Union mass meetings, "will vociferously demand 'reform,' as if it were some concrete substance which could be handed out
to them in slices, and will then disband with a feeling of the most serene
self-satisfaction, and the belief that they have done their entire duty as
citizens and members of the community." No doubt Roosevelt's words
contained an element of payback for the constant drubbing he and
Lodge had received from members of their own social set. Roosevelt
declared the vast majority of wealthy and educated men ignorant of
even the basics of politics, such as the purpose of a caucus or primary.
These men did not understand that they had to join political parties
in order to have any sort of influence, rather than shrinking from the
fight. Roosevelt took dead aim at the effete, shrill, and toothless reformers who in the end accomplished nothing. Certainly he attempted
to set himself apart from such men. Yet what was Roosevelt himself

doing in January 1885 but writing calls for action while remaining in self-imposed exile nearly 2,000 miles away? Perhaps Roosevelt did not see the irony. Or, perhaps, being back in New York and observing politics firsthand, he questioned whether he was, in fact, shrinking from the struggle.

During the spring and summer of 1885, as Roosevelt rode the roundup, politics was never far from his mind. Although it was an off-year with no federal elections, in New York State Democrat David Hill was running for reelection as governor. In early June, Roosevelt's old Assembly colleague Walter Sage Hubbell wrote to inquire whether Roosevelt would seek a spot on the Republican ticket that fall. Hubbell was really fishing for information: he also asked whether someone called "H"—possibly Roosevelt's friend Walter Howe from New York—was seeking the nomination for lieutenant governor. Hubbell sought Roosevelt's support for his own possible bid for office as well. Roosevelt stated in response that he had no information about "H's" plans, but he hoped there would be no rivalry among the younger members. In the end, Hubbell received no nomination for the state ticket, although Roosevelt's old friend William O'Neil was briefly considered for the party nomination for state treasurer. Of his own plans, Roosevelt wrote, "I really have not given a single thought to my taking a place on the state ticket this fall . . . but I do'nt [sic] think it all probable unless for some reason it should seem best to outsiders." By "outsiders," Roosevelt apparently meant those "outside the Republican machine." If independents, such as the ones who had elected William Grace mayor, drafted Roosevelt, only then would he run. This seemed unlikely.

Still, by the time Roosevelt wrote Hubbell that June, things were looking up for him politically. Just before Roosevelt had left New York that April, he had organized a new slate of reform delegates to the various conventions from the Twenty-First District and prepared for the inevitable battle with Hess. Much to his surprise, his forces came to an agreement with the Hess men, and a union ticket of delegates was organized with Roosevelt at its head. With Roosevelt out of town and out of touch that political season, being named head of the delegates constituted, as he wrote Lodge, "a posthumous political victory." "I am really sorry," he continued, "for I can not spend the time necessary to take much personal part in politics now." No doubt Roosevelt was truly sorry, as attending the various conventions that spring and summer might have been an avenue back into city and state politics. It was a good sign, however. He had begun the slow process of patching things up with the New York bosses.

Just as Roosevelt kept New York politics in mind, New York politicians evidently kept Roosevelt in mind. Even as he supervised a new herd arriving at his ranches in Dakota in early May, Roosevelt was appointed a member of a Republican state committee to evaluate new rules for picking convention delegates. The very next day, on May 7, 1885, the annual meeting of the Civil Service Association named Roosevelt to its executive committee. Although these were hardly positions that could draw him back to New York, a more interesting offer came from Mayor Grace in June. Grace was endeavoring to oust the corrupt president of the Board of Health, Alexander Shaler, and he offered the spot to Roosevelt. Roosevelt expressed his uncertainty to Lodge that June, yet decided to take the position. Shaler was indicted for bribe-taking at the end of the year. From then until the following summer, Roosevelt wrote letters back east asking people how long the court case would last and when he should ready himself to return to New York. Shaler's case, however, lasted until 1891, as he was ably defended by old Roosevelt family friend Elihu Root. Only then was Shaler finally removed from office, much to Roosevelt's disappointment. Here had been a real chance to return to New York, and it evaporated before his eyes.

After only five weeks back out west, Roosevelt again returned to New York in early July. This time he stayed for two months, spending most of that time at Sagamore Hill, the home he had built at Oyster Bay—originally for Alice, though she had never lived there. Indeed, he had nearly stopped construction on the house after her death, but had changed his mind at the urging of relatives who believed he should have a home for his daughter. The home was not yet completed in the summer of 1885, but it was close enough for him to host guests there. It was at this time that he first held his brother's infant daughter, future First Lady Eleanor Roosevelt. And he increasingly bonded with his own daughter, who was now almost one and a half years old. On July 23, as a captain in the New York State Militia, he marched in the funeral parade of former president General Ulysses S. Grant. At the end of August, Roosevelt readied once again to reprise his commute to his ranch, although this time he planned to stay only a month. He reached Medora, North Dakota, on August 25, and within four weeks, turned around and set off for the Republican state convention at Saratoga.

Roosevelt's appearance at Saratoga was significant for several reasons. First, he was *there*. In the spring, he had been unsure whom to support for governor, and appeared ready to settle into cowherding until the big beef roundup in October. By mid-September, though, he was heading back to New York. Second, Roosevelt went to Saratoga as part of the New York delegation that included Jake Hess. Although they did not enter the convention hand-in-hand, rapprochement was the order of the day. "The general disposition," one journalist observed in the *New York Times*, "was for the cultivation of harmony." Third, by entering the fight against David Hill, who had succeeded Cleveland as governor, Roosevelt sought to strike a blow in favor of his career-long passion, civil service reform. Hill was a vocal supporter of the spoils system and did not shrink from declaring his opposition to civil service reform, as it prevented any administration, even at the federal level, from rewarding faithful service to the party. In Hill, Roosevelt found a deserving foe.

To counter Hill, Roosevelt looked to Cornelius Bliss, a successful businessman and independent Republican much like himself. For Roosevelt, Bliss had the additional advantage of not being the choice of machine politicians. This put Roosevelt in much the same position as only a year before, when he had backed Vermonter George Edmunds against Blaine at the Republican National Convention. Roosevelt energetically politicked for Bliss's nomination, conferring with all the lesser candidates and former governor Alonzo Cornell. When other party leaders refused even to speak to Roosevelt about Bliss, Roosevelt stubbornly continued his canvass. After Bliss lost the nomination to a compromise candidate, Ira Davenport, Roosevelt stumped for the party choice that fall.

At Saratoga, Roosevelt had been an active participant, doing more than just routine work, especially considering his tenuous position in the party over the past year. On the Resolutions Committee, Roosevelt helped shape the very wording of the platform dealing with civil service reform. The platform also included another interest of Roosevelt's, protecting black suffrage in the South. For Roosevelt and other Republicans, this was as much about breaking the Democrats' stranglehold on the South's 153 electoral votes as it was about social and racial justice. In drafting the strong language for the platform, Roosevelt actually found himself on the same side as his old Assembly nemesis, who was now state senator and the convention's temporary chairman, Warner Miller. Just as when he had attacked corruption in Tammany-controlled New York, Roosevelt had found a cause that appealed to him both personally and politically.

Finally, Roosevelt had not simply arrived at Saratoga anonymously. He made an entrance. The time out west had dramatically changed his physical appearance, something that often shocked people who knew him. Gone forever, it seemed, was the pale and sickly young man. Roosevelt returned east healthy, bronzed, and carrying as much as thirty extra pounds. Moreover, Roosevelt understood the effect his changed appearance had on people, and he exploited it. To the riverside town of Saratoga, now filled to bursting with all manner of political hacks smoking cigars and plotting strategy, Roosevelt wore a large straw sombrero. It got him noticed. Men hollered, "Hello, where's the rest of the cowboys?" Roosevelt explained the hat with a great story. "A bucking mustang stood on my head, and when I got to my feet I found that my best hat encircled my neck like a courtier's collar," he said. "This was the next best thing I could find to wear, and I've had to wait till I could get back to civilization to buy a substitute." Why Roosevelt would have been wearing his best derby while riding a bucking bronco, he did not explain. While likely apocryphal, the story indicated how Roosevelt could use his time in the West to disarm a roomful of cigar-chomping eastern politicos. And hats would feature prominently in this performance. After his time in Cuba, Colonel Roosevelt would make sure to wear his Rough Rider hat to political gatherings—including the 1900 convention that nominated him for vice president. In Roosevelt's case, the hat made the man.

With the convention over and Davenport nominated, Roosevelt turned to campaigning. He addressed the Young Republican Club of Brooklyn accompanied by a surprise guest, Henry Cabot Lodge. Reflecting the Saratoga platform he had helped to write, Roosevelt hammered the Democrats on civil service and their coercive political monopoly in the South. The next day, he attended a meeting that was billed as a conference of Republican leaders, then visited Republican headquarters. Roosevelt not only meant to take an active part in Republican Party politics that fall; he meant to have an influence and get noticed. To address an even wider audience, that October Roosevelt published an article in *The North American Review*, "The President's Policy." This article later attracted the attention of Roosevelt biographers because in it Roosevelt compared Jefferson Davis to Benedict Arnold, prompting Davis to send a letter of protest to Roosevelt. But these historians overlooked other details in the article, such as Roosevelt's characterizations of the Democrats, his appeal to independent Republicans who had bolted the party the previous year, and references to his own Assembly career. In other words, Roosevelt was still working hard at making up for his actions of 1884 and reestablishing himself in the Republican Party. Such things would have been unnecessary, had he been planning to stay out west.

One final lure dangled in front of Roosevelt that October, and he bit eagerly. He became reacquainted with his childhood chum and onetime love interest Edith Carow. They were children no longer. At twenty-four, Edith was refined and intelligent. She was as sophisticated and cosmopolitan as Roosevelt, having spent time living with her family in Europe. And she was beautiful, with a long, graceful neck, slim waist, wide brown eyes, and an ample mouth. The attraction was immediate and mutual. Already, Roosevelt's cowboy persona was fading away, the draw of the Badlands ranch receding into the distance.

Roosevelt had one more major event to attend that October, but it was far away from the political carnival gripping Manhattan. On October 26, the day before his twenty-seventh birthday, Roosevelt took to the hounds and rode with Long Island's Meadowbrook Hunt.

Rather than galloping across open ranchland, as in Dakota, the horses on this hunt had to maneuver through dense woodlands and make enormous jumps over fallen trees. Riding his large and powerful horse Frank, Roosevelt led all the riders. Behind him, the hunt was taking its toll in the form of broken bones and torn skin. It was too much for Frank, who started to go lame. As the hunt approached a stone wall about five feet high, Frank hesitated. Roosevelt drove his spurs into Frank's sides to make the jump. With no power in his lame leg, however, Frank tripped on the wall, and horse and rider went down. With his face covered with blood and an arm broken, Roosevelt remounted Frank and took off after the hounds. "It's a mere trifle," he told a reporter for the *Times* who asked about it. To Lodge a few days later, he wrote, "I don't grudge the broken arm a bit. . . . I am always willing to pay the piper when I have a good dance; and every now and then I like to drink the wine of life with brandy in it." Except for the forced inactivity, the arm seemed to bother him little.

There may have been another reason why Roosevelt felt so happy. After his arm was set and his scraped nose bandaged, he hosted the Hunt Ball at Sagamore Hill. Edith was the guest of honor. Although Roosevelt had built the house for Alice, now another woman strode across the wooden floors. Edith danced and laughed as if the house had been built for her. With his freshly broken arm, and not a little pain, Roosevelt may not have been the most attentive host to Edith. But seeing her at Sagamore Hill must have awoken something inside him. She fit there, with him, and with his daughter. Within three weeks they would be engaged, and their marriage would last thirty-two years.

AS THE CLOCK STRUCK MIDNIGHT out on Long Island after the Meadowbrook Hunt, Roosevelt turned twenty-seven. Although he had spent many months out west, the events of the past few weeks made him eye a future in New York. Politics had been the foremost reason for returning, and Roosevelt had thrown himself into the election season with gusto. He had made up with Jacob Hess in the Twenty-First District. He had played an important role at the Republican state convention at Saratoga. He had been publicly recognized as one of the leaders of the Republican Party. And he had done good work for the

party, campaigning for the nominee for governor and writing a piece
for an influential journal that criticized the Democrats and sought to
draw back independent bolters. With Mayor Grace offering him the
position of president of the Board of Health, there even seemed to be a
real chance of returning to New York in order to take a relatively important job. It had taken some work to undo the damage done in June
1884, but by October 1885, much of that work seemed complete.

As well as the political, the personal constituted a strong draw to
New York. Roosevelt wrote often to Lodge expressing his affection for
him and his "cara sposa," Nannie Lodge. His brother and sisters were
married and having their own families. And little Alice was a baby no
longer, but a toddler of nearly two. Now there was Edith, well-read
and well-bred, unlikely to become a housewife on a cattle ranch. A life
with her meant returning to New York City and again taking up politics. With their engagement secret, because so little time had passed
since Alice's death, Roosevelt was free, for the time being, to return to
Dakota. This last stretch of seven months on his ranch would be one
of his longest. Perhaps this was because Roosevelt knew it would be
his last.

SIX

"Into the Yawning Gulf"
Roosevelt's 1886 Bid for Mayor

THE NEW YORK MAYORAL CONTEST of 1886 reflected the continuing contrasts of a city split between wealthy financiers and the laboring poor. That brownstone-born Theodore Roosevelt ran against Henry George, a united labor candidate, exemplified the contrast.

Roosevelt returned to New York from the West only on October 8, as Henry George, recently nominated by the Central Labor Union (CLU), gave his first stump speech to a crowd of 2,000. Republicans and Democrats scrambled to find challengers to take on the labor candidate. Significantly, Roosevelt had just passed through Chicago on the very day the men convicted of the Haymarket bombing were sentenced to be hanged. The May 3 bombing, which left seven police officers dead, helped redraw the social and political landscape of 1886, as reflected by George's candidacy and the frightened reaction of New Yorkers of both parties. Roosevelt would eventually lose the race, but he helped to unite city Republicans on the eve of the 1888 national election.

Roosevelt ran as a reforming Republican who pledged to clean up city government. For the first time, the former assemblyman addressed a citywide audience rather than just a safe Republican district. The mayoral race against George in a year of labor radicalism deepened Roosevelt's understanding of the stark social and economic divisions in the city. Within a decade, Roosevelt would write to urban reformer Jacob Riis of the need for New York to have a "working-man's mayor." But Roosevelt was not quite there yet. When he used the term "yawning gulf" to describe the hopeless contest he faced, he might also have been talking about the gap between New York's very rich and very poor.

Under the leadership of Terence Powderly, the Knights of Labor had grown tremendously in the mid-1880s and scored a number of successes. In 1884 and 1885, the national labor organization had achieved victories in the Union Pacific Railroad and Wabash Railroad strikes. By 1886, its membership had swelled to 700,000. In New York City, labor organized into the Central Labor Union, representing about 50,000 workers. This meant that even when small groups of poorly organized workers went on strike for shorter hours or increased pay, they received the backing of both the CLU and sympathetic working-class communities.

In March 1886, the streetcar drivers and conductors of the Dry Dock Line along Grand Street went on strike for reduced hours. The drivers regularly worked sixteen- and seventeen-hour days without time off for dinner. They asked to work only twelve hours a day. When policemen escorted scab workers to operate the streetcars, neighborhood crowds blocked the tracks with barricades of garbage. The police chief responded by sending 750 men, a quarter of his force, to protect the streetcars as they inched across Lower Manhattan through hostile crowds. Policemen clubbed rioters as angry mobs overturned and set fire to the cars. The CLU called for a sympathy strike on every streetcar line, and 16,000 drivers, conductors, and stablemen answered the call. New York City traffic came to a standstill until the Dry Dock Company gave in to its employees' demands.

Theodore Roosevelt missed the strike and the ensuing riots, as he was in residence at his Dakota ranch. While Roosevelt's time in the West gained him numerous enriching experiences as a ranchman and hunter, he missed a crucial moment in New York history. By living away from the city for much of the time between the spring of 1884 and the fall of 1886, he missed the rise of labor militancy in New York. After the Chicago Haymarket bombing of May 3, Roosevelt wrote his sister Anna a fairly violent response with reference to his own cowboys. He noted that his men worked just as hard or harder than many of the strikers, and for little money. "But they are Americans through and through," Roosevelt wrote. "I believe nothing would give them greater pleasure than a chance with their rifles at one of those mobs." If only East could meet West in some showdown between cowboys and radical labor: "My men shoot well and fear very little," he said. Although this statement could be interpreted as hostility to organized labor, in reality it reflected the way Roosevelt distinguished between orderly protest and riotous mobs. Nearly a decade later, when Roosevelt became police commissioner, he made that distinction clear. "We shall guard as zealously the rights of the striker as those of the employer," Roosevelt said in a statement quoted by the *Evening Post*. "But when riot is menaced it is different. The mob takes its own chances. Order will be kept at whatever cost. If it comes to shooting we shall shoot to hit. No blank cartridges or firing over the head of anybody." Violent disorder would not be tolerated.

Late nineteenth-century mob violence reflected a new reality of modern, urban America. Riots during the Revolutionary period had been communal activities directed against perceived wrongs. More recent riots, however, derived not from shared ideas, but from the very divisions facing a vastly growing, polyglot city confronted with sharp social and economic distinctions. One contemporary New York writer referred to this situation as the "volcano under the city." In 1887, William Osborn Stoddard, onetime secretary to Abraham Lincoln, wrote, "They carry guns, pistols, axes, hatchets, crowbars, pitchforks, knives, bludgeons, the Red Flag. Much of their shouting is done in other Tongues, but the cry is in English: 'Down with the rich men! Down with property! Down with the police!'" Stoddard called it "an insurrection of evil against law, an uprising of suppressed hellish forces against order." His words reflected well much of the fear shared by New Yorkers in the late nineteenth century as they witnessed the rapid and massive changes to their city. Men such as Stoddard and Roosevelt worried about more than just damage to private property or higher taxes, a common complaint against upper-class New Yorkers, who were often regarded as being merely self-serving. They honestly worried that the next riot would rip the city asunder as a new civil war played itself out on the streets of New York.

Roosevelt's own words revealed the changing times as well. In campaign speeches in 1884 and 1885, he spoke about civil service reform and the disenfranchisement of blacks in the South. By 1886, he was forced to address questions of labor. When a Henry George campaign club sent Roosevelt a letter labeling him part of "the employing and landlord class," Roosevelt attacked its "reckless misstatements and crude and vicious theories." In a letter Roosevelt noted that he owned no land except that on which he lived. "I have worked both with hands and with head," he commented, "probably quite as hard as any member of your body. The only place where I employ many 'wage-workers' is on my ranch in the West." He mocked the idea that one group of Americans was responsible for the economic conditions of another group. It was like saying they were responsible for some people being shorter, or more nearsighted. Roosevelt also took umbrage at the very use of the word "classes," so much in vogue in American cities by 1886. "If you had any conception of the true American spirit," Roosevelt lectured, "you would know we do not have 'classes' at all on this side of the water." From George's theories of wealth redistribution by means of a land tax, to the language of labor militancy, Roosevelt showed himself firmly on the conservative side of the debate.

As he had since the fall of 1884, Roosevelt made sure he was back in New York City by October and the start of the 1886 election season. With his secret engagement to Edith and his growing longing for his two-and-a-half-year-old daughter Alice, Roosevelt had been actively looking for a way back into New York City life and politics. The opportunity came when Republicans asked him to run for mayor against Union Labor Party candidate Henry George and Democrat Abram Hewitt. "It is of course a perfectly hopeless contest," Roosevelt wrote after receiving the Republican nomination on October 15, "the chance for success being so very small that it may be left out of account."

If he knew he was going to lose, why did Roosevelt agree to run? The Republicans' slim chances that year had already led Elihu Root to turn down the nomination. Certainly Roosevelt sought a more active role in the New York political scene after his time out west. Throughout 1884 and 1885, Roosevelt had attended district and state conventions, and by the spring of 1886 he was active in the city in a number of areas. He had been elected to the executive committee of the Civil Service Reform Association, and he was even on the Citizens' Auxiliary Committee of the Grand Army of the Republic, making arrangements for Memorial Day. More importantly, even during his absence he had scored an important political victory, having been elected president of the Twenty-First District Association. It represented a final victory over Jake Hess, who was "put out to pasture" by being named a commissioner to the Board of Electrical Control.

Right from the beginning of the 1886 mayor's race, Roosevelt understood that he was being asked to run as a sacrifice for the Republican Party. Moreover, he knew that at that point in his career, it was a sacrifice he had to make. The year 1884 had been not only a tragic one for Roosevelt personally, but also a disastrous one for him politically. After opposing Blaine as the party's nominee, then opting to campaign for the party that fall, Roosevelt had succeeded in alienating both party leaders and independents, who bolted for Cleveland. The split Republican Party in New York that year had cost Blaine the election. Now, in 1886, New York party leaders sought a reform candidate who could stand as the nominee of a united Republican Party, thus healing the split of 1884. It was widely understood that any Republican nominee that year would be a "sacrifice candidate." During the election campaign, Republican leaders would continually stress party unity with an eye toward the 1888 presidential election. The 1886 mayoral race allowed Roosevelt to return to the party's good graces while campaigning on the reform issues that would mark his entire political career. In the end, Roosevelt lost the election, but it was a necessary defeat that reestablished him in the city and state from which he would launch his career. Moreover, the election continued to illustrate the kind of Republican Roosevelt was: both a loyal party man and a progressive reformer. This continued ability to bridge the great divide in the Republican Party would make Roosevelt a successful politician over the next quarter century.

Roosevelt attended the Republican County Convention held in the Grand Opera House on October 15. He would later say he attended simply because he was "curious" to see who the Republicans would choose to battle George and Hewitt. It seems just as likely that Roosevelt hoped to get the nomination himself, or at least to make sure party leaders knew he was back in town. Although he later expressed surprise that he was asked to run, this seems a bit disingenuous. After all, for many months he had been waiting for Mayor Grace to come through with an appointed position in city government. Moreover, Roosevelt had been writing to Lodge about his friend's hand in writing the party platform for Massachusetts Republicans, as well as Lodge's new attempt to win a seat in Congress. Roosevelt referred to this as Lodge's "political reappearance." No doubt Roosevelt's own political reappearance was much on his mind. In Roosevelt, Republican Party leaders found a candidate who could unite the two wings of the party.

In 1886, power within the New York City Republican Party was divided between machine politicians such as Thomas Platt and wealthy "Swallowtail" Republicans such as Elihu Root. Republican reformers tended to stay aloof from the party machine, preferring instead to influence city politics through citizens' committees and reform clubs. In 1886, Roosevelt received the backing of the district managers controlled by party boss Thomas Platt. This would be the first of many such reconciliations between Roosevelt and the party boss. Both men had already shown their common belief in party harmony. The former Republican boss, Roscoe Conkling, had overseen the state party machine at a time when the national party was riven by factions. Such divisions, Platt believed, only led to the party's defeat. The Easy Boss valued party harmony as the key to electoral victory. Hence, Platt had seconded the nomination of Blaine in 1884, although Conkling was dead set against it. In backing the Republican nominee in 1884, Platt and Roosevelt had acted together to defeat the Democrats. Now, in 1886, they did so again.

Roosevelt also received backing from the reformers. He was nominated by a Citizens' Committee of One Hundred that represented the reform wing of the party. Reformers were pleased at Roosevelt's nomination, but surprised. *The Nation*, in an article on Roosevelt's selection by the party bosses, asked, "How is it possible for him to think the 'Johnnies' and 'Jakes' and 'Mikes' sincere, when the investigations and reformatory legislation which he carried through were bitterly opposed and resisted by these very men?" Probably the party bosses were not sincere, but saw Roosevelt's nomination as a mere convenience serving a larger purpose. Just as Roosevelt barely mentioned the mayoral race in his autobiography, Republican boss Platt made no mention of Roosevelt's nomination in his own autobiography. For a man like Platt, such compromise with the reformers—leading to an election loss—was best forgotten.

In September, George had been overwhelmingly nominated at a trades union meeting that represented more than 40,000 workingmen. A black engineer named James Ferrol seconded the nomination, warning that if the people did not do their duty and vote for George, "shame be on their own heads for making their children slaves." Labor enthusiasm aside, the story came down to numbers: if George could secure the workingman's vote, he stood a chance at being elected. To answer his nomination, the Democrats had put forward Abram Hewitt, a popular and reforming former congressman whom Republicans could support with a clear conscience.

By the time Roosevelt officially accepted the nomination for mayor, only two weeks before the election, he had missed the momentum of the campaign. Reports of his nomination were overshadowed by a public debate between Hewitt and George that appeared in the city's newspapers. Indeed, the two other candidates largely ignored Roosevelt's candidacy, as did the city's labor press. By the end of Roosevelt's first week as a candidate, even the *New York Herald*, which supported Hewitt, had ignored Roosevelt, focusing instead on George as Hewitt's main opponent. It was a rare moment in New York City history when the Republican nominee was essentially a third-party candidate. Perhaps accepting his inevitable defeat, Roosevelt contributed to his own marginalization by running a lackluster campaign. He avoided attacking either of his opponents, including George, who adhered to a radical philosophy, and did not try to attract voters from outside the party. Roosevelt understood his role as a reform Republican uniting the party, and he spoke solely to the party. This made for some rather dry reading, as reflected by his official letter of acceptance. In discussing municipal reform, Roosevelt wrote, "It is practically impossible for any member of the party now, and for so long past, dominant in our local affairs to work a real reform therein, for, no matter how good his aims, he would find himself at every step trammeled by a thousand personal and political ties." It had all the sizzle of a good government pamphlet.

On October 20, Roosevelt addressed the Republican Club of the City of New York. Introducing Roosevelt as "a man of national reputation, noted for his independence and aggressiveness," Elihu Root seemed more concerned with the Republican organization than with the candidate, remarking that the meeting of the club represented the "grand spirit of organized Republicanism." "It makes a difference," he declared, "between the breaking up of the party and the building up of the party." Roosevelt, characteristically for this campaign, spoke briefly, noting his Assembly career and the need to register Republicans to vote. He barely mentioned George and Hewitt, leaving it to others, such as Root, to attack the George movement and the Democratic machine. The following day, the Republican Union League endorsed Roosevelt, with Joseph Choate calling him "the one man . . . who will reform our municipal government." Over the next several days, the same themes of a united Republican Party backing a reform candidate were repeated throughout the city and in newspapers that supported Roosevelt.

Roosevelt himself stressed the importance of his candidacy in fostering party unity. Speaking to the executive committee of his party, Roosevelt stated his belief, said the *Tribune*, that "whatever the result of the election might be, he was satisfied that the party would be more firmly unified for the active work of the present campaign." Expressing public doubt about the outcome of an election is usually suicidal for any candidate. But Roosevelt expressed such doubts privately to his friends. To longtime friend Frances Theodora Dana, author of botanical books for children, Roosevelt predicted his overwhelming defeat. "The simple fact is that I had to play Curtius and leap into the gulf that was yawning before the Republican party," Roosevelt wrote. "Had the chances been better I would probably not have been asked." Curtius was the Roman youth who, according to myth, rode his horse into a chasm that appeared in the middle of Rome, thus saving the city. Roosevelt saw himself in the same vein—as helping to end the divide in the Republican Party, and sacrificing himself in the process.

Still, reform Republicans had long memories. They remembered that Roosevelt had backed Blaine in 1884, and now he was being backed by Platt and the machine. Whose side was Roosevelt on? The *Evening Post* described Roosevelt as a "straw man" put up by the machine. In *The Nation*, Godkin echoed the *Post*: Roosevelt was merely selected by "a corrupt clique of Republican machine politicians so they could secure concessions from Tammany by seeing that Roosevelt does not run too well." Later, Godkin worried that the vote for Roosevelt would "bring the Anarchists and Socialists and Strikers . . . within 10,000 or 20,000 of full possession of the city government." Even Hewitt picked up on this theme. "He is a bright young man," the Democratic nominee said in a speech at Cooper Union. "But he has made a mistake. He has allowed himself to be made the tool of designing men." As a result, he might open the election to Henry George. If this occurred, "Mr. Roosevelt would lament in sackcloth and ashes, and ask for forgiveness of his fellow citizens for the calamity he had helped to bring about." That Roosevelt was young and ambitious, no one could deny. For many, this combination seemed to translate into a candidate who compromised his ideals and was open to manipulation.

Roosevelt had to perform a sensitive balancing act. He had to claim, on the one hand, that his candidacy represented a united Republican Party, while, on the other, asserting his independence from any boss or faction. Roosevelt began an October 25 speech to New York dry-goods merchants by affirming his dedication to beating his opponents and the possibility that he could still do so. By this late date, with so many in the press and in his own party having written him off, Roosevelt had to argue for the continued relevancy of his candidacy. "I don't think any one who knows me will say that I am not in this race to beat George," Roosevelt declared. "I'm in to beat both him and Mr. Hewitt." Then Roosevelt urged that people "not lose sight of the greater issue," as "there are municipal reforms to be effected," and Hewitt would be hampered by his obligation to Tammany Hall. "If elected," Roosevelt said, "I shall go to the City Hall unpledged to any one." The same day he spoke to the dry-goods men, Roosevelt penned a letter to one of his supporters, Charles Miller, who had echoed the concerns of the *Post*. Did Roosevelt stand by his 1884 decision to back Blaine? Roosevelt replied that not only did he stand by it, he would do so again even if it meant losing the current election. The *Times* published both Miller's letter and Roosevelt's reply. Two years later, Roosevelt was still fighting the battles of 1884.

Other prominent Republicans openly bolted the party for Hewitt that fall. On October 26, top New York independent Republican Carl Schurz wrote Hewitt saying, "A good many of my acquaintances are hesitating as to whether to vote for you or for Mr. Roosevelt." Schurz worried that what Roosevelt claimed was true—that Tammany's support of Hewitt would come at the price of the Democratic machine's power over mayoral appointments. Roosevelt's own Assembly investigating committee in 1884 had exposed the quid pro quo between Tammany boss John Kelly and Mayor Frank Edson. Schurz asked Hewitt whether he had made any promises to Tammany for its backing. When Hewitt replied that he had made no pledges to Tammany concerning appointments, that was good enough for Schurz, who was not only a leading Republican, but also one of the most prominent German Americans in New York—and German Americans usually voted Republican. That same week, Schurz addressed a large meeting of German Americans in Cooper Union and urged the election of Hewitt. Roosevelt he referred to as "an excellent gentleman who had done excellent work in the Legislature and had a splendid record." But, in the end, Schurz saw Hewitt as a "man of experience, and a statesman as well as a politician" who could poll more votes than Roosevelt. This would not be the last time fellow reforming Republicans looked askance at Roosevelt's cooperation with the machine.

The climax of Roosevelt's campaign came on October 27, his twenty-eighth birthday, at a large meeting of Republicans at Cooper Union Hall. Drawing on comments that Mayor Grace had made in supporting Hewitt, Roosevelt referred to himself as a "radical reformer" and promised to clean up city government. Yet, in addition to underscoring his reforming tendencies, Roosevelt made plain that he was, in his words, "a strong party man." As had happened at other large Republican meetings during the campaign, someone called out "Three Cheers for James G. Blaine!" Only the day before, at a meeting of Ninth District Republicans, the cry had been answered by cheers that shook the building. The mention of Blaine, who was still seen as a possible presidential candidate in 1888, was a double-edged sword for Roosevelt. On the one hand, it reminded party regulars of Roosevelt's divisive actions during the 1884 Republican National Convention. On the other hand, it reminded independents that Roosevelt, both in 1884 and in the current campaign, had opted for the party machine. The *New York Herald* sought to exploit the latter sentiment, frequently declaring that Roosevelt was the "Blaine candidate for mayor," or that "the republican vote is not to be a vote for New York, but a vote for Blaine." For his part, Roosevelt avoided referring to 1884.

Despite the optimistic headlines of the *Times* ("Roosevelt's Great Army," "Flocking to Roosevelt") and Elihu Root's assertion that Roosevelt might attract as many as 100,000 votes, Election Day saw the Republican candidate cross the finish line in a distant third place, with only about 60,000 votes. Hewitt was the victor. Roosevelt seems to have taken the loss in stride. He took great delight in the fact that Lodge had won a seat in Congress, and he busied himself with his travel plans to England for his coming nuptials. The day before the election, Roosevelt seemed more concerned with wishing Lodge luck, and then finally telling his closest friend of his engagement. Roosevelt said there had been little chance of his election, placing the blame on independents who would vote for Hewitt. This was the common understanding of the election results: that Roosevelt in 1886 was being punished in the same way Lodge had been punished by Massachusetts independents in 1884, when he had lost his first bid for Congress. Roosevelt's friend Joseph Bucklin Bishop would later write that Roosevelt lost the election because independent Republicans were "unable to forgive Roosevelt for his advocacy of Blaine" in 1884.

True, many independents must have voted for Hewitt, yet Roosevelt and other observers probably overstated their defection in 1886. In fact, many regular Republicans stampeded to Hewitt in order

to avoid a George victory—the potential "calamity" Hewitt had mentioned. Samuel Gompers, who had led Assemblyman Roosevelt on a
tour of the tenements, was active in the George campaign. In his autobiography, he recalled the rumor that Republican headquarters had actually instructed party members to vote for Hewitt in order to ensure
George's defeat. Although this seems a ludicrous rumor, Gompers was
inclined to believe it. Decades later, a contemporary of Roosevelt's, the
critic Brander Matthews, recalled being as much afraid of Roosevelt's
youth and impetuosity as George's advocacy of a land tax. "I do not
believe that we, the aristocracy of New York," Matthews told inter-
viewer J. F. French in 1922, "were really any more afraid of Henry
George with his radical doctrines than we were of Roosevelt's youth
and radical opinions. Hence, many Republicans voted for Hewitt."
What these "radical opinions" were, Matthews did not say, and he may
have been referring more to Roosevelt's later ideas, as expressed in his
New Nationalism, than to anything he said in the campaign of 1886.
Finally, other Republicans, especially businessmen, were so afraid of
George's ideas that many were angry with the Republican bosses for
putting up a candidate at all, and not throwing in their lot with Hewitt
to defeat George outright. After the election, New York journals agreed.
The *New York Tribune* said it was "evident at a glance" that Roosevelt
had been knifed in the back by the Republican machine and deserted
by members of his own party. *The Nation* believed that the wealthy
uptown districts had abandoned Roosevelt, and that he had failed
"to command the support of the most intelligent element of his own
party." Not just independents, but thousands of regular Republicans,
had bolted to Hewitt to defeat George.

Still, despite his third-place finish, Roosevelt could take some
pride in the outcome of the race. Previous mayoral elections in New
York had shown that in a three-way contest involving a reforming Democrat, the Republican candidate stood little chance of winning. In 1886, Roosevelt won 16,000 fewer votes than Republican
Alan Campbell had in 1882 in a two-way contest against Democrat
Franklin Edson, a midterm election marked by low voter turnout. Yet
Roosevelt won 16,000 more votes than Republican Frederick Gibbs
had in 1884 in a three-way contest with Tammany candidate Hugh

Grant and independent William Grace. In a state or federal election, those 16,000 votes were crucial in New York, a state that had swung to the Democrats in 1884 by fewer than 1,200 votes. With only one state-wide contest in New York that year, the city's 1886 mayoral race took on extra importance as an indication of Republican voting for 1888. By running as the Republican candidate endorsed by both machine bosses and independent reformers, Roosevelt did much to ensure the election of a Republican president only two years later.

While privately blaming the same independent Republicans who had turned against him and Lodge in 1884, Roosevelt publicly characterized his defeat in the same terms as he had when he accepted the nomination—as a Curtius-like sacrifice for party unity. He even gave an interview to this effect on the very night of his defeat, calling his candidacy "the means of holding the Republican party in the city together." Here, again, Roosevelt underscored the real significance of his failed candidacy. He had been defeated in a greater cause, that of re-uniting the Republican factions behind a single candidate. Moreover, he had campaigned as both a loyal party man and a reformer promising to clean up municipal politics. Appealing to both machine and independent Republicans in this way contributed to Roosevelt's later political success, both as Republican nominee for governor in 1898 and as vice presidential nominee in 1900. In fact, the 1886 campaign can be seen as a microcosm of Roosevelt's career. As he had in 1884, Roosevelt opted to work with the party bosses as the only way to be effective. This led to Mugwump skepticism, as displayed by the attacks of Godkin, the *Post*, and *The Nation*. Even that old Republican Carl Schurz endorsed Hewitt. Being abandoned by reformers in his own party infuriated Roosevelt. He complained to Lodge that they had acted with "unscrupulous meanness and a low, partisan dishonesty and untruthfulness which would disgrace the veriest machine heelers." Roosevelt would have ample opportunity to repeat such complaints in the years to come.

Aside from his own election defeat, Lodge's victory, and his coming December 2 marriage to Edith in London, money was on Roosevelt's mind. He had put $600 into his mayoral campaign, and the Roosevelt uncles had contributed another $1,400. With half his net worth tied up in his Dakota ranch and owing a pile of debt on Sagamore Hill, he could hardly afford even this small sum. Even during his European honeymoon, as the newlyweds traveled first class across the continent, Roosevelt worried about money. He wrote to his brother-in-law Douglas Robinson, Corinne's husband, asking him to sell his favorite horse, noting, "If I stay east I must cut down tremendously along the whole line." He even contemplated giving up his New York residence, doubting his political future in the city and complaining of the city's high personal tax. He would make the same calculation while residing in Washington, DC, a few years hence.

Worse was yet to come. Roosevelt expressed his financial concerns even before the terrible winter of 1886–1887 ripped into the Plains, killing half the cattle in Montana and the Dakotas. Only in February did eastern papers start carrying the terrible news from the West. "Cattle Dying for Want of Food," came one report from Bismarck. "Stockment Say Fifty Per Cent. Have Been Lost," roared another headline in the *Times*. The losses helped Roosevelt make up his mind: opting for the East, he put the ranches up for sale. But he was finally able to sell them only in 1898 at a further tremendous loss.

Income from his investments and royalties from his books were not enough. What Roosevelt needed was a regular paying job, and he looked ahead to the presidential election of 1888 to help him secure it. If he could continue to serve his party by campaigning for the successful Republican candidate, Roosevelt could count on an appointed government position, perhaps even in Washington, DC. For a prominent civil service reformer, Roosevelt found himself in an awkward position: depending for his livelihood on the very spoils system he opposed.

SEVEN

"*With Fidelity and Integrity*"
Roosevelt as Civil Service Commissioner

FOR NEW YORK CIVIL SERVICE reformers such as Theodore Roosevelt, the city police had long been the prime example of corrupt public officials. For those religiously minded, graft aided and abetted a sinister array of evils, from drinking to gambling and prostitution. The 29th Street police station was ground zero as it oversaw the center of New York's nightlife. Around the station blazed thousands of electric lights. Enormous signs heralded the city's grandest hotels, theaters, and dance halls. The patrons of such entertainment were served by an array of gambling houses and bordellos. Before Captain Alexander "Clubber" Williams transferred to the precinct, he had been stationed downtown, where he had little to do, and little opportunity to take bribes. "The pickings were lean" there, Henry Collins Brown recalled in his book *New York in the Elegant Eighties*, meaning that Williams had less opportunity to take graft downtown. When he received his promotion to inspector and his transfer uptown, Williams remarked, "Ah! No more chuck steak for me; now I'll get a little of the Tenderloin." By the middle of the 1880s, New York's Tenderloin District had become notorious. By one estimate, half of the businesses in "Satan's Circus" were connected with vice. It became the target of temperance advocates and every kind of social reformer. As New York's Finest openly accommodated the vice trade, lining their pockets in the process, other reformers focused on police reform. They faced an enormous task.

Appointments to the police department were based on political connections, not qualifications. Once one received a badge, there was little oversight. Aside from graft, abuse of civilians was common. Clubber Williams received his moniker because of his dexterity with his patrolman's club. Nighttime meant heavier weaponry. "The night stick was a miniature baseball bat," Brown remembered, "far longer and heavier than the 'billy' or club attached to every policeman's belt in the day time." Without whistles as standard issue, policemen summoned help by beating the club on the sidewalk. "The police courts were filled with cases against policemen who clubbed peaceable citizens," Brown wrote. He also remembered that policemen had yet to be trained in the arts of politeness. "If you told the old time policeman that he should say 'please' and 'thank you' to a mere citizen," Brown recalled, "he would have torn off his badge, thrown it in your face and resigned forthwith from what he would have inferred was a bible class." The 4,000 police officers on New York's streets in the 1880s had, at best, a tense relationship with its citizens.

For Theodore Roosevelt and other good-government advocates, the answer lay with civil service reform. Policemen should be hired and fired, and promoted and disciplined, based on merit rather than political influence. And if the police force could be cleaned up, this would pave the way toward cleaning the city of its numerous illegal ventures. Civil service reform always remained a cornerstone of Roosevelt's political ideology. While in the state Assembly, he had worked to create a bill making New York the first state to have a merit-based civil service. He had also helped usher in a bill that would establish such a system for the state's largest cities. Roosevelt joined the civil service reform organizations and maintained close contact with other advocates. By the mid-1880s, civil service reformers were heartened by the implementation of the 1883 Pendleton Act, which created a national Civil Service Commission in Washington, DC, to oversee about one-quarter of federal jobs. Even while out of political office after 1884, Roosevelt continued to preach the gospel of reform. By early 1887, Roosevelt the Republican politician was dedicated to two related goals: defeating President Grover Cleveland and the Democrats in 1888, and furthering the cause of civil service reform. He was about to play an active and successful role in both.

THEODORE AND EDITH ROOSEVELT returned to New York from their lengthy European honeymoon in March 1887. For most of their trip through London and the great cities of Italy, they had not been entirely alone. Soon after their December 2 wedding, Edith had become pregnant with the first of the five children she and Theodore would have together. But what of little Alice? She was now a full three years old, had seen her father only sporadically her entire life, had never known her own mother, and was about to meet her "new" mother. Indeed, her Aunt Bamie was the closest thing she had to a mother, and really the only full-time guardian of any kind that she had known. It was this very question that led to perhaps the first serious disagreement in the new marriage. Thinking he was being sensitive to all three women— Edith, his sister Anna, and little Alice—Theodore assured Anna that Alice would remain in her care. Edith would have none of it. She insisted that Alice was now her child and would reside with her and her father and new sibling at Sagamore Hill. Anna was sent south for a short vacation while Roosevelt headed west to investigate the condition of his ranch. In leaving New York, he left behind one settled conflict only to face another enormous problem.

The winter of 1886–1887 had devastated western agriculture. In the Dakota Territory, farmers and cattlemen were ruined. For Roosevelt, it was the beginning of the end of his western experiment. "I am bluer than indigo about the cattle," Roosevelt wrote Anna. "It is even worse than I feared." He wrote that he expected to lose at least half of his initial investment of $80,000, but he knew it was the end: "I am planning how to get out of it," he said. To Lodge, too, he showed he was in the process of turning his face firmly back toward New York. "The losses are crippling," he wrote. "For the first time I have been utterly unable to enjoy a visit to my ranch. I shall be glad to get home." Significantly, Roosevelt used the word "visit" for his stays on his ranch, while referring to New York as "home." One assumes that his absence from Edith and Alice added to his homesickness. Returning east and supporting a family meant reviving his political career, especially on the eve of the 1888 presidential election. Whether living at Oyster Bay or not, for Roosevelt New York was the place to start. New York would oblige.

That April, Republicans of Roosevelt's own Twenty-First Assembly District had banded together to form a new social club of politically like-minded young men. In his November 1886 *Century* article, Roosevelt had underscored the role that socializing played in politics. Now he and his friends had set out to create exactly what Roosevelt had discussed, "a social club of young men of the same political faith," as the *Times* said. The very name "Federal Club" echoed the more established and influential "Union League."

Upon his return, in May Roosevelt was feted at Delmonico's by the new Federal Club. It was almost as if New York Republicans had come out to celebrate Roosevelt's return to the city and to New York politics. Although only 60 to 80 people had been expected, the number quickly swelled to 150. The list of names was a "Who's Who" of city Republicans, including top New York Republicans Chauncey Depew and Levi Morton, for whom Morton Hall was named, and leading New York City lawyers Joseph Choate and Elihu Root. There was a senator-elect, a former assistant secretary of the treasury, future mayor William Strong, several aldermen, representatives of both the New York and Brooklyn Republican committees, and B. F. Jones of the Republican National Committee. Even Henry Cabot Lodge came down from Massachusetts to support his friend. That the Federal Club chose Roosevelt as its first guest of honor, having incorporated only the month before, reflected his standing in the city. Allowing himself to be a sacrifice candidate in 1886 had been a shrewd political move. The ghost of 1884 had been exorcised.

On the night of the banquet, according to a reporter from the *Times*, the tables at Delmonico's "literally groaned beneath the weight of the good things on them." It was probably a good thing for Roosevelt that the wine had been flowing freely before he spoke to the gathering, for the speech was not his best. He was supposed to talk about

"The Republican Party: Its Professions and Practices." Instead, he gave a vague address that discussed the outside threats to the party—prohibitionists, labor, and independents—more than the Republican Party itself. Rather than touch on the specifics of what the party stood for, he averred only that in the past few years, "the cause of right was supported by a majority of our party, [and] the cause of wrong was championed by the majority of our foes." Only a few weeks before, he had observed that Lodge was right to begin the campaign of 1888 early. But Lodge, sitting at Roosevelt's table, could not have been pleased with Roosevelt's own opening shot of the campaign. Roosevelt finished by looking at the Cleveland administration. Again, though, rather than pointing to any specific faults of Democratic government, he referred to "a distinct falling off from what it was during Republican rule." While Delmonico's offered its patrons strong drink, Roosevelt offered his audience a very watery brew.

The year 1887 ended with two events that greatly affected Roosevelt's life, political career, and eventual legacy as president of the United States. The first event resulted from his autumn western hunting trip. Over the previous few years, Roosevelt had noticed the increasing scarcity of native wildlife, from small animals, such as beavers, to the large bison. Upon returning to New York, he had joined with other wealthy outdoors enthusiasts to form the Boone and Crockett Club. With Roosevelt as its first president, the club sought to work for the preservation of large game and of forest regions. Within only a few years, the club would score a number of triumphs, helping to found the National Zoo in Washington and aiding the passage of the 1894 Park Protection Act that saved Yellowstone National Park. All this was achieved years before Roosevelt became president, and it clearly marked the beginning of his preservation efforts, one of his greatest legacies as president. Significantly, these actions were not taken on his ranch, surrounded by cowboys. The first organizing meeting of the Boone and Crockett Club took place at the fashionable Roosevelt home at 689 Madison Avenue—which served as Theodore and Edith's New York City residence, although it was owned by his sister Anna. It was because they were city dwellers that Roosevelt and his New York friends took steps to preserve America's flora and fauna treasures. Western forests and plains served as important symbols for urbanites, antidotes to industrializing and urbanizing America. Moreover, few westerners had the pull to influence government policy that New Yorkers had. Roosevelt and his ilk had the power and prestige to lobby congressmen, cabinet secretaries, and presidents.

The second event helped Roosevelt secure the position he would hold in Washington for the next six years. With reformers giving Cleveland fairly high marks on civil service, that issue would likely not affect the upcoming presidential contest. Cleveland himself provided another issue in his State of the Union Address in December 1887. He dedicated his entire speech to that third rail of nineteenth-century politics, tariff reform. Republicans and many northern Democrats had long favored a high tariff to protect American industry. By the mid-1880s, however, the tariff was bringing in so much revenue that the federal government was running a surplus. Cleveland and most Democrats thought it unjust to needlessly raise consumer prices. In his speech, the president declared the national tariff to be too high, calling on Congress to initiate steep reductions. Cleveland's speech galvanized Republicans, who began immediately preparing for the 1888 election. In January, Roosevelt presented to the Union League Club a report that affirmed the Republican Party's commitment to the tariff. In March, he corresponded with Louis Theodore Michener, chairman of the Indiana Republican Party and Benjamin Harrison's political manager. Without firmly committing himself, Roosevelt shrewdly expressed his inclination to support Harrison for the presidential nomination. Blaine was refusing to be nominated. Harrison, a former general, was the favorite son of a battleground state. He had been a US senator from 1881 to 1887, but had been defeated by a Democrat, David Turpie, in the previous election. He was also the grandson of William Henry Harrison, who had been president briefly in 1841 before dying of pneumonia. Cleveland had effectively split the Democratic Party over the tariff issue, a blunder he would repeat several years later on the issue of the gold standard. Meanwhile, Republicans were closing ranks after their near-miss with Blaine four years before. Roosevelt's 1886 mayoral campaign had served this purpose, uniting New York Republicans while resuscitating his own political career in the city. In an important election year, Roosevelt's name once again had great worth for the party.

That fall of 1888, Roosevelt was tapped to give campaign speeches not only in New York, but also in Harrison's Indiana. New York campaign managers reluctantly gave up Roosevelt for additional stints in Minnesota and Michigan, the latter having gone to Blaine in 1884 by a mere 3,300 votes. While he was campaigning for Harrison, there came another sign that Roosevelt had revived himself politically in New York. As city Republicans looked for a candidate to challenge Abram Hewitt in the fall mayoral election, Roosevelt's name sparked great interest. After all, it was noted, he had polled quite well in 1886, notwithstanding the stampede of Republicans to the Democrats in their fear of Henry George. Two years after Roosevelt's defeat, here was further evidence that he had served the Republican Party's interests well. In the end, Roosevelt was not nominated, and the eventual Republican challenger to Hewitt, Joel Erhardt, suffered a large defeat. Roosevelt, however, had already done his work in uniting the party in 1886. Republicans had lost both Indiana and New York in 1884. Now they had placed an Indianan on the ticket to win back that state—and old Levi Morton from New York as Harrison's running mate. Meanwhile, Roosevelt's own actions in 1886 and 1888 did much to ensure that New York slid back into the Republican column.

Election Day gave Harrison a solid electoral victory, although he lost the popular vote to Cleveland by 100,000 votes. Republicans also gained control of both the House and the Senate. In Washington, Harrison tapped for secretary of state James Blaine, who had resigned that post soon after Garfield's death in 1881. In Massachusetts, Henry Cabot Lodge had been easily reelected to Congress. Defeated New York City mayoral candidate Erhardt was rewarded with that perennial plum position: collector of the New York Custom House.

In March 1889, Blaine wrote to Lodge's wife, Nannie, asking, "Do you happen to know a young gentleman—*gentleman* strongly accented—not over forty-five, well educated, speaking French well, preferably German also (with an accomplished wife thoroughly accustomed to society) and able to spend ten to fifteen thousand—twenty still better, beyond the salary he might receive?" Blaine was looking for an assistant secretary of state, whose duties would include throwing lavish parties for Washington's diplomatic corps. For the Lodges, their close friend Theodore Roosevelt matched the description almost exactly. True, the Roosevelts would probably have some difficulty matching the extra expenses needed for socializing in Washington, especially as the salary for the post was only $4,500. But Roosevelt had shown he was a loyal Republican, and they felt he deserved some recognition for his work during the previous fall's campaign.

Communicating with Blaine through Nannie, Lodge pressed his friend's claim, but to no avail. Blaine remembered the convention of 1884, and his wafer-thin loss of New York. Had it not been for Theodore Roosevelt, Blaine might have been just beginning his second term as president. To the Lodges, Blaine was blunt: "My real trouble in regard to Mr. Roosevelt is that I fear he lacks the repose and the patient endurance required in an Assistant Secretary. Mr. Roosevelt is amazingly quick in apprehension. Is there not danger that he might be too quick in execution?" Blaine indicated that he would be home in Maine much of the time, leaving his assistant in charge of America's foreign affairs. Did the Lodges really think Roosevelt had the temperament for the job? "I do somehow fear that my sleep at Augusta or Bar Harbor would not be quite so easy and refreshing if so brilliant and aggressive a man had hold of the helm. Matters are constantly occurring which require the most thoughtful concentration and the most stubborn inaction. Do *you* think that Mr. T. R.'s temperament would give guaranty of that course?" Possibly Blaine was right, at least that Roosevelt, having only just turned thirty in October, was incapable of "stubborn inaction." But Blaine had secured a small bit of revenge for 1884.

Lodge continued to advocate for a place for Roosevelt in Washington, visiting the White House and soliciting the support of House Speaker Thomas Reed. The value of Lodge's friendship to Roosevelt at this point in their respective careers cannot be overestimated. Here was Lodge, eight years Roosevelt's senior, firmly established in Massachusetts politics and Washington's upper circles, and just reelected to Congress, pressing the case of the younger Roosevelt, whose entire political career consisted of just three years in the state legislature and a failed mayoral bid. By early 1889, Lodge's star was clearly on an upward trajectory, whereas Roosevelt's future was decidedly uncertain.

In March and April, Roosevelt was unhappy with Harrison's appointment of Republican machine men to key New York posts. The villain was Conkling's successor as party boss, Thomas Platt. In helping to deliver New York to Harrison, Platt had expected to be named secretary of the treasury, an appointment that never materialized. Instead he kept firm control of state patronage, much to Roosevelt's chagrin. Roosevelt, writing to Lodge about the situation, suggested one possible antidote to the spreading "Platt machine" in New York: "I do hope the President will appoint good civil service commissioners," Roosevelt wrote. Roosevelt's letter gave Lodge the idea of suggesting Roosevelt for the post. Probably that was Roosevelt's intention all along.

And so Roosevelt was named one of three United States civil service commissioners. It was a mixed blessing. This had little to do with the fact that the Civil Service Commission oversaw only about 28,000 of the 140,000 federal jobs, or that the commission had only the power to investigate, and not prosecute, any malfeasance. Roosevelt had been closely identified with civil service reform, and had gone after patronage and corruption in New York while serving in the state assembly. No doubt his fellow civil service reformers, such as Lodge, rejoiced at his appointment. But it was an appointed, not an elected, position, and indeed, was the first of a succession of appointed jobs he served in until his election as governor in 1898. In other words, Roosevelt would win no election, and hold no elected office, for fifteen long years during the prime of his life. Moreover, as commissioner, he would be investigating government officials of his own party, loyal Republicans who in some cases had been appointed by the president himself. For any young man with political ambitions, this was not a healthy place to be. Would serving as civil service commissioner really lead to a seat in the New York State Senate, or next to Lodge in the US House of Representatives? Or was the new job a foreshadowing of Roosevelt's future: a series of appointed positions while spending his free time writing books? There was even another, darker, and more ironic way of looking at his situation: Was Roosevelt's livelihood about to become dependent upon the very system of party patronage that he fought against?

Until he became president, Roosevelt's six years as civil service commissioner would constitute his longest tenure in any job. His time in Washington would provide him with significant experience, however. While in the capital, he became intimate with some of the most important figures in Washington political and social circles, men such as historian Henry Adams, descendant of the Adams presidents; old New York family friend John Hay; British diplomat Cecil Spring-Rice; German diplomat Hermann Speck von Sternburg; an old Harvard friend, Winthrop Chanler; Assistant Secretary of State William Wharton; naval intelligence officer Charles Henry Davis; and naval theorist Alfred Thayer Mahan. He solidified his friendship and political alliance with Henry Cabot Lodge. He sharpened his political and administrative skills, and he showed he could navigate Washington's treacherous waters. Roosevelt even survived being the target of one of Washington's favorite career-killers, the Congressional Investigating Committee. His walks frequently took him past the White House, and it was at this time, he later admitted, that he had his first thought of becoming president. During his time as civil service commissioner, he moved his family back and forth between Washington and New York, and two children born during this time—Kermit in 1889 and Ethel in 1891—were born at Sagamore Hill. Roosevelt continued to write, and he published, among other things, many western-themed books, such as *The Winning of the West, American Big-Game Hunting, The Wilderness Hunter,* and *Hunting in the Bad Lands.* Yet through all of his endeavors—family, writing, and work—ran the theme of New York. Even when he was in Washington, the city of his birth remained an important Roosevelt touchstone.

DARK SHADOWS HAD ALWAYS cast themselves across Roosevelt's life. In his youth he had been small and sickly. By age twenty-five, Roosevelt had grieved the loss of the three people who were dearest to him: his father, his mother, and his first wife. Another shadow that loomed was the declining mental and physical health of his beloved brother Elliott. Born less than two years apart, as boys "Ellie" and "Teedie" had been constant companions. As they grew older their differences became apparent. Elliott was handsome, charming, and a born athlete.

Theodore was the introverted naturalist who was destined for Harvard. All the Roosevelt children seemed to have been born with some illness, whether it was Anna's spinal deformity or Theodore's asthma. From a young age, Elliott had learned to control his periodic fits of convulsions with large quantities of alcohol. In 1880, when he took his brother west on a hunting trip just before Theodore married Alice, Roosevelt wrote home about Elliott's drinking. "As soon as we got here he took some ale to get the dust out of his throat," Roosevelt wrote his sister Corinne, trying to be funny. "Then a milkpunch because he was thirsty; a mint julep because it was so hot; a brandy smash 'to keep the cold out of his stomach;' and then sherry and bitters to give him an appetite." At dinner, Roosevelt recounted, Elliott then imbibed "beer, later claret and in the evening shandigaff [*sic*]," the last better known as a shandy, or beer mixed with lemonade. Between the end of the hunt and bedtime, then, Elliott drank an unknown quantity of about eight different alcoholic beverages. He was only twenty years old at the time.

By the time Roosevelt left for Washington to become civil service commissioner, Elliott's health was in steep decline. Roosevelt knew that Elliott's alcoholic lifestyle contributed to his constant need for medical care, but he could do little but offer aid and compassion. During the summer of 1888, when Elliott was bedridden with simultaneous attacks of rheumatic gout, inflammatory rheumatism, and neck abscesses that prevented him from swallowing, Roosevelt expressed his displeasure at his younger brother's debauched lifestyle at his own Oyster Bay estate, Hempstead. "I do hate his Hempstead life," he wrote their sister. "I do'n't [sic] know whether he could get along without the excitement now, but it is certainly very unhealthy, and it leads to nothing." By July 1889, Roosevelt was begging Elliott to seek round-the-clock professional help at an institution of some kind, but to no avail. A complete breakdown later that year prompted a move with the family to Europe, where Elliott eventually checked himself into a fashionable German asylum. His wife, Anna, was pregnant with their third child; their first child, Anna Eleanor, who would later marry Franklin Delano Roosevelt and become First Lady, was then not quite five years old. Back in America, a servant girl named Katy Mann was also pregnant with Elliott's baby. Armed with gifts and letters that Elliott had sent her, she wrote to Theodore Roosevelt for adequate compensation, well aware that Elliott's brother was a prominent federal official. Elliott pleaded innocence, and Roosevelt wanted to believe his sick brother. Even if Elliott was the father, Roosevelt reasoned, clearly he had been drunk and out of his mind at the time. With one hand Roosevelt paid off Katy Mann, or asked his uncles to do so to save the Roosevelt name from disgrace. With the other hand he filed a writ of lunacy to strip Elliott of control of his finances.

On August 17, 1891, every major newspaper in New York reported Theodore Roosevelt's move to have his brother declared insane. For the yellow press of the 1890s, this was a juicy story of insanity and back-stabbing within one of New York's top families. The only thing that might have made the story more sensational was if the protagonists' names were Astor or Vanderbilt rather than Roosevelt. Still, the tanta-lizing glimpse inside the old knickerbocker family must have made a million New Yorkers shudder with a kind of schadenfreude. Roosevelt's aunts and uncles shuddered from rage and shame. "Elliott Roosevelt Insane" screamed one *Times* headline. Newspaper stories recounted word-for-word Roosevelt's testimony before the court about his brother, including passages about Elliott's drinking, his violent behavior, and his threats, on several occasions, to commit suicide. The writ humbled Elliott, and Roosevelt certainly used it as a tool with which to control his brother. It would only be lifted, Roosevelt carefully explained to Elliott in Paris, where he had moved with his new mistress, if Elliott returned to the United States and checked himself into another dry-ing-out asylum for his alcoholism. Without much choice, Elliott obliged. Roosevelt even found his brother a job managing the Virginia estates of their brother-in-law Douglas Robinson. But he also cautioned the family that they had done all they could and must now stay aloof from Elliott's problems.

Roosevelt understood that a lifetime of heavy drinking had taken a heavy physical toll on Elliott, one not easily reversed by simply taking "the cure." Roosevelt's father, mother, and first wife, Alice, had died at fairly young ages. Roosevelt was devastated, although perhaps not com-pletely surprised, when his closest friend and playmate from childhood finally succumbed on August 14, 1894. Elliott was only thirty-four.

For the third time in Roosevelt's life, a telegram summoned him back to New York to be at the bedside of a dying family member. As on the day of his father's death, however, Roosevelt did not make it in time; he missed the moment of Elliott's death. He could only gaze down on his brother, who was seemingly transformed by death into a younger, more handsome man, like the one Roosevelt had known before alcohol had destroyed his body and mind. Bamie, their older sister, had been in England at the time of Elliott's death, and their other sister, Corinne, wrote to her that Theodore wept like a child. Elliott was interred with his father, mother, and Theodore's first wife, Alice Lee, out at Green-Wood Cemetery in Brooklyn.

FAMILY OBLIGATIONS KEPT Theodore Roosevelt returning to New York, but his job as civil service commissioner, beginning in 1889, also gave him ample opportunity to visit his hometown. The civil service reform movement had long targeted the New York Custom House as the corrupt repository of powerful politicians. Chester Arthur's reputation certainly had not been aided by the fact that he had held the collectorship at the bequest of his party boss, Roscoe Conkling. When presidents tried to assert control over this richest and most powerful of patronage plums, they inevitably tangled with the Republican machine of New York. Rutherford Hayes had tried to oust Arthur and replace him with honest reformer Theodore Roosevelt Sr. Only months before the elder Roosevelt's death, Harvard undergraduate Theodore Roosevelt had avidly read newspaper accounts of the sordid fight between Hayes and Conkling, with his own beloved father stuck in the middle. When Roosevelt Sr. failed to clear Conkling's own committee, it was a bitter lesson for the young Roosevelt. Within only a few years, Roosevelt would be one of New York's leading advocates of civil service reform and good government. Now, at age thirty, he was in a position to attack the spoils system in the custom house in a way that even a president could not.

Local bosses, hacks, and heelers were not about to let civil service laws stand in the way of their control over patronage. A set of examinations was introduced to standardize and remove patronage in applications to the federal civil service, including the New York Custom House.

For machine politicians who still wanted to use the custom-house posts as political patronage, the solution was simple: either have someone more qualified than the actual candidate take the exam, or attain an advance copy of the questions. Roosevelt had taken up his new post in Washington in mid-May 1889, and within a week he was heading to downtown Manhattan to investigate charges of irregularity in the custom house brought by deputy naval officer John Comstock. He heard testimony and took the affidavits of two employees, Nathaniel Fowler and Thomas Jordan. Roosevelt collected a large amount of supporting documents, including job applications and examinations for admission and promotion. Based on this preliminary investigation, conducted solely by Roosevelt, the entire Civil Service Commission returned to the custom house on May 28 for a full hearing.

Roosevelt's two fellow members on the commission were Charles Lyman and Hugh S. Thompson. Both men were older than Roosevelt and were veterans of the Civil War—Lyman from the North and Thompson from the South. Months before the attack on Fort Sumter, Thompson had led a battalion of Citadel students who had fired on a Union warship entering Charleston Harbor—the very first shots of the war. After the war, he served two terms as governor of South Carolina before being named assistant secretary of the treasury by President Cleveland in 1886. Thompson and Roosevelt were appointed by Harrison at the same time; Lyman had been appointed earlier by Cleveland. Lyman was an old civil service hand, having served as civil service examiner in the Treasury Department since 1872. Both were more than willing to give Roosevelt free rein in pursuing his investigations, although Lyman was nominally the commission's president. While Roosevelt initially liked the two older men, he quickly grew impatient with them because they failed to match his level of activity and enthusiasm. But who could? By October, Roosevelt was complaining to Lodge that he could not trust Thompson in the work that needed to be done, while Lyman he characterized as "utterly useless."

In May 1889, however, when Roosevelt brought the full commission to Manhattan, the commissioners were still enjoying their honeymoon. With reporters in attendance, Roosevelt took center stage on May 28 and read a preliminary report before examining witnesses.

Roosevelt recounted the story of Thomas Jordan, who desired to acquire the questions before he sat for the civil service exam. As the same exam was given three days in a row—"in itself a very unfortunate state of things," Roosevelt observed—another man, Nathaniel Fowler, sat at the back of the examining room copying the questions, which were later passed, along with the answers, to Jordan. The next day, Jordan took and passed the exam. As a reward, Fowler had been promised a place in the custom house, which required no examination. When no reward was forthcoming, Fowler took to showing up drunk at the custom house, demanding a position. Jordan and a custom-house employee who had helped in the scheme, Charles Terhune, pretended that they could get Fowler a night inspectorship job, but that it required taking the exam. Jordan and Terhune said they would give Fowler the questions and answers for the hefty sum of $50. "That's a nice howdy-do," Fowler told the commissioners. "Here I ain't got 50 cents; I ain't working, and they're asking for $50." Fowler offered to pay the money after he received the position, but Terhune replied, "No; got to have the dust. There are three or four in on this, and got to have the dust." Since Fowler could not get "the dust"—the money—he decided to turn state's evidence. Fowler, a *Times* reporter, noted, "was not a very favorable appearing specimen of young manhood." But he was Roosevelt's key witness against the other men.

Roosevelt also reported his findings in another case, that of custom-house employee Saul Hollander, having taken a close look at Hollander's application and exam papers. The *Times* reporter observed that Hollander did not want to testify, "and his cringing was both pitiful and amusing." Roosevelt pointed out to Hollander that not only did his handwriting greatly differ on his application and two examination papers, one for admission and one for promotion, but three completely different dates had been entered for his birthday. Even the year had changed: on one paper it was 1843, on the next 1840, and on the most recent, Hollander had suddenly become five years younger with a birth year of 1845. Hollander replied not by proclaiming his innocence, but by pleading his ignorance. "Gentlemen," he said to the three commissioners, "I couldn't get the date of my birth. No one knew when I was born except my mother, and she was an aged woman and she couldn't tell me. She had forgotten. So I put it down as near as I could. Afterwards some of my friends told me when it was. I have got the day of the month right. It was May 10." Someone reminded Hollander that although his friends had supposedly given him the correct date, he had not stuck to it on subsequent exam papers.

When the question of his changing handwriting was raised, Hollander claimed an injured arm. When Roosevelt asked Hollander to describe the room in which he had taken the examination, Hollander's memory failed him. "I ought not to be asked to answer technicalities," he protested. Commissioner Lyman, an old hand at civil service exams, asked Hollander to write an equation on a piece of paper. He was not asked to solve the equation, just to write down what Lyman said. But Hollander could not think of how to write a minus sign. The equation also included fractions and the multiplication symbol. "He has been studying those signs since I tested him the other day," Roosevelt commented. The commissioners produced his examination for admission, in which all of the mathematical questions were answered correctly. "Read .0005," said Commissioner Thompson, showing Hollander the exam paper. "Hollander looked at it as one might look at a Chinese letter print," the *Times* reporter observed. In reply to Thompson, Hollander said, "Three oughts and a five."

> THOMPSON: "I know, but read it mathematically."
> HOLLANDER: "That's what it is; ought, ought, ought, and five."
> THOMPSON: "Why no; it is five ten-thousandths."
> HOLLANDER: "That's what I said."

When Commissioner Lyman finally asked Hollander who had written the exam for him, Hollander replied, "Nobody." He then broke down crying, saying he had a wife and family to support. The commissioners let him go. When he had left, Thompson observed, "That man is the biggest liar I ever saw."

In the end, Hollander and Terhune were dismissed from their offices, and Terhune was indicted by a grand jury for violating the civil service law.

This was the first time Roosevelt had ever used such unsavory fellows as Jordan and Fowler as witnesses. In order to get their testimony, Roosevelt had been forced to make them promises. Even though Jordan had obtained his position fraudulently, Roosevelt worked to protect his job at the custom house. This meant asking Collector Erhardt—whom Abram Hewitt had defeated for mayor the previous fall—to keep Jordan on. In an 1890 letter to Erhardt, Roosevelt recalled the shady deal. After Jordan turned state's evidence, Roosevelt recalled, "I had told him that so far as I could I would protect him against being turned out for testifying—he having been one of the beneficiaries of Terhune's wrong doing—and on my representing the case to you you said he should not be molested in his then position." By the time Roosevelt wrote to Erhardt, Jordan had been implicated in election fraud in Jersey City; Commissioner Roosevelt apparently penned the letter to Erhardt on the very same day he read about the charges in the newspapers. Roosevelt also wrote custom-house naval officer Comstock, who had initiated the proceedings the previous year. Since Comstock had been a witness to Roosevelt's dealings with Jordan and Fowler, the civil service commissioner wanted to ascertain whether Comstock's recollections matched his own. "Before making their statements they asked me, in substance, if I would not see that they were protected, or were not molested, for testifying, and I told them I would do what I could to protect them," Roosevelt wrote in his letter. "As I recollect it, you were in the room, and within earshot, the whole time. Is that so? And is your recollection substantially as above?" Roosevelt was worried that his deal with Jordan and Fowler was about to be made public, and he was trying to line up witnesses who would back his version of events. Simply put, he was covering himself.

Roosevelt had reason for concern. Although he had been in the job only a short time, Roosevelt had already made many powerful enemies in Washington. After his investigation into the New York Custom House, he had tackled corruption under the local postmaster of Indianapolis, William Wallace. This was Roosevelt back in crusading form, mindless of the political consequences, as Indianapolis was President Harrison's hometown, and Wallace was the president's friend. Roosevelt's investigation led to further dismissals and the humiliation of Wallace. Roosevelt could not hide his delight. "We had only a week's trip but we stirred things up well," he wrote Lodge. "The President has made a great mistake in appointing a well-meaning, weak old fellow in Indianapolis, but I think we have administered a galvanic shock that will re-inforce his virtue for the future." Knowing Roosevelt better than just about anybody else, even the Massachusetts congressman must have shuddered at Roosevelt's hubris in thinking a civil service commissioner could influence the president's nominations. The Midwestern tour had then taken Roosevelt to Milwaukee, revealing more scoundrelism in the postmaster's office there. Roosevelt's actions were not making him many friends among Republican leaders, including the president. Moreover, Roosevelt, always careful to cultivate public opinion, made sure to leak his findings to the press. He also gave some frank interviews, something Lodge cautioned him strongly against. "Edith thoroughly agrees with you about the interviews," Roosevelt wrote Lodge, "so I cry peccavi ["I have sinned"] and will assume a statesmanlike reserve of manner whenever reporters come near me." Unfortunately, the damage had already been done.

By the end of 1889, opposition to Roosevelt was mounting, and it found an outlet in the attacks of Frank Hatton, editor of the *Washington Post* and himself a former postmaster general. Hatton had discovered an apparent bit of hypocrisy on Roosevelt's part in investigating the Milwaukee postmaster, George Paul. As he had in New York, Roosevelt relied on the testimony of a dubious character, Hamilton Shidy, a postal supervisor who testified that Paul had rigged the civil service exams to ensure the hiring of party members. After Paul retaliated by firing Shidy, Roosevelt personally intervened with the superintendent of census to secure Shidy a place in the Census Bureau. For opponents of civil service reform and for Roosevelt's enemies, this was a clear case of Roosevelt utilizing the sort of political influence he was ostensibly fighting. In the *Washington Post*, Hatton called for a House investigation and the removal of Roosevelt, "this pampered pink of inherited wealth." In January 1890, the House of Representatives announced an investigation of Roosevelt and the creation of a commission led by Congressman Hamilton Ewart of North Carolina, a leading opponent of civil service reform. As Roosevelt, Shidy, Postmaster Paul, and Postmaster General John Wannamaker all testified before the committee, Hatton targeted Roosevelt in the headlines of the *Post*. "Roosevelt Knowing His Infamous Character, Forced Him into an Important Position." "Dr. Jekyll and Mr. Hyde Impersonated by the Reformers." "The Most Shameful Testimony Ever Offered." "Even Roosevelt Hung His Head in Shame." Only a few years before, Roosevelt had been at war with fellow reformers over deciding to back Blaine in 1884. Now Roosevelt was being attacked from the other side.

Still, everyone knew Ewart and Hatton's agenda, both in Washington and back in New York. Outside of those two cities, few newspapers bothered to dedicate any ink to the House investigation. For every negative headline in Hatton's *Post*, New York papers favored Roosevelt and the commission with favorable press. The *Times* even portrayed the House investigation as "A Tribute to Civil Service Reform." "Hypocrisy is said to be the tribute that vice pays to virtue," began an editorial, "and the attack made by such vulgar champions of the spoils system as Messrs. Hatton and Ewart upon the Civil Service Commissioners, under the pretense that they have failed in their duty, may be taken as a conspicuous tribute to the cause of civil service reform." From President Harrison's own state, the president of the Indiana Civil Service Reform Association, William Dudley Foulke, wrote a long letter to the *Times* that the paper reprinted in full. Foulke said that the appointment of Roosevelt to the Civil Service Commission had made that body a real agent of reform. He called Roosevelt "more active, energetic, and aggressive than any who had been upon the board before" and said he enjoyed "the confidence of those who believe in reform everywhere." Removing Roosevelt, Foulke warned the Harrison administration, would drive the reform element from the Republican Party entirely. This was an important moment for Roosevelt. Since the presidential election of 1884 and the mayoral election of 1886, Roosevelt had had a frosty relationship with reformers in his party. Now that he was under withering attack from the Republican Old Guard, reformers rallied to Roosevelt's defense.

When the investigating committee finally issued its report, it completely vindicated Roosevelt and the Civil Service Commission.

Commissioner Roosevelt, the report stated, had executed his duties "with entire fidelity and integrity." What had begun as a witch hunt directed at Roosevelt turned into a personal and political triumph for him. Roosevelt not only kept his job, but, back in his hometown, newspapers used the investigating committee report to single out Commissioner Roosevelt for praise. Reformers made the commissioner's cause their own. Here was an important result of Roosevelt's tenure as civil service commissioner. It allowed him to once again don the mantle of active reformer, something he had not been able to do while out of office since 1884. By investigating malfeasance in the federal civil service in the face of stiff opposition, often from members of Harrison's own cabinet, Roosevelt once again attracted to himself the support of the reform wing of the party.

Roosevelt's time as civil service commissioner could have ended in complete disaster. He had acted with great hubris, thinking he could "shock" the president into acting in line with his wishes. Roosevelt had also taken on powerful interests within his own party, a move that might have completely disqualified him for future positions. It should be remembered that Roosevelt became commissioner after James Blaine rejected Roosevelt for assistant secretary of state, saying Roosevelt lacked "repose" and "patient endurance." Roosevelt's actions as civil service commissioner undoubtedly left many other top Republicans sharing Blaine's assessment of the young man from New York. In the end, however, Roosevelt was not fired from the commission. His time in Washington once again illustrated his ability to perform that most difficult of tightrope acts, as he maneuvered between the two factions of the Republican Party. This was an ability that few men could match, and even fewer in the most important battleground state of New York. Roosevelt's ability to bridge these two parts of his party was crucial to his future success at the state and national levels.

ROOSEVELT'S YEARS AS CIVIL SERVICE commissioner coincided with his coming into his own as an American historian. There is some irony in the appearance of so many of his western writings while serving as a government official in Washington, DC. In 1891, as part of the

Historic Towns series, Longmans, Green and Company published Roosevelt's history of his hometown, entitled simply *New York*. The early chapters are a straightforward narration of Manhattan's discovery by Henry Hudson, the years of Dutch rule, the growth of the British colony, and New York's first hundred years as America's premier city. The final chapter, on "Recent History," however, provides insight into Roosevelt's views of the city.

Roosevelt always wrote history with a clear message that was relevant to nineteenth-century America. His western writings lauded masculinity, Anglo-Saxon superiority, and continental manifest destiny. His *New York* observations sounded much like his previous writings on machine politics and his work in the Assembly. "There are shoals of base, ignorant, vicious 'heelers' and 'ward workers,'" Roosevelt wrote, hardly sounding like a historian, "who form a solid, well-disciplined army of evil, led on by abler men whose very ability renders them dangerous." Referring to the well-oiled urban political machine as an "army of evil" was a classic Roosevelt line. He was far from finished. "Some of these leaders are personally corrupt," Roosevelt continued. "Others are not, but do almost as much harm as if they were, because they divorce political from private morality." This was also classic Roosevelt. He was calling for a kind of civic morality that could only be brought about by pulling the best of men into city politics.

Roosevelt's *New York* even had some echo of his Federal Club speech of May 1887. Roosevelt still seemed baffled by the independents' willingness to side with the evil heelers and manipulators of Tammany Hall rather than with the better sort of men in the Republican Party. "Neither the unintelligent and rancorous partisan," Roosevelt wrote, "nor the unintelligent and rancorous independent, is a desirable member of the body politic; and it is unfortunately true of each of them that he seems to regard with special and sour hatred, not the bad man, but the good man with whom he politically differs." Again, what this all had to do with the "Recent History" of New York City is unclear. But just as Roosevelt used his *Thomas Hart Benton*, a biography of America's leading antebellum advocate of western expansion, to comment on the tariff system in the United States, so he used *New York* to critique the current political situation in the city, dominated as it was by Tammany and those Mugwumps who were willing to side with the Democrats. Roosevelt was not just a historian, he was a good *Republican* historian.

In later years, especially during World War I, Roosevelt would worry about the dual identities of recent immigrants, such as German Americans and Italian Americans. In *New York*, however, Roosevelt only saw the great, underlying patriotism of the city's immigrant community. The 1889 centennial celebration of the US Constitution had illustrated this patriotism: even in the poorest of the tenement districts, foreign-born New Yorkers displayed the Stars and Stripes and portraits of Washington. "Thus," concluded Roosevelt, "there is no doubt that in case of any important foreign war or domestic disturbance New York would back up the general movement with men and money to a practically unlimited extent." *New York* was published just on the cusp of the great turn-of-the-century wave of immigration that would transform the city and the nation. Roosevelt had yet to witness the unprecedented millions who were about to step onto the streets of Manhattan. *New York* was published in 1891. Ellis Island opened the following year.

In his memoirs, Roosevelt would extol the outdoors and the western experience he had enjoyed as a young man in the 1880s. In 1891, however, Roosevelt praised the opportunities of America's largest city. New York's life, he wrote, "is so intense and so varied, and so full of manifold possibilities, that it has a special and peculiar fascination for ambitious and high-spirited men of every kind, whether they wish to enjoy the fruits of past toil, or whether they have yet their fortunes to make, and feel confident that they can swim in troubled waters—for weaklings have small chance of forging to the front against the turbulent tide of our city life." New York, then, rivaled the West for instilling and fostering in a young man the fighting spirit and the vigor of life. "The truth is," Roosevelt concluded, "that every man worth his salt has open to him in New York a career of boundless usefulness and interest."

Would Roosevelt have ever uttered anything like Horace Greeley's famous advice, "Go West, young man, and grow up with the country"? It seems unlikely, especially as Roosevelt himself was witnessing

America's astonishing growth from an urban perspective. Go West? No, the boundless opportunities were in the East. "Go East, young man," Roosevelt seemed to be saying in 1891. "Go to New York and grow up with the country."

As his history of New York indicated, the city was still very much on Roosevelt's mind. After Grover Cleveland won back the White House in the 1892 election, it appeared that the civil service commissioner might be heading back there very soon. Would the Democrat keep the Republican Roosevelt?

In late December and early January, Roosevelt used sixty-three-year-old Carl Schurz as an intermediary with the newly elected president. Roosevelt and Schurz had a tense relationship going back to the election of 1884. Schurz no longer spoke to Henry Cabot Lodge, because Lodge had eventually backed James Blaine for the presidency. In 1886, Schurz had failed to back Roosevelt for mayor. A New York Mugwump, Schurz was exactly the sort of casual Republican that Roosevelt loathed. But in 1892, Schurz had succeeded George William Curtis as president of the National Civil Service Reform League. Although politically, Roosevelt was frequently at odds with such men as editor E. L. Godkin and Schurz, when it came to civil service reform, they were all allies. On January 4, 1893, Schurz wrote Roosevelt to say that Cleveland "wishes *very much* to see you." Two weeks later, Schurz accompanied Roosevelt to a meeting with Cleveland, where the men discussed civil service reform. But Cleveland was slow in asking Roosevelt to stay. When he finally did in April, it came as a tremendous relief to Roosevelt. With the Democrats in office, Roosevelt had faced the very real possibility of becoming unemployed.

Serving another term as civil service commissioner had its drawbacks, however. First of all, Cleveland asked Roosevelt to stay on for only another year or two. By 1894, Roosevelt would need to start looking for another post. Second, as Roosevelt noted to Schurz, he was now in the odd position of being "a Republican fighting Democratic colleagues over the actions of Democratic spoilsmen under a Democratic administration." Although Roosevelt might gain some favor with

Republican leaders for going after Cleveland appointees, he risked having people doubt his motives. Moreover, serving the cause of reform under a Democratic president seemed like something Carl Schurz would do. There was something of the Mugwump in it, and Roosevelt was no Mugwump. Finally, staying in Washington for five or six years in an appointed position was not the best stepping-stone to higher office. His friend Henry Cabot Lodge was proof to the contrary: Lodge had never served in a Washington post, but had found advancement through the Massachusetts Republican Party. Just as Roosevelt secured another year or two on the Civil Service Commission, Lodge was elected to the US Senate. The junior senator from Massachusetts would not have to worry about reelection until nearly the end of the century. Roosevelt, though, was already worrying about 1894, and beyond that, the presidential election year of 1896.

With President Cleveland serving his second, nonconsecutive term, the 1896 presidential contest would be wide open. Republicans were already lining up behind their candidates, such as old Levi Morton of New York, House Speaker Tom Reed, and Ohio's William McKinley. Cleveland had been reelected in 1892 largely on the issue of tariff reform, which was a major national issue for much of the late nineteenth century. Earthshaking global events, however, were about to change the very language of American politics.

By the 1880s, the railroad industry was suffering from overbuilding and bad financing. Just days before Cleveland's second inauguration, the Philadelphia and Reading Railroad went bankrupt. Banks and other businesses soon followed. As the economic crisis worsened, people withdrew their money from banks, and credit virtually dried up. Many on Wall Street, and the new president himself, fixed blame on the Sherman Silver Purchase Act of 1890. This act, backed by farming and mining interests, required the government to purchase massive amounts of silver every month. Special Treasury notes were issued for the silver purchases, notes that could be redeemed for either silver or gold. The plan backfired when investors turned in the Treasury notes for gold, depleting the nation's gold supply. Soon after taking office, Cleveland convened a special session of Congress and called for repeal of the Sherman Act. The president pointed out that in the three years since the act was passed, gold bullion reserves had decreased by more than $132 million, while silver reserves had increased during the same time by more than $147 million. Repealing the act would send a strong message about the soundness of the US dollar and, Cleveland hoped, revive the economy. Back in December 1887, in calling for steep tariff reductions, Cleveland had kicked over a hornets' nest. Only days into his new term, he had done it again.

American politics had changed radically in the past few years. In 1892, delegates from various labor and farmers' groups had formed the People's Party, known as the Populists. The Populist platform included many remedies to the perceived inequalities in the American market-place that agrarian and labor advocates had been backing for years: the eight-hour workday, redistribution of wealth through a graduated income tax, direct election of US senators, and government ownership of railroads, for example. Such ideas would form the cornerstone of the Progressive Era. Another key idea of the Populists related to the money supply. By 1893, the United States had been on the gold standard for twenty years. Every paper dollar circulating in the country was backed by an equal value of gold. Business leaders liked the gold standard because it placed the US dollar, and thus the whole economy, on a firm foundation—a solid-gold foundation. Gold kept inflation down and reassured European lenders of the dollar's stability. After all, the building of American railroads and industry was largely financed by European banks, as the United States remained the largest debtor nation on earth until the Great War.

Farmers hated the gold standard. A tight money supply kept crop prices down and placed a stranglehold on credit. Loosening the money supply by printing more money allowed moderate inflation to occur, pushing up crop prices and land values and allowing banks to give out more credit. Populists and others did not advocate abandoning the gold standard completely, but rather, backing the dollar with both gold and silver. Democratic congressman William Jennings Bryan of Nebraska was a leading bimetallist. When Cleveland called for repeal of the Sherman Act, Bryan, serving his second term in the House, replied with a rousing speech. "Whence comes this irresistible demand for un-conditional repeal?" Bryan asked. "Not from the workshops and farms, not from the working men of this country, who create the wealth in time of peace and protect its flag in time of war, but from the middle-men, from what are termed the 'business interests,' and largely from that class which can force Congress to let it issue money at a pecuni-ary profit to itself if silver is abandoned." The president, Bryan said, had been deceived by these interests, the alliance between government, banks, and corporations that he would later call "The Money Power." The "Boy Orator" was unsuccessful, and the Sherman Act was repealed. Cleveland won the day but split his party in the process, creating a new issue—"free silver" vs. the gold standard—that would play out in the 1896 election.

ROOSEVELT HAD TO GET BACK to New York before 1896. Ideally, he would be asked to run for office in the 1894 congressional or city elections. Everything seemed to be falling into place when Roosevelt was approached about once again running for mayor in 1894. Edith opposed the idea, however, believing the family could not afford the expense of the campaign. Roosevelt deferred to his wife, yet instantly regretted the decision. City Republicans chose another reform candi-date, businessman William Strong. "I made a mistake in not trying my luck in the mayoralty race," Roosevelt wrote his sister Anna. "The prize was very great; the expense would have been trivial; and the chances of success were good. I would have run better than Strong." Always one to look and move forward, this was a rare expression of regret by Roosevelt. His regret must have only increased when Strong won. Until now, Roosevelt had been only a state assemblyman and a US civil ser-vice commissioner. Being the chief executive of the nation's largest and most important city would have suited Roosevelt well. He had been a good-government advocate for years, dedicated to battling Tammany Hall and the corruption and inefficiency that plagued American cit-ies. While in the Assembly, he had been responsible for making New York's mayor a powerful office, answerable more to the voters than to political bosses or aldermen. A Roosevelt mayoralty in 1895 might have ushered in a period of great reform for New York City. Moreover, he could have returned to the city of his birth and lived with his family at Sagamore Hill. The chance had slipped through his fingers.

Yes, with the election of 1896 looming, Roosevelt needed to return to New York. The city—its politics, its people, its problems, and even its long history—was never far from his mind.

EIGHT

"There'll Be a Hot Time in the Old Town Tonight"

Roosevelt as Police Commissioner

ALTHOUGH ROOSEVELT MISSED his chance to become mayor of New York City in 1894, he still aimed to return to his hometown prior to the national election of 1896. In the meantime, he was still trying to influence events in New York. So he arranged a meeting between the reform-minded Republican mayor-elect, William Strong, and his friend Jacob Riis. In 1890, Riis had published *How the Other Half Lives*, a book chronicling the terrible living conditions of the city's working poor, complete with haunting pictures. "It is very important to the city to have a businessman's mayor," Roosevelt wrote Riis as he tried to set up the meeting. "But it is more important to have a workingman's mayor." This is a remarkable passage. Here was brownstone-born, Harvard-educated Theodore Roosevelt expressing his belief in New York's need for "a workingman's mayor." To Riis, Roosevelt wrote about the needs of the working poor living in tenements. These were the neighborhoods Roosevelt had visited briefly with Samuel Gompers in the early 1880s. True, Roosevelt was not advocating work programs for the unemployed, or even tenement reform, but only a better chance for respectability and usefulness. Roosevelt was more than a touch condescending. Still, voicing the need for something to be done for New York's poor was a radical notion in 1894. Here was Roosevelt displaying an understanding of urban social problems, and his belief in government's responsibility for addressing them. Henry George or William Jennings Bryan could not have said it any better.

In his letter to Riis, Roosevelt also indicated his high hopes for Strong's term in office. Might it not be a good thing to be associated with a reform Republican administration back in New York? In fact, Strong did offer Roosevelt a place in his administration—as head of the Street Cleaning Commission. On the one hand, this was the very matter that had brought Roosevelt into politics nearly fifteen years before. On the other hand, had he accepted, the ambitious Roosevelt would have been responsible for hauling away the city's garbage. When Roosevelt declined the offer, he worried that he was shutting an avenue of opportunity. He wrote Riis that he would have liked to have been Strong's street cleaning commissioner, but that he was simply not familiar with the mechanics of hauling garbage and sweeping streets. Declining the position was a smart move, and in the end his decision was also good for New York. Strong next asked Colonel George Waring to fill the post, and Waring accepted. He brought to the job an unprecedented level of efficiency and professionalism.

Roosevelt was still uncertain when Strong then asked him to serve on the four-man police commission. Far from being chief of New York's Finest, a police commissioner sat on an oversight committee meant to ensure that hiring and firing, promotion and discipline were all based on merit rather than political connections. In other words, it was a sort of civil service commission for New York's police. Roosevelt had spent six years on the federal Civil Service Commission, so he worried that such a job would be a step backward for him. Could he turn down a second offer from Strong? If Roosevelt did not accept this job, what position could he possibly attain back in New York before 1896? Roosevelt was completely at a loss. He wrote to Lodge, "It is very puzzling!" Always the savvy politician, Lodge told his friend to accept the offer. Roosevelt became head of the commission, with the title "president." After accepting, excitement overshadowed his previous hesitation. "I think it is a good thing to be definitely identified with my city once more," Roosevelt wrote his sister Anna. "I would like to do my share in governing the city after our great victory; and so far as may be I would like once more to have my voice in political matters." Here exactly were the twin reasons for taking the position of police commissioner: it allowed Roosevelt to return to New York—"my city"—and it allowed him to take an active role in city government and politics.

Such a move was key on the eve of the 1896 elections. If the midterm elections just past were an indication, 1896 was shaping up to be a Republican year. In the House, Republicans had gained 117 seats, while the Democrats had lost 113. It was the largest transfer of power between parties in American history. In twenty-four states in 1894, no Democrats were elected to national office. Added to this were the economic downturn, the split within the Democratic Party over bimetallism, and the fact that after his two terms, Cleveland would not be running again for president. The eventual Republican nominee would not have to face a Democratic incumbent and could assail a divided Democratic Party on the economy. As was often the case, a strong electoral showing for the Republican presidential ticket would trickle down to affect state and local elections. Roosevelt might just be the beneficiary of this in 1896.

As ever, Lodge understood the situation better than this friend did. He warned Roosevelt that, while doing his job as police commissioner, he should not lose sight of national party politics. Lodge had warned Roosevelt of essentially the same thing when the New Yorker was civil service commissioner, as Roosevelt's reforming righteousness often tested the patience of Republican leaders. In attacking police corruption, Lodge warned, Roosevelt should be practical and avoid burning his bridges before 1896. "You need not have the slightest fear about my losing interest in National Politics," Roosevelt reassured Lodge. "In a couple years or less I shall have finished the work here for which I am specially fitted, and in which I take a special interest." He added, "I shall then be quite ready to take up a new job." Roosevelt seemed to understand what Lodge undoubtedly knew perfectly: that preparing for the next step up the political ladder required a modicum of restraint and prudence on Roosevelt's part. Events would quickly show that such qualities were beyond Roosevelt's ability.

ROOSEVELT OWED HIS JOB in part to the efforts of Dr. Charles Parkhurst, president of the Society for the Prevention of Crime. Under Parkhurst, the society had aggressively targeted all manner of vice in New York City. The society hired private detectives who raided brothels and gambling dens, collecting evidence of police corruption. Under pressure from the press and public opinion, the New York State Senate had appointed a special committee to investigate the notoriously corrupt police department. Named after its chairman, Clarence Lexow, the Lexow Committee met in the Tweed Courthouse, itself the greatest symbol of Tammany corruption. The committee collected more than 10,000 pages of testimony that chronicled the alliance between the police and Tammany Hall in controlling elections and collecting protection money from illicit operations. In its January 1895 report, issued only months before Roosevelt took office as commissioner, the committee described the "brutal treatment of Republican voters" by police on Election Day, portraying cops as essentially "agents of Tammany Hall." In shocking detail, the committee had heard endless stories of police brutality, especially against, as it recounted, "the poor, ignorant foreigner residing on the great east side of the city." One story involved a Mrs. Urchittel, "a humble Russian Jewess, ignorant of our tongue, an honest and impoverished widow with three small children whom she was striving to support." A precinct detective had falsely accused her of keeping a brothel in the back room of her store where her children slept. The detective demanded money, and when the woman could not pay, he secured false testimony from witnesses under his control—his "miserable tools," the report said—and had her convicted. Her children were taken from her, and she had to sell her store to pay the resulting fine. When she was released from jail, she fell seriously ill. "When she recovered," the report recounted, "her home was gone, her children were gone, and she was penniless."

The record of police abuse and corruption seemed endless. Police purchased their appointments for the standard rate of $300, and one

Captain Creedon confessed to paying $15,000 to secure his promotion. The police organized widespread protection rackets that netted tens of thousands of dollars. To open a new brothel, the brothel operator had to pay the police $500, while protection for existing brothels ran from $25 to $50 per month. The system had been perfected over the years. Police charged the proprietors of the brothels according to certain formulas, such as by the number of women working in them, or the number of rooms occupied. Individual prostitutes paid the local patrolmen a fee for permission to ply their trade along city highways. Operators of the approximately six hundred "policy shops" that controlled New York gambling each paid the police a fixed sum of $15 a month, and police made sure to protect the territory of each "policy king." Not only criminals paid the police. "It has been abundantly proven," concluded the committee,

> that bootblacks, push-cart and fruit venders, as well as keepers of soda water stands, corner grocerymen, sailmakers, . . . boxmakers, provision dealers, wholesale drygoods merchants and builders . . . steamboat and steamship companies, who require police service on their docks, those who give public exhibitions, and in fact all persons, and all classes of persons whose business is subject to the observation of the police, or who may be reported as violating ordinances, or who may require the aid of police, all have to contribute in substantial sums to the vast amounts which flow into the station-houses.

In other words, at one time or another, just about every citizen of New York was subject to, or the victim of, police extortion. As many businesses listed payoffs to police as part of their cost of doing business, all New Yorkers paid a price for police corruption.

Police brutality was also common, yet only one dismissal in three years had been ordered "for the clubbing of a private citizen." Even during the committee's proceedings, witnesses were brought into the hall bruised and bloody from recent police beatings. "The eye of one man," read the committee's report, "punched out by a patrolman's club, hung on his cheek." The police themselves had become a special criminal class in New York, "a separate and highly privileged class, armed with the authority and the machinery for oppression and punishment, but practically free themselves from the operation of the criminal law."

The chief of police had little executive power over his own department. Instead, the police commissioners, appointed by the party in power, were vested with vast authority, including "power of appointment, of promotion, of assignment, and of discipline, with respect to a force of 4,000 men." Moreover, commissioners oversaw police equipment, station houses, and disbursement of $5 million of appropriations plus $600,000 in pensions annually. Commissioners also sat in judgment over police officers, with the number of police trials averaging 5,000 per year. Finally, police commissioners were charged with overseeing the inspection of elections—from certifying candidates for office to taking custody of the actual election returns. If commissioners so chose, they could "exert a potent influence" in favor of a particular candidate or political party. With Tammany usually in firm control of New York's mayoralty, the Lexow Committee's report was a damning indictment of the Democratic machine's criminal alliance with the police. The committee recommended a separate civil service exam for police officers. It also recommended making the Board of Police Commissioners bipartisan. With the two parties equally represented, it was thought, politics would cease to control police commissioners' actions. On this last point, Roosevelt was about to find out how wrong the Lexow Committee was.

UPON TAKING OFFICE in May 1895, Roosevelt began to clean house. He was able to force the chief of police and other corrupt officers to resign. With his friend Jacob Riis, a former police reporter, he began his famed midnight inspection tours, making sure police officers were on duty when and where they were supposed to be, rather than asleep, or spending time in brothels or saloons. Arguably, in tackling corruption among New York City's 4,000 policemen and their countless allies in the criminal and political classes, Roosevelt faced a task more vast and complex than overseeing America's federal civil service.

At the center of much of the corruption lay the weekly violation of the Sunday excise law, which prohibited alcohol sales on Sundays. This state law had been backed by the rural, upstate temperance vote and imposed on the city, where it was routinely ignored. Worse, it was selectively enforced. Payoffs to the police allowed a saloon to remain open on Sunday, yet police could choose to enforce closure of, say, a saloon that competed with one owned by a local political figure. Many saloonkeepers were also Tammany bosses, and their saloons often doubled as unofficial Tammany headquarters. Like his Assembly investigating committee of 1884, Roosevelt's enforcement of the Sunday excise law not only served to attack vice and corruption, but also appeared to serve the interests of the Republican Party. Republican leaders would soon have reason to dispute this.

When Roosevelt took office in early 1895, between 12,000 and 15,000 saloons were operating in New York City. Within a few months, Roosevelt had been successful in closing 97 percent of them on Sundays, stopping the flow of some 3 million glasses of beer. As a result, by the summer of 1895, Roosevelt had become the most unpopular man in New York City. Inevitably, he was attacked by opposition politicians in the Democratic Party. But Roosevelt was also attacked by German Americans, who usually voted Republican. In the 1895 elections for state assembly, German Americans switched their votes to the Democrats, and Republican leaders blamed Roosevelt for their disastrous showing at the polls that year. Someone even sent Roosevelt a letter bomb that a postal clerk opened to find loaded only with sawdust. When a US senator from New York, Democrat David Hill, attacked Roosevelt for wasting police resources on this crusade rather than fighting crime, Roosevelt chose to reply to Hill by giving a speech to a German American audience. The Sunday excise law, Roosevelt said, was never meant to be honestly enforced. "It was meant to be used to blackmail and browbeat the saloon keepers who were not the slaves of Tammany Hall," he declared to a hostile audience, "while the big Tammany Hall bosses who owned saloons were allowed to violate the law with impunity and to corrupt the police force at will." Here was the clearest explanation for Roosevelt's crusade against the saloons. It was not a temperance crusade against the evil of drink, nor an attempt to save drunken immigrants from themselves. Instead, by simply enforcing a statute already on the books, Roosevelt sought to break the powerful and corrupt alliance between Tammany Hall and New York's police.

Always aware of the power of the press and public opinion, Roosevelt made a great effort to explain his actions and motivations to reporters. When at the beginning of his Sunday excise crusade the *New York Sun* had questioned why Roosevelt would act against public sentiment, Roosevelt had replied, "I do not deal with public sentiment. I deal with the law." Roosevelt also pointed out that lax enforcement resulted in a system in which saloonkeepers bribed policemen or hid behind political influence. For Roosevelt, the problem was having a law "which is not strictly enforced, which certain people are allowed to violate with impunity for corrupt reasons, while other offenders who lack their political influence are mercilessly harassed." He made a promise: "All our resources will be strained to prevent any such discrimination and to secure the equal punishment of all offenders." Equal enforcement of the law, and equal treatment of all citizens by the government, were hallmarks of Roosevelt's thought. They underlay many of his beliefs about good government, the evils of the spoils system, the benefits of basing civil service solely on merit, and, in New York, the need for police promotions based on meritorious service rather than political influence.

The year 1896 found a new addition to the anti-saloon crusade in the form of the Raines law, which made it illegal to serve free lunches as a way of drawing in midday drinkers, who usually ended up being the working poor. Hence the saying, "There is no such thing as a free lunch." The law also allowed Sunday liquor-selling in hotels only. This provision resulted in every saloonkeeper renting out the upstairs rooms in the tenement or building that his saloon occupied. By the summer of 1896, such new "Raines Law Hotels" were springing up daily, and they were widely seen as seedy and unwelcome. Renting out the rooms above saloons struck many as a throwback to the days when prostitutes plied their trade only a stairway's climb from the saloon floor. Others saw the rooms as encouraging gambling and other liquor-related vices. In an August 6 editorial, the *New York Times* complained that in one precinct where there had been only two hotels before passage of the Raines law, there now existed fifty-one "hotels" that sold liquor on Sundays, "and [at] all hours of the night with impunity and with a noticeable increase of drunkenness and disorder." The *New York Evening Post* complained of the "Raines law humbug."

The political backlash to his saloon-closing crusade and the Raines law were blows to Roosevelt. With the best of intentions, he had enforced an incredibly unpopular law. As a result, he had been attacked by both Republican and Democratic politicians, by German Americans, and by the press. In a recent development, tailors on the Lower East Side had gone on strike, and this had resulted in frequent, violent clashes between them and the contractors who were trying to keep their shops open with scab labor. Some in New York now blamed Roosevelt for this violence, saying that all the police were tied up in the anti-liquor crusade rather than maintaining law and order. In the end, the Sunday saloon-closing effort was largely a failure and meant the end of any future career in New York City politics for Roosevelt.

In this defeat, however, were sown the seeds of future political victory and his role as a Progressive Era reformer. After the 1895 Republican losses of city Assembly seats—losses that party leaders had blamed on him—Roosevelt had written to Lodge saying that party leaders were distancing themselves from him. They had not even allowed him to campaign and make speeches for Republican candidates. In his reply, Lodge advised Roosevelt: "You are making a great place and reputation for yourself which will lead surely to even better things. Remember too that apart from the great principle of enforcing all laws there is a very large and powerful body of Republicans in the State who will stand by you and behind you because you are enforcing that particular law." In other words, Roosevelt might be losing support in the city, but he was gaining support statewide, perhaps for the next political office. Lodge even talked about Roosevelt's path soon leading to a seat next to his in the United States Senate. Lodge was close to being correct. Within only two years of his anti-saloon crusade, Roosevelt would indeed be elected to statewide office, not as senator, as Lodge had speculated, but as governor of New York.

But at the moment, upper-class, brownstone-born Roosevelt was clearly oblivious to the role saloons played in New York City working-class culture. Saloons were not just places to get a beer, but also alternative communal spaces for men, often organized around ethnicity or occupation. Saloons provided the workingman many free things, not just a free lunch. They also provided newspapers, check-cashing services, and job information. At a time when laborers worked six days a week, enforcing the Sunday excise law deprived workers of the community and comfort provided by saloons. If Irish and German immigrants could not partake of a beer on Sunday, what other day could they head down to their local saloon? This was the irony of Roosevelt's battle to close saloons on Sunday: while it was meant to help the "humbler class" throw off Tammany's yoke, it also punished the very people Roosevelt thought he was aiding. These working-class immigrants, crowded into Lower East Side tenements, were exactly the same people he would seek to help once more during one of the worst natural disasters in New York history.

THE KILLER HEAT WAVE of 1896 began on August 4, with an official high temperature in the city of 87 degrees and 90 percent humidity. The combination was deadly. Before it was over, the heat wave would claim 1,300 lives, mostly immigrant laborers living in tenements. New Yorkers literally worked themselves to death. Across the river in Brooklyn, Mayor Seth Low opened that city's parks to citizens at night so they could sleep outdoors. Such a simple move allowed thousands in Brooklyn to catch at least a breath of fresh air and some rest before returning to work the next day. In New York City, with the ban on sleeping in the parks still in effect, people slept on rooftops, on fire escapes, at the piers, and even on the streets. A place on top of a garbage bin was highly prized, as it allowed the sleeper to rise above the searing, stinking asphalt. Rooftop sleeping just added to the tragedy, as some people fell to their deaths. Others fell asleep on piers, rolled into the river, and drowned.

Death certificates from the ten-day heat wave chronicled the unfolding tragedy. The first victim may have been fifteen-month-old Hyman Goldman, newly arrived in the city with his family. For three weeks a doctor had been seeing little Hyman for "cholera infantium"—a common diarrhea suffered by children during summer months that led to dehydration, and frequently death. By the time the heat wave settled over the Goldman family's tenement at 55 Broome Street, the toddler had already been severely weakened. His doctor wrote a one-word cause of death: "Exhaustion." The heat wave took a terrible toll on the city's very young, as indicated by the batch of death certificates filed by doctors at the New York Foundling Hospital. The hospital had been established to care for abandoned babies and to address the nineteenth-century practice of infanticide of unwanted children. The heat wave felled the little babies one after another. But in addition to the very young, the elderly were at great risk during the heat wave. Katherine Brennan was a sixty-six-year-old widow originally from Ireland who lived in a tenement. Her death certificate said she died of "Weakness of old age" exacerbated by "hot weather." Sometimes, the heat caused death indirectly. One baby died after his mother went into labor prematurely. Often a doctor would measure the victim's body temperature at the time of death. Readings of 111 degrees were common.

During the heat wave, horses died by the hundreds, and their carcasses were left to fester on the city's streets. Often, days would go by before a dead horse could be removed, and, all the while, it baked in the sun and began to emit a horrible smell, causing great discomfort for those nearby. "The heated term was the worst and most fatal we have ever known," Roosevelt wrote his sister Anna. "The death-rate trebled until it approached the ratio of a cholera epidemic; the horses died by the hundred, so that it was impossible to remove their carcasses, and they added a genuine flavor of pestilence." A *New York Herald* reporter noted a dead horse on every city block, and many businesses had to close because the stench kept away customers. The managers of the Anchor Steam Brewing Company sent Mayor Strong a letter of complaint about the dead horses, asserting that "in no small town or City . . . would a dead animal be allowed to decompose for four days as occurred under our office window last week, notwithstanding the fact that it was three times reported to the 'Board of Health.'"

Roosevelt's position as president of the Board of Police Commissioners also gave him a place on the Board of Health. He recalled one storekeeper who wrote continually to the board, asking for a dead horse in front of his store to be removed. The smell was deterring customers. The board finally sent a cart to remove the horse, but it was a large wagon already stacked with the carcasses of eleven other dead horses. When the cart stopped in front of the man's store, it broke down. Now the storekeeper wrote back to the Board of Health, asking it, as Roosevelt remembered, to "remove either the horses, or his shop, he didn't care which."

It was probably complaints like that one from Anchor Steam Brewing that prompted Mayor Strong on August 13 to call an emergency meeting of department heads. Up until then, the city had made no concerted effort to relieve the plight of New Yorkers during the heat wave. If he had been mayor, would Roosevelt have done anything differently? With his comment to Jacob Riis that New York needed "a workingman's mayor," and his decision to target saloons as a way to lift Tammany's yoke from the neck of the workingman, it seems likely he would have. At the very least, Mayor Roosevelt might have begun to coordinate the efforts to remove dead horses much earlier. He might have cooled down the streets by having them "flushed" with hoses; kept the "floating baths," constructed with pontoons in the rivers, open longer; and changed the work hours for city employees. All of these remedies had been undertaken individually by department heads without orders from the mayor's office. Roosevelt might have also ordered the city parks to be thrown open at night. As police commissioner, he had already ordered that police wagons be pressed into service as ambulances to carry the prostrated to hospitals. One order Roosevelt did not issue, however, was any modification to the police dress code of heavy blue wool. As first responders during the heat wave, many policemen suffered heat exhaustion; hundreds were hospitalized, and six died. Roosevelt did press his police department into service to aid the stricken poor in the tenement districts, where the heat wave hit hardest. The police commissioner suggested a scheme for the city to distribute free ice through the police station houses.

Before electric refrigeration, people used "ice boxes": wooden boxes lined by tin or zinc, and requiring the purchase of a large block of ice. In every major American city, ice vendors were some of the largest businesses. In New York, an ice magnate named Charles Morse controlled most of the ice distribution. The resulting trust—a group of firms that combined to reduce competition and raise prices—kept prices high and ice out of reach of the city's poor. In a heat wave like that of August 1896, this practice had deadly consequences. Private charities responded by raising money for ice giveaways, but never before in the city's history had the government distributed free ice to the poor. On August 13, Roosevelt instructed his policemen to inform local residents of the ice giveaway scheduled for later that evening. Everyone was shocked at the massive turnout. Hours before the ice even arrived in precinct houses, hundreds of men, women, and children crowded around the police stations clamoring for free ice. "It was to them better than bread to the starving," the *New York Journal* reported. "Mothers with sickly babes in their arms jostled with weary men, while children begged for a piece of ice to take home to the sick room." The *Times* estimated that 20,000 people were served ice that first night, yet that was only a tiny fraction of the residents of one of the most densely packed tenement districts. Roosevelt recommended the giveaway be doubled the following evening. Seeing that some better-off residents received free ice at the expense of some of the poorest, Roosevelt devised a system whereby police gave tickets to the poorest families along their beats. Moreover, he personally explored the darkest back alleys of the tenement districts to see how families used the ice. He observed firsthand fathers chipping off pieces of ice for children to suck, and a mother wrapping ice in a handkerchief to tie around the forehead of an ailing infant in her arms. Few New Yorkers of Roosevelt's class had ever had such intimate contact with the city's poorest residents. Almost twenty years later in his memoirs, Roosevelt still remembered the "strange and pathetic scenes" from the heat wave.

ROOSEVELT GAINED NO political advantage from helping the immigrant poor of the Lower East Side. Such New Yorkers voted Democrat. Because of the crusade to enforce the Sunday excise law, Roosevelt's city career was at an end. As Republicans readied in 1896 to battle William Jennings Bryan as the "Popocrat" candidate—nominated by both the Populists and Democrats—Roosevelt made sure to visit Republican headquarters in New York and offer his services to William McKinley's campaign manager, Mark Hanna. In the event of a Republican win that fall, Roosevelt and Lodge hoped that Roosevelt's efforts on behalf of McKinley would be rewarded with a post in Washington. Still, the heat wave and Roosevelt's contact with the urban poor helped shape his ideas about government responsibility for workers and immigrants. Roosevelt had been one of the few city department heads to take concrete steps to aid the residents of the tenements. He had advocated and carried out a scheme to give away a commodity that had been priced out of reach for many New Yorkers because of the existence of a trust. Roosevelt's actions helped "bust" the trust, which would become a hallmark of Roosevelt's presidency. He had expressed not only great sympathy for the poor, but also government's responsibility to take action to alleviate their suffering. From his words to Jacob Riis calling for a "workingman's mayor" to his actions during the heat wave, Roosevelt displayed an amazing sensitivity to the plight of even the humblest of New Yorkers.

Roosevelt's understanding of the problems facing urban America went far beyond mere sympathy, however. His time as police commissioner allowed him to acquire a broad view of the entire city. Tackling police corruption and closing saloons on Sundays were not isolated phenomena, but part of a vast, interconnected web of evils plaguing New York. Although he was head of only one city department during his two years as president of the Board of Police Commissioners, Roosevelt understood that battling police corruption touched on just about every other problem in the city: the exploitation of immigrants; the exploitation of women; the problems facing labor; the blackmail of small business owners; corruption among city officials; high taxes; ineffective, if not brutal, police; rigged elections; vice, including gambling and prostitution; failure to enforce, or selective enforcement of, the law; the inadequacy of the courts; the dangers of tenement dwelling; and the filth, dirt, and disease that plagued the city and its denizens. Roosevelt's advocacy of good government and his implementation and expansion of civil service might appear as a tiny sliver of the immense total reform agenda being advocated at the dawn of the Progressive Era. But Roosevelt understood that having clear government oversight, enforcing the law equitably, and increasing executive power—whether of a mayor or police chief—led to more livable cities and the alleviation of the plight of the poor, especially the working-class immigrants living in tenements. Being police commissioner gave Roosevelt an almost holistic understanding of the American city, both the problems it faced and the solutions available.

By the late nineteenth century, city problems were quickly becoming national problems. On the streets of New York, Roosevelt received an education that would serve him well as he rose to become chief executive, first of the nation's largest state, then of the nation itself.

NINE

"The Ritz Riders"
Assistant Secretary of the Navy,
War in Cuba, and Roosevelt's
Path to Albany

IF BAD WEATHER ON ELECTION DAY favors the underdog, in November 1896 New York Democrats were hoping for a hurricane. Instead they got a beautiful late fall day, the kind New Yorkers savor before the onset of winter. People happily walked or rode carriages to the nearly 1,400 polling places in New York County. Election officers commented on the rush to vote early. Before the polls even opened, voters lined up to cast their ballots, and until noon large crowds could be seen at most polling places. The turnout was enormous. In some city districts, nearly every registered voter cast a ballot. In the Twelfth District, George McClellan Jr., son of the famed Army of the Potomac commander, ran as a Democrat against Charles Hess, brother of Jake Hess, Roosevelt's old nemesis in the Twenty-First Assembly District. For most New Yorkers, voting took mere seconds. For those voting a straight ticket, only a single box needed to be checked. In addition to the presidential, state, and local elections, a single measure appeared on the ballot, a proposed amendment to the New York State Constitution. Theodore Roosevelt had a keen interest in the outcome of all of these votes.

The proposed amendment had to do with the preservation of the Adirondacks. President Harrison had signed the Forest Reserve Act into law in March 1891, while Roosevelt was civil service commissioner. But Roosevelt's Boone and Crockett Club had played a key role in the passage of the bill, as it had lobbied Congress, the secretary of the interior, and the White House about the dangers of deforestation and the need for federal action. The act authorized the president to set aside public lands as forest reserves. After signing the bill, Harrison almost immediately set aside 13 million acres of protected forest, all of it in the West. From the beginning, however, Roosevelt had also envisioned protecting the Adirondacks, and a state Adirondack Park was established by Albany the following year. The initial law, though, allowed the state to lease parklands for camps and cottages. Roosevelt and other conservationists championed the "Forever Wild" movement, which opposed allowing any selling or leasing of land set aside as parks or reserves. In 1894, a covenant was added to the state constitution declaring Adirondack Park "forever wild." Henceforth, any change to the "forever wild" clause would require the approval of a majority of the state's population and two successive legislatures. Attempts were made to do this in 1895 and 1896. Returning to Oyster Bay to vote in 1896, Roosevelt undoubtedly checked only two boxes: one to vote a straight Republican ticket, and a second to oppose the constitutional amendment allowing campsites in Adirondack Park. The amendment was defeated.

So, too, were the Democrats. While William Jennings Bryan won the solid South and much of the West, he lost to McKinley in those states where Roosevelt had traveled that summer and fall: Minnesota, Michigan, Illinois, and North Dakota, which had become a state in 1889. In New York State and in the city, Republicans scored massive victories. New York's Republican boss Thomas Platt's man Frank Black was elected governor with a plurality of more than 200,000 votes. Republicans gained a majority in the state legislature. In the city, for the first time since the organization of the Republican Party in 1856, New Yorkers gave a majority of their votes to the Republican presidential candidate. In New York State, McKinley secured the greatest plurality ever given to any candidate: he beat Bryan by about 270,000 votes, greater even than Cleveland's record-setting plurality when he was elected governor in 1882. For anyone paying close attention, McKinley's great electoral victory illustrated how the success of the national ticket could trickle down to state and local elections. In an editorial, the *Times* noted that the result "has been quite independent of the record of the Republican Party in State affairs and of the character of its candidates." This was a slap at Platt, and the Republican machine in New York, but it is unlikely Platt much cared what the paper said. Although he was not running for office in 1896, on Election Day Platt emerged as New York's greatest victor.

Almost immediately, speculation began as to the constitution of McKinley's new cabinet. New York was the largest and most politically important state in the Union, so at least some of those posts were expected to go to prominent New Yorkers. Early on, top New York Republican Cornelius Bliss was rumored to be under consideration for Treasury, although he ended up at the Department of the Interior. Eventually, New Yorkers John Hay and Elihu Root would find top spots in the McKinley administration. One prominent New York Republican not mentioned amid the speculation was Theodore Roosevelt, who had lobbied hard for a position. He had hosted close McKinley confidant Mrs. Bellamy Storer at Sagamore Hill; had paid homage to this year's Republican kingmaker, Mark Hanna; had campaigned wherever Hanna and the Republican National Committee had sent him; and had even called on McKinley at his home in Canton, Ohio. Now much hinged on the efforts of Lodge and other prominent Republicans.

Within a month of the election, Lodge visited McKinley in Canton. The visit was likely meant to mend fences with the president-elect. Lodge and Roosevelt had opposed the 1890 McKinley Tariff and McKinley's 1896 nomination for the presidency. In a two-hour conversation, McKinley touched upon a variety of subjects, including the new Cuban revolution against Spanish colonial rule, tariffs, and possible nominees for secretary of state. Talk then turned to Theodore Roosevelt's suitability for the Navy Department. Just as Blaine had worried about Roosevelt's temperament back in 1888, McKinley worried that the police commissioner would have, as Lodge recounted, "preconceived plans which he would wish to drive through the moment he got in." Lodge reassured McKinley that was not the case, and he pressed a Roosevelt appointment as the one personal favor the president-elect could do the Massachusetts senator. Outside observers assumed that Lodge had gone to Canton to seek an office for himself. Probably no one imagined that such a senior American statesman as Lodge, crafter of America's new foreign policy as a world power, was pressing the case for a mere New York civil servant.

McKinley was not the only person who needed convincing about Roosevelt's suitability for the Navy Department. Lodge and Roosevelt still had to contend with Boss Platt. For a decade, Platt had shown his power to block or ease federal actions in New York State. The 1896 elections had only increased his power. By December, Platt was readying for the following month's Republican state caucus, which would almost unanimously support him for a seat in the US Senate. A week after visiting McKinley, Lodge called Platt on the telephone and asked for his support of Roosevelt for assistant secretary of the navy. The Easy Boss was as coy as ever. Platt told Lodge he worried that from the Navy Department Roosevelt would "make war" on the party organization. Lodge was perplexed. How could an assistant secretary of the navy come into conflict with the Republican state machine? "There is the Brooklyn Navy Yard," Platt replied. He referred to federal appointments there, but as Lodge pointed out later in a letter to Roosevelt, new rules had made such appointments "perfectly trivial" and under the purview of the navy secretary, not the assistant secretary. Lodge told Roosevelt he thought Platt did not realize that the "matter of Navy Yard patronage died out of the Navy Department some years ago." But Lodge did not know Platt. Of course Platt knew by heart every position of federal patronage in New York State. Platt used the pretended concern as a smokescreen to keep both Lodge and Roosevelt off balance and under his sway. Such prevaricating was classic Platt, as Roosevelt would soon find out.

Every day Roosevelt must have thanked heaven for a friend like Lodge. The Massachusetts senator secured further support for a

Roosevelt appointment from John Hay; McKinley's new secretary of the interior, Cornelius Bliss; fellow US senators Edward Wolcott of Colorado and Cushman Davis of Minnesota; Speaker of the House Thomas Reed; McKinley's secretary, John Addison Porter; and even the vice president–elect, Garret Hobart. By March, it was clear that John Long, former governor of Massachusetts, was to be the new navy secretary. Lodge met with Long, who spoke "in the highest terms of you," as he told Roosevelt. "The only thing resembling criticism was this queer one: 'Roosevelt has the character, standing, ability and reputation to entitle him to a Cabinet Minister. Is not this job too small for him?'" This was a nice bit of dissembling by Long. Still, Long was not the problem; Platt was still withholding his support. Roosevelt asked a couple of New York machine Republicans to talk to Platt, but he received a depressing response. Platt noted the appointment to McKinley's cabinet of New Yorkers opposed to the machine, men like Cornelius Bliss. All further appointments, Platt asserted, should therefore go to organization men, and Roosevelt's appointment would mean, as Lodge wrote to Roosevelt, "one place less for the organization people, to which he could not well consent." The conversation with the Platt men left Roosevelt temporarily downcast. Within two days, however, he heard from top Platt lieutenants that the machine now favored his appointment. It was enough to give a man whiplash. But Platt's support made sense, as it was a way to get Roosevelt out of his current job in New York. The turn of events gave Roosevelt pause. He wondered to Lodge whether Platt's previous opposition "was not merely said with the hope of making me give him something in connection with this office, or else to establish a ground for holding off, so as to get something from the Administration." Roosevelt was learning.

In April 1897, Roosevelt finally received the much-coveted appointment as assistant secretary of the navy. New York's reformers received the news of Roosevelt's imminent departure as they might a death in the family. Charles Parkhurst, who had long called for reform of the New York City Police Department, wrote to Roosevelt, "I consider your departure a municipal affliction" and "a personal bereavement." Father Alexander P. Doyle, editor of *Catholic World* magazine, said he felt sorry for the city of New York. "You have planted the standard of municipal honor further ahead and higher up," he wrote. "I cannot contemplate the loss of your fearless honest spirit to this municipality without some regret." Even Roosevelt's Mugwump nemesis E. L. Godkin wrote to say "how very sorry I was to hear of you leaving the New York police." "In New York," Godkin added, "you were doing the greatest work of which any American today is capable, and exhibiting to the young men of the country, the spectacle of a very important office administered by a man of high character in the most efficient way." These were warm sentiments from a man who mocked Roosevelt in his journals. New York reformers saw Roosevelt's departure from their city as a grave loss.

If Roosevelt had not taken the post in Washington, however, Platt and other Republicans would have likely found some other way to remove him from the police commission, voluntarily or not. After years serving the city—whether in the Assembly, running for mayor, or as police commissioner—Roosevelt was finished with New York City posts. This did not mean New York City no longer served as an important base of Roosevelt's power, or that his New York City identity diminished in any way. As the geographical considerations of cabinet appointments illustrated, Roosevelt's "New Yorkness" remained an important political characteristic. In Roosevelt's future possibly lay more New York positions, perhaps in Congress, or in a statewide position such as governor or US senator.

Returning to Washington presented the Roosevelts with a serious problem. It was expensive. In August, Roosevelt wrote his Uncle Jim that his personal tax "is put on me much heavier than it used to be in New York [City], and I adhere to New York as my place of abode, so I shan't pay any in Oyster Bay. I have been voting in New York for the past two years, and that has been my residence." It was an interesting comment from Roosevelt. One important reason he claimed New York as his residence was so that he could vote in the city and affect the outcome of city and state elections. For anyone who has tried to characterize Roosevelt as a kind of "country gentleman" who preferred Oyster Bay to Manhattan, Roosevelt himself made plain that his connection to the city remained important. But it was also costly. Because of this, Roosevelt's lawyer would eventually suggest a way to reduce the assistant secretary's tax burden. All Roosevelt had to do was to swear an affidavit repudiating his residence in New York since moving to Washington in April 1897. Roosevelt would do this in March 1898, stating, "Since 1897, I have not had any domicile or residence in New York City." Although his political opponents would soon make much of this, the importance of such a statement should not be exaggerated. After all, it was not Roosevelt's idea, and he did it for tax reasons only. Had Roosevelt even imagined that it might disqualify him from any new office, either in the city or in the state, he would not have made such a statement. The affidavit reflected penny-pinching more than any rejection of the city of his birth, the place he constantly referred to as "my city."

ROOSEVELT'S SINGLE YEAR in the Navy Department was a momentous one. With war with Spain a distinct possibility, and with Secretary Long frequently out of the office, Roosevelt had much latitude in implementing ideas for a larger and more modern navy. He saw Lodge all the time and dined frequently with the president. By September 1897, Roosevelt had developed detailed plans as to the US Navy's deployment in both the Caribbean off Cuba and the Pacific off the Spanish Empire's other major holding, the Philippines. For someone so in the thick of things in Washington, his connection to and concerns about New York remained surprisingly strong. He kept up correspondence with New York newspaper editors, such as Paul Dana at the *Sun*, and continued his public jousting with the *Post* and the *Journal*. His friend on the police commission, Avery Andrews, kept Roosevelt abreast of developments in the police force, and in August 1897, he offered his congratulations to the new chief of police. The next month, Roosevelt published, in *The Atlantic Monthly*, an article entitled "Municipal Administration: The New York Police Force," in which he defended his enforcement of the Sunday excise law in the face of widespread opposition. It was a nice chance for Roosevelt not only to defend his record, but also to keep his name before New Yorkers. As Lodge had noted during the Sunday excise fight, residents of upstate New York supported the law and Roosevelt's enforcement of it. By 1897, it was they who would have to vote Roosevelt into any future statewide position.

As of now, Roosevelt was keeping his New York residence in order to play a role in city elections, but the elections of 1897 proved a maddening affair. As assistant secretary of the navy, Roosevelt had the luxury of observing the Republican disaster that autumn from a safe distance in Washington. Indeed, the elections that year probably made Roosevelt doubly happy that he had left behind him the problematic position of president of the New York City Board of Police Commissioners, and New York politics in general.

In 1897, wealthy city reformers made another effort to undermine the power of the machine by founding the independent Citizens' Union. By running candidates for elected positions in the city, both for mayor and for seats in the state legislature, the Citizens' Union hoped to separate city politics from the state and national party organizations. This was a direct attack on Platt's power as Republican boss. That fall, the Citizens' Union ran former mayor of Brooklyn and Columbia University president Seth Low for mayor of New York City. Since the spring, Platt had called for an alliance of independent and machine Republicans to defeat Tammany Hall, and he approached Low about accepting both the Citizens' Union and Republican nominations. Low refused. In return, Platt refused to endorse Low.

Right from the beginning, it appeared obvious that Low would simply split the Republican vote and allow the election of a Tammany mayor. A week before Low's nomination, Roosevelt wrote to Lodge to complain about the "idiotic conduct of the Citizens' Union." At the same time, throughout the October campaign Roosevelt continuously reached out to Low and his supporters. After Cornelius Bliss came out publicly for Republican candidate Benjamin Tracy, Roosevelt wrote to Low saying that President McKinley had expressly told him he should not voice his support for Low. "I only wish I could be on the stump for you," Roosevelt wrote to Low, "for I have hardly ever felt more interested in anyone's success. All I could do on the quiet has been done." Apparently this included making his support for Low as widely known as possible among New York acquaintances. Roosevelt indicated his support to Carl Schurz, Jacob Riis, New York financier John Kennedy Todd, publisher George Putnam, and E. L. Godkin. He told Putnam that he had given money to the Citizens' Union, and indicated to Todd and Schurz that he had contemplated resigning his post to campaign for Low. To friend Lodge, however, he excoriated both Low and the Citizens' Union. The day after he wrote to Low, Roosevelt told Lodge that he could not "with self respect" support the Citizens' Union. "I am glad I am out of it," Roosevelt wrote his friend. Roosevelt and Lodge spent a great quantity of ink tearing down Low and the Citizens' Union. On October 29, Roosevelt replied to Lodge, agreeing with the senator's assessment that, in not seeking fusion with the Republicans, "the conduct of the Low people and of Low . . . was not merely stupid, but from the civic standpoint almost criminal." "What a grim comedy the whole canvass is!" Roosevelt concluded. Roosevelt was hardly laughing.

Democrat Robert A. Van Wyck won the mayoral election handily, with 80,000 more votes than Seth Low, and more than double the votes of Benjamin Tracy. Labor candidate Henry George had died of a stroke during the campaign; his son replaced him on the ballot and finished a distant fourth. Tracy even polled fewer votes than Roosevelt had in 1886, when Brooklyn was still a separate city. Platt and the Low people had achieved pyrrhic victories of a sort. Platt had shown Citizens' Union supporters that they could not win without regular Republican support, but the Citizens' Union supporters had shown Platt that they could deny Republicans election in the city. The Citizens' Union had also managed to deny the Republicans victory in the elections for the state Assembly. Of the city's thirty-five seats, only two were won by Republicans, as opposed to thirty-one by Democrats. By running independent candidates in city districts as well as for mayor, the Citizens' Union had secured two of its own seats in the Assembly while ensuring a reduced Republican majority in Albany. It was this outcome that caused Roosevelt to refer to the election results as a "disaster." "I don't see much hope in the situation in New York," the assistant secretary wrote Lodge from Washington. "The Citizens' Union people are very foolish, and the unspeakable scoundrelism as well as folly of the machine has alienated decent republicans more deeply than you could imagine." During the campaign, Roosevelt had followed a pattern of publicly reaching out to both wings of the party while privately condemning both. No matter how much he may have criticized Platt, Roosevelt was learning some valuable political tactics from the Easy Boss.

The 1897 elections made a deep impression on Roosevelt. Writing in his 1913 *Autobiography*, he remembered the results of those elections as having "brought the Republican party to a smash, not only in New York City, but in the State." Roosevelt had long seen the dangers of a split Republican Party. The 1897 elections proved once again to Roosevelt the absolute necessity of a united Republican Party. As he indicated to Lodge, only fools would advocate otherwise. Platt, too, seemed chastened by the result. He would soon look for a candidate for governor who would be palatable to both machine and reform Republicans.

By early 1898, however, great events were overshadowing New York City politics. Three years after Cubans had once again revolted against Spanish imperial rule, an American war with Spain seemed imminent. Since the birth of the republic, American presidents had tried unsuccessfully to acquire the island of Cuba, a mere ninety miles off the coast of Florida. As Latin American revolutions stripped Spain of its holdings, the once-great empire gripped its only remaining New World colonies—Cuba and Puerto Rico—ever more tightly. This irritated a United States that was growing in both political and economic power—and that was increasingly willing to assert that power in the Western Hemisphere. By the time of the latest Cuban insurrection, Americans had invested $50 million in the island's sugar fields, while Britain and European powers increasingly bowed to American interests in the hemisphere. A Cuban junta had established offices in New York City and fed propaganda of Spanish atrocities to the yellow press. By 1896, Congress had passed a resolution recognizing the Cuban belligerency. Throughout the country, Americans took up the cry of *Cuba Libre!*

Under pressure to make some sort of firm gesture toward Spain, and to ensure the safety of American lives and property in Cuba, in January 1898 President McKinley dispatched the battleship *Maine* to Havana harbor. Early the next month, William Randolph Hearst's *New York Journal* published a letter from the Spanish minister to Washington, Enrique Dupuy de Lôme, criticizing McKinley. The De Lôme letter led to the minister's return to Spain and inflamed American opinion.

Worse was yet to come. On February 15, the *Maine* blew up in Havana harbor, killing more than 250 American sailors. War fever gripped the yellow press and Americans in general. Even as McKinley tried to negotiate Cuban autonomy with Madrid, pressure on the president mounted to ask Congress for a declaration of war. On April 11, McKinley relented. By the end of the month, America was at war.

Roosevelt, Lodge, and others wanted war with Spain not because of any mindless love of war, but to kick the brutal, decrepit, and Catholic Spanish Empire out from America's hemisphere. Roosevelt did his part by preparing the navy for war, including sending orders to Commodore George Dewey to prepare the Pacific Squadron to move against the Philippines. From New York came unwanted advice. Republican operator Benjamin Tracy, defeated for mayor the previous year, and so close to Platt that he was law partner with Platt's son Frank, sent both President McKinley and the Navy Department strongly worded suggestions as to the building and deployment of America's fleet. As secretary of the navy under Benjamin Harrison, Tracy thought he had the right to proffer advice. On April 2, before McKinley asked Congress for a declaration of war, Tracy urged moving the fleet toward St. Thomas. On April 15, as Congress debated declaring war, Tracy wrote again to criticize the navy's preparations. Why, he asked, were five battleships still under construction? Why had a fleet of "torpedo boats" not been ordered? "Buying yachts and tugs may be well," he scoffed, "but it is not an adequate provision for a naval conflict, and to longer delay the construction of torpedo boats is little less than criminal." Roosevelt wrote cordial replies, pointing out his position subordinate to Secretary Long. While still carrying out the business of the Navy Department, Roosevelt was likely distracted by other concerns. Only a week later, it was announced that Roosevelt had resigned his post to become second-in-command of the First US Volunteer Cavalry. Via San Antonio, Texas, and Tampa, Florida, Roosevelt was bound for Cuba.

In New York, Katherine Duer was not happy. Although her wedding day was supposed to be the most special day of her life—or so everyone told her—it was not as special as it should have been. Katherine could not complain about the arrangements. Her parents' house at

17 West 21st Street had been transformed for the occasion. White lilies and apple blossoms formed a grotto at one end of the drawing room, where the ceremony would take place. The mantel above the fireplace had been completely covered with bougainvillea, specially grown for the wedding. Long branches of blooming apple blossoms concealed the doors of the drawing room and the library next door. In the hallway, roses were everywhere, except in the places where there were palms instead, to conceal the orchestra. Neither could Katherine complain about her dress, a simply tailored affair of heavy satin with a long veil. She could even take pride in the fact that she was marrying into royalty. Her husband, Clarence Mackay, although untitled himself, was related by blood to Italian royalty. Attending the ceremony were Mackay's aunt, the Countess Telfener, and his sister, the Princess Colonna. This made Katherine herself a sort of princess, did it not? Having royalty at her wedding was a great social coup. But so many invited guests and members of the wedding party were conspicuous by their absence. Katherine blamed the war.

A May 17 wedding was considered late in the wedding season, and the Mackay-Duer nuptials were among the very last of the year for their New York social set. Had the ceremony taken place only a week earlier, many of the absent young men would have been able to attend. Craig Wadsworth, a leader of cotillions and a star polo player, was supposed to have been one of Mackay's ushers. Worse, the best man was supposed to have been Reginald Ronalds, former Yale football star, member of the Knickerbocker Club, and descendant of tobacco magnate Pierre Lorillard. Both members of the wedding party were absent. So, too, were many of the invited guests, young men who were the cream of New York society. Although the elder Tiffanys attended, their son William did not. Hamilton Fish, former Speaker of the Assembly and son of President Grant's secretary of state, was present. His nephew, also named Hamilton Fish, was not. Only the week before, shortly after the United States declared war on Spain, all the young men had traveled to Washington, DC, where they had been inducted into the army. Almost immediately, they left Washington for training in San Antonio under the leadership of their new lieutenant colonel, a former assistant secretary of the navy and, like them, member of New York's social elite, Theodore Roosevelt. Instead of attending Katherine Duer's wedding, Wadsworth, Ronalds, Tiffany, and Fish were all now part of the First US Volunteer Cavalry, a regiment that would soon be known as "The Rough Riders."

It is often forgotten that Roosevelt initially served as second-in-command to Leonard Wood, a full colonel with battlefield experience. More importantly, Wood had played a key role in some of the last skirmishes with Native Americans in the West, including the capture of Geronimo. As America was preparing for war in April 1898, Wood received the Medal of Honor for his western efforts. His citation reads: "Voluntarily carried dispatches through a region infested with hostile Indians, making a journey of 70 miles in one night and walking 30 miles the next day. Also for several weeks, while in close pursuit of Geronimo's band and constantly expecting an encounter, commanded a detachment of Infantry, which was then without an officer, and to the command of which he was assigned upon his own request." Roosevelt is often credited with attracting western cowboys to the regiment, because of his stint in North Dakota, but little credit is given to Wood. However, Wood not only was a combat veteran, army officer, Medal of Honor winner, and famed Indian fighter, but had also served in America's Southwest, along the border between the United States and Mexico. Most of the cowboys who joined the Rough Riders did not hail from North Dakota. In fact, only three members of Roosevelt's regiment were listed as being from that state. Instead, they came to Texas by the trainload from the neighboring Arizona, New Mexico, Oklahoma, and Indian Territories. This was where Wood's name, not Theodore Roosevelt's, had prominence. It was Wood who detailed men he knew in all of those places as recruiting officers. It was Wood who chose San Antonio as the regiment's point of assemblage, because it was adjacent to Fort Sam Houston. It was Wood who arranged the purchase of horses in Texas. Finally, it was Wood who left Roosevelt behind in Washington to ensure that the Ordnance and Quartermaster's departments delivered promised supplies, while Wood established the camp in the State Fair Grounds on the outskirts of San Antonio. Roosevelt was a stranger to Texas and the Territories. In Wood, the Southwest welcomed home a hero.

Theodore Roosevelt's name still carried much weight in New York, however, and New Yorkers joined the regiment by the score. Aside from Texas, New Mexico, and the Indian Territories, no part of the United States sent more soldiers to the Rough Riders than New York State. Most of these men hailed from the city. There were poor Katherine Duer's missing wedding guests—Craig Wadsworth, William Tiffany, Hamilton Fish, and Reginald Ronalds. Kenneth Robinson, brother to Roosevelt's brother-in-law Douglas Robinson, also joined. So, too, did a football star and son of a New York millionaire, I. Townsend Burden Jr. In addition, Woody Kane, only two years behind Roosevelt at Harvard, joined, along with former Princeton football star Horace Devereux. Bob Ferguson, whose brother Ronald was a British member of Parliament, was a close friend of Roosevelt's from New York; he became a second lieutenant. The list of prominent New Yorkers who joined Roosevelt was lengthy. The Bull brothers, Charles and Henry, had rowed crew at Harvard and were sons of a wealthy New York broker. David M. Goodrich, of the Goodrich rubber family, had captained crew at Harvard and would later become chairman of the B. F. Goodrich Company in Akron, Ohio. Sumner Gerard, like Kenneth Ferguson, was a champion golfer. Dozens more New York men joined, listing as their home addresses houses along Fifth Avenue or various social clubs. They were joined by other prominent young men from Newport, Rhode Island, and New Haven, Connecticut. Four New York City policemen joined, along with Edwin Emerson of *Collier's* magazine. New York newspapers identified this local contingent as "College and Club Men," while others referred to them as "The Fifth Avenue Boys." They might have been called "The Ritz Riders."

Young men growing up in Manhattan's elite society necessarily had much in common with even the roughest of western cowboys. Like Roosevelt, they had learned to ride and shoot, and both Craig Wadsworth and Hamilton Fish were champion polo players. Young men of the Victorian era were expected to be manly and athletic, which is why Roosevelt had taken up boxing and wrestling, promising his father that he would stay fit. Like Roosevelt, a few had even gone west to work on cattle ranches. Basil Ricketts, son of Civil War general James Ricketts, had worked for two years on a ranch in Colorado, as had William Tiffany. They received no special treatment either in camp or in battle. A few were given commissions, but most served as troopers in Troop K, which might be called the "Club Troop." The elite young men from Manhattan served side-by-side with cowboys and Indians, became friends with them, and died with them. The most dramatic example of this was the short military career of Hamilton Fish.

Fish, who stood six feet two inches, had captained crew at Columbia College. After graduation, he had spent a few years as a man about town before heading west to try his hand at being a cowboy. Roosevelt knew Fish's uncle well. A longtime Republican member of the Assembly, the elder Hamilton Fish was a former Speaker and a Platt man. And as both Hamilton Fishes were members of the Union Club, it is likely Roosevelt had been acquainted with young Ham Fish before the war. When the call went out for volunteers, Fish eagerly enlisted. He almost did not make it to Cuba. In April 1898, the United States found itself so ill-prepared for war that it did not have enough transports to get its army to Cuba. Fish's I Troop had been ordered to stay behind at the embarkation point in Tampa. Captain Allyn K. Capron of L Troop asked Colonel Wood if Fish could be transferred to his troop and promoted to sergeant. Fish, then, found a place on a transport to Cuba sporting an extra stripe, but without a horse. Because of the lack of space, the First US Volunteer Cavalry regiment had to leave its horses behind.

Fish became friends with Ed Culver, part Cherokee, who had been raised on the cattle ranges of the Indian Territories. In Cuba on June 23, during a soaking rain, Fish and Culver stood under a tree together trying to stay dry. "Old boy," said the club man, "this is soldiering." When the rain stopped, the two made a fire, and Culver made coffee as Fish watched. Colonel Roosevelt and Captain Capron sauntered over. Roosevelt later remembered the moment in his account of the campaign. "As we stood around the flickering blaze that night," Roosevelt recalled in *The Rough Riders*, "I caught myself admiring the splendid bodily vigor of Capron and Fish—the captain and the sergeant. Their frames seemed of steel, to withstand all fatigue; they were flushed with health; in their eyes shone high resolve and fiery desire. Two finer types of the fighting man, two better representatives of the American soldier, there were not in the whole army." Within twenty-four hours, both men would be dead.

The next day, June 24, at Las Guásimas, the Rough Riders came into contact with the Spanish. Culver dropped behind a rock, and Fish crawled up beside him. "Got a good place?" Fish asked. "Yeh," Culver replied. Fish fired four or five shots before a single Spanish bullet tore through both Fish and Culver. Fish was shot through the heart and died. Culver was also shot through the chest, but he was able to stagger to the rear, one hand clutching the wound as blood soaked the front of his uniform. Later the journalist Richard Harding Davis came across Fish's body. Reaching into the dead trooper's clothes, Davis pulled out an expensive watch engraved with the words "God gives." Roosevelt next passed Fish and stopped a moment to contemplate the young man's body. It had been a costly skirmish, taking the lives of eight of the Rough Riders. Fish's military career had lasted only three weeks. Roosevelt called him "one of the best non-commissioned officers we had."

After the skirmish of Las Guásimas, the Rough Riders settled into camp as the American high command planned the battle that would bring the war to a speedy end. The US Navy had bottled up the Spanish fleet in Santiago Harbor, while Spanish troops occupied the heights above the city. If the Americans could take the heights, they could besiege the city and make continued Spanish occupation of Cuba untenable. Roosevelt and his men were ordered to attack the San Juan Heights on July 1. Just before the battle, Colonel Wood was given command of the brigade, replacing a general felled by yellow fever. This left Colonel Roosevelt in full command of the regiment. In front of the San Juan Heights sat a small hill called Kettle Hill. On Roosevelt's order, his men charged up the hill, a bullet grazing Roosevelt's elbow while he shot a Spanish soldier with his revolver. From the top of Kettle Hill, Roosevelt could see American infantry making painstakingly slow progress up the San Juan Heights. Almost on instinct, Roosevelt ran to support the attack, nearly forgetting to issue a command to the men behind him. Roosevelt turned back and shouted, "Forward march!" The Rough Riders ran up the heights as Spanish soldiers deserted their positions at the top. When Roosevelt and his men reached the crest, they could gaze down onto Santiago. Two weeks later, the Santiago garrison surrendered, signaling the end to Spanish power in the Western Hemisphere. With the exploits of Roosevelt and the Rough Riders already making headlines across the country, the Battle of San Juan also signaled the beginning of a new chapter in Roosevelt's political career. Already, messages were arriving in Cuba asking Roosevelt to run for governor of New York.

For the time being, Colonel Roosevelt was too busy tending to his wounded and sick. New Yorkers continued to figure prominently among the casualties of the war. Ken Robinson, Charles Bull, and Horace Devereux were wounded, and Bob Ferguson and William Tiffany fell ill. Becoming sick with malaria, typhoid, or yellow fever often posed a greater threat to a soldier than a physical wound. Fewer than four hundred American soldiers died in combat during the war, but ten times as many succumbed to disease. William Tiffany contracted yellow fever in Cuba. In August, the transport *Olivette* delivered him to Boston, where Tiffany checked into the Parker House hotel "in a sadly emaciated condition," the hotel staff observed. He died the very next day. It was said that his last words were "Colonel Roosevelt is a brick." Roosevelt attended the funeral in Newport, Rhode Island, riding there on John Jacob Astor's private yacht.

The Rough Riders departed Cuba on August 8, and after four days' quarantine aboard ship, on August 15 made camp at Montauk Point on Long Island. The New Yorkers in the regiment took the opportunity to visit home. A sickly Craig Wadsworth stopped by the Knickerbocker Club, the hall porter failing to recognize the sunburned figure wearing a battered army hat and discolored canvas clothes. On Sunday, August 21, the Reverend Henry Brown, chaplain of the Rough Riders, gave the sermon at Grace Episcopal Church, declaring the men "more respectful of religion than any other regiment." Roosevelt's camp attracted visitors, too. President McKinley came, accompanied by Vice President Garret Hobart, Secretary of War Russell Alger, and Attorney General John Griggs. Considering Roosevelt's future career, perhaps the most important visitor to Montauk Point was Lemuel Quigg. Republican boss Thomas Platt had sent his lieutenant to sound out Roosevelt about running for governor of New York.

DID THEODORE ROOSEVELT's heroism in Cuba make him governor of New York? Roosevelt himself certainly thought so. Later, as president, as he traveled through North Dakota with naturalist John Burroughs, Roosevelt commented that had he not raised the regiment of Rough Riders and gone to war, he would not have been made governor of New York—and that it was becoming governor of New York that made his rise to the presidency almost inevitable. Burroughs rightly observed that Roosevelt "would have got there someday," but perhaps it would not have been quite as quickly without the war with Spain. Roosevelt was not nominated for governor in a vacuum, however. Nearly twenty years of public service in New York, Albany, and Washington had made him a well-known figure in the Empire State well before the Rough Riders set foot on Cuban soil. And, although it is natural to focus on Roosevelt's dramatic actions as a soldier during the war, the war should not distract attention from political events closer to home that played a role in his election. Roosevelt's nomination was not in his own hands, or even in the hands of New York voters. It is better to ask another question: Did Roosevelt's Cuban actions gain him the support of Republican boss Thomas Platt? The answer is no.

Almost as soon as McKinley won the White House in 1896, Platt had worried about the Republican Party losing support among independents. An ominous sign came when independent Republicans in New York backed Joseph Choate for the US Senate seat sought by Platt in early 1897. With US senators still chosen by state legislatures, and with an enormous Republican majority in Albany after the 1896 elections, Platt won election easily, but the independent bolt continued. The November 1897 New York City elections proved a stunning blow to Platt and a catastrophe for the Republicans. From Washington, Theodore Roosevelt had watched as Platt refused to back Seth Low for mayor, and the split among anti-Tammany forces allowed the election of a Democrat as the first mayor of Greater New York. In the large cities outside of New York, the picture was equally grim. Albany,

Binghamton, Syracuse, Rochester, and Buffalo all elected Democratic mayors. In the New York Assembly, Democrats nearly doubled their seats from the year before, an increase from 38 to 68. Throughout New York, politicians of all stripes blamed Platt. "There's a hot time in the old State tonight," Senator David Hill telegraphed New York's new mayor, Alton Parker. Top Republican and editor of the *New York Tribune* Whitelaw Reid said, "Platt's 'leadership' is a costly handicap to the Republican party." Madison Grant, a Wall Street lawyer, wrote Roosevelt at the time, "We are all stunned here by the catastrophe which has overwhelmed us, but a few of us are emerging from the debris with the determination to cut Mr. Platt's throat for his share." Platt said nothing, and contemporary observers noted that he seemed depressed for months, "loaded with the consciousness," New York Congressman De Alva S. Alexander said, "of being solely responsible for the overwhelming defeat of his party." Alexander also observed, "The belief existed that his subsequent acquiescence in Roosevelt's nomination for Governor sourced in an unwillingness to chance the repetition of such another disaster." The elections of 1897, then, had more to do with Roosevelt's rise to the governorship than the war of 1898 did.

Although 1898 found Platt still chief of the party, and also a US senator, the problems continued for the Easy Boss. His man in the governor's mansion, Frank Black, had further alienated independents by his adoption of, in his words, "starchless"—in other words, more flexible, and under the sway of the party machine—civil service that swept out of the state bureaucracy nearly all Democratic officeholders. This action received the condemnation of Roosevelt's friends in the New York Civil Service Reform Association. The tide continued to turn against Republicans in the 1898 spring town elections for supervisors. In twenty-five counties, Democrats elected seventy-five supervisors, including in Platt's own hometown of Oswego, where a Democrat had not been elected town supervisor for years. With 1898 an important state election year, Platt could not ignore the signs. In his autobiography he later wrote, "Independent threats caused me to do a heap of thinking. Cognizant of the revolts which . . . deprived Blaine of the Presidency and placed the National and State governments in the custody of the Democrats for eight years and ten years respectively,

I began to formulate plans for holding our enemies in leash." His own lieutenants must have prompted much of this thinking. Benjamin Odell, who had just become the new chairman of the Republican State Committee, actually wrote to Roosevelt about the possibility of running for governor—without Platt's knowledge—while Roosevelt was still in Cuba. Odell and Quigg pestered Platt about backing Roosevelt's nomination until Platt finally relented and sent Quigg to meet with Roosevelt at Montauk Point.

The conversation between Roosevelt and Quigg, who was acting as the mouthpiece for Platt and the Republican state machine, reveals much about why Roosevelt received the nomination. Little was said about Roosevelt's heroism during the Cuban campaign, although that was certainly icing on the cake for placing Roosevelt before New York voters. Mainly, Quigg and Roosevelt spoke about Roosevelt's close association with the Republican Party and his ability to unite machine and reform Republicans. A dozen years after Roosevelt's nomination for New York mayor in 1886, Republicans still saw in him a candidate able to bridge the divide between the two factions of the party.

When Quigg visited Roosevelt, Platt was still trying to get Governor Black to withdraw as a candidate for renomination in favor of Roosevelt. Black replied by tearing into Roosevelt, calling him "impulsive and erratic" and likely to "play devil with the organization." Quigg wrote to Roosevelt saying that Platt's reply was that "you have always been a sturdy thoroughgoing Republican, and that while you have not identified yourself with the machine, you have never done anything to its injury; that you have promised to act in all important matter [sic] after full consultation and in view of the interests of the organization as such, as well as the party and public interest." For Quigg and Platt, Roosevelt's Republicanism was more important than his Cuban heroism.

Right from the beginning, however, the machine politicians understood the pitfalls of having Roosevelt as governor. If a popular figure such as Roosevelt could unite the party behind him, what would stop Roosevelt from challenging Platt for the leadership of the state Republican Party? In other words, Roosevelt's very success in carrying out Platt's goals of party unity would pose a direct threat to Platt.

Quigg worked hard to dissuade Colonel Roosevelt from becoming enmeshed in "Mugwump"—independent Republican—schemes, and from seeking to become a figure greater than Platt. Roosevelt needed to persuade Platt that he would not seek to displace him as the state party leader and that he would work with the Easy Boss for a united party and strong organization. Quigg's long September 10, 1898, letter to Roosevelt was almost like a contract between the Colonel and the Easy Boss. Roosevelt wanted the nomination and agreed. As would so many letters from Quigg, Odell, and Platt over the next two years, the September 10 letter ended with a summons to Platt's offices in the Fifth Avenue Hotel in New York. There, as much as in Albany, lay the real power of the state Republican Party.

TEN

"Governor of the Entire Party"
Roosevelt, Thomas Platt, and the New York Governorship

BY SEPTEMBER 1898, it seemed likely that Theodore Roosevelt would receive the Republican nomination for governor of New York. Still, Governor Black and his supporters made clear that Roosevelt would not secure the nomination without a fight. Black planned to seek renomination at the coming Republican state convention due to be held at Saratoga. Among Black's staunchest supporters was State Superintendent of Insurance Louis Payn. Payn freely gave interviews in which he claimed loyalty to Black. "Under no circumstances will Governor Black yield," Payn told the *Times*. "He will enter the lists, and there is good reason to believe that he will meet with the success which he deserves." Later, Payn said that he would "stake his head" on Black's renomination. At the time, some in the Republican Party wondered why Payn, a friend and ally of Thomas Platt, would so adamantly back Black in the face of mounting support for Roosevelt. By September 23, the reason had become clear. For days, Payn and other top Republicans had been discussing the March 1898 affidavit that Roosevelt had sworn to while he was assistant secretary of the navy, affirming his residence in Washington, DC. This, Payn and other Black supporters claimed, made Roosevelt ineligible to be governor of New York.

With the Saratoga convention set for September 27, Roosevelt, Platt, and other Republican leaders had only days to deal with this bombshell. In public, Platt calmly replied to reporters' questions, "There is nothing in it." But Platt's nonchalance masked a flurry of activity behind the scenes. After a meeting at Republican headquarters in the Fifth Avenue Hotel, Platt placed Elihu Root in charge of sorting out the affair. In the end, it was not difficult to establish Roosevelt's New York residency. He had many documents showing residency in New York, from tax rolls to military records. Roosevelt enlisted in the army as a New York resident, and the War Department listed him as such. When he received his promotion to full colonel in July, Roosevelt wrote to the army adjutant-general, "I was born in New York on October 27th 1858 and have resided in New York ever since." Roosevelt even had an August 24 affidavit claiming New York residency. He had sworn this affidavit for the same reason he had made trips back to New York from his ranch during every election season—he wanted to keep a hand in New York politics. As he explained to educator and future Columbia University president Nicholas Murray Butler, "I wished to continue my residence in New York, among other reasons, because I thought it possible we could, by some kind of union ticket, carry the city." Such a ticket might have offered Roosevelt a chance to return to New York to take an important position. "I thought it best to keep my residence," Roosevelt wrote Butler, "so that if the chance of work there *did* seem to be much bigger than in Washington, I might take it."

At Saratoga on September 27, after top New York Republican Chauncey Depew, who was about to be elected US senator, nominated Roosevelt for governor, Elihu Root stood to refute the charges that Roosevelt had given up his residence in New York. Root provided documentation in the form of letters, affidavits, and Roosevelt's army promotion. Roosevelt, Root concluded, "would not give up his State, and I take it, gentlemen, that the people of the State of New York would not willingly surrender the priceless possession of his citizenship." Root's forceful speech forced the Black supporters to abandon their ploy, as

even they conceded Roosevelt's New York residence. Within a few minutes of Root's resuming his seat, the matter was finished: Roosevelt was
nominated by 753 votes to Black's 218.

The Democrats, guided by Tammany boss Richard Croker, chose
as their candidate Judge Augustus Van Wyck, brother of the mayor of
New York City. Roosevelt turned the election into one between himself and Croker rather than between himself and Van Wyck, spelling
out the dangers of electing, in his words, "Mr. Croker's Governor."
Roosevelt won on November 8 by a slim majority of 18,000 votes,
losing some independent votes because of Platt's support. Roosevelt's
presentation of himself as governor of the entire party was reflected in
the congratulatory letter John Hay wrote to Roosevelt after the election. "While you are Governor," Hay wrote, "I believe the party can
be made solid as never before. You have already shown that a man may
be absolutely honest and yet practical; a reformer by instinct and a wise
politician; brave, bold, and uncompromising, and yet not a wild ass of
the desert." The description of Roosevelt as both reformer and practical
politician was an apt one. Roosevelt himself surely agreed with Hay's
depiction of the lunatic fringe reformer as "a wild ass of the desert."

To secure the nomination, Roosevelt had assured Platt lieutenant
Lemuel Quigg that as governor he would not make war on Platt, and
would confer with the machine. His short inaugural address on January 2,
1899, confirmed his intention to work through the Republican organization. Roosevelt told the New York State Assembly that nothing could be
accomplished unless the work was done through practical methods. He
confirmed his dedication to the party by asserting, "It is only through
the party system that free governments are now successfully carried on."
Roosevelt's Annual Message of the same day reflected his career-long effort to maintain balance between a reform agenda and practical politics.
The new governor suggested an overhaul of the tax system, but warned
against "driving property out of the State by unwise taxation." He urged
reform of the civil service system, but only in order to make it practical,
not as an attack on patronage. Although he brought up the question of
instituting biennial sessions for the legislature, he quietly let that topic
drop. Finally, he opened the door to a scheme of Platt's by targeting
the New York City police. In all, his first annual address was a modest

document. It may have covered a wide range of issues, but it did not put forward an extreme reform agenda. Moreover, Roosevelt singled out matters that helped the Republican Party, such as reform of New York's police. Roosevelt was diligently carrying out the agenda of Platt and the party.

ON DECEMBER 30, the entire Roosevelt family left the Madison Avenue house for Grand Central Station and the train ride to Albany. The last time Roosevelt had lived in Albany, he had been a twenty-five-year-old assemblyman, married to Alice, and living in a boarding-house. At the very end of 1898, forty-year-old Roosevelt returned to Albany as New York State's chief executive–elect, with his wife Edith and all six of their children, including fourteen-year-old Alice Lee; eleven-year-old Theodore Roosevelt Jr. (technically Theodore Roosevelt III), who was clutching a box of guinea pigs; and Quentin, who, at one year old, was the youngest. The large family moved into the Executive Mansion, a short walk from the new Capitol building, where Governor Roosevelt would draw a handsome salary of $10,000. Only four years before, Edith had asked her husband not to run for mayor of New York City as they could not afford the expense. Now, after years of debt and the expense of maintaining homes in two cities, Roosevelt had finally achieved financial stability and could live—free of charge—with his entire family in one place.

New York City and its politics came to dominate much of Governor Roosevelt's time in office. Independents and the Republican machine still fought for the soul of the party in the city, which made a repeat of the 1897 disaster increasingly likely. Much of the conflict centered on urban reform Republicans much like Roosevelt, men on whom the governor counted for support in Albany. One of these was Robert Mazet, the assemblyman for the Nineteenth District and chairman of the Cities Committee, which continued to shape legislation for New York City. In an echo of Roosevelt's actions in the Assembly, early in Roosevelt's term Mazet chaired an investigating committee to look into New York's governance under Tammany Hall. The Mazet Committee took particular aim at the Building Department and its close relation-ship with Tammany, a relationship that prevented tenement reform and enriched Democratic bosses. As Mazet called boss Richard Croker and his son Frank before the committee, Roosevelt and Platt rejoiced, satisfied at the anti-Tammany headlines that resulted from the investigation. Mazet, however, failed to call Platt before the committee, or to look into his many financial interests in the city. That omission immediately made Mazet a target of the Citizens' Union in the upcoming 1899 elections.

Still, Platt and Roosevelt were more than pleased with Mazet and his committee's final report, which labeled Croker a "dictator." In September 1899, on the eve of the fall elections, Roosevelt wrote Lodge that he believed Tammany was currently in disfavor, thanks in part to the work done by the Mazet Committee. Yet, in the same letter, Roosevelt pointed out the trouble facing a divided Republican Party. "It is a dreadful task to try to keep the republican party united here," he told Lodge after returning from his summer swing through the agricultural fairs in upstate New York. "Aside from the deep-seated causes of division between the two wings, which shade off into the irrational and unscrupulous machine men on the one hand and the quite as irrational and unscrupulous independents on the other, there are the bitter factional fights and splits," Roosevelt said, echoing his comments to Lodge about the disastrous 1897 elections. As he had then, Roosevelt reserved special scorn for the independents, whose tactics again seemed likely to hand Tammany an electoral victory.

The governor had reason for concern. With 1899 an "off year"— with no national or statewide contests to bring out the upstate rural vote—the Republican Party already expected to see its twenty-four-seat Assembly majority erode. The elections of 1897 had illustrated the ability of the Citizens' Union to split the Republicans and, in only a single election, swing representation from one party to the other. The 1896 elections, which included successful Republican presidential and New York gubernatorial bids, had given the Republicans an eighty-seat majority in the Assembly. One year later, that number was down to only six. By all accounts, the Citizens' Union was gearing up for a repeat of 1897, running its own men against Republican candidates in city districts. Already five or six names were being considered for Citizens' Union candidates, including one to run against Robert Mazet in the Nineteenth District. It was reported that Republican attempts to bring about an alliance with independents, including in Mazet's district, had failed. In fact, the possibility existed that the Citizens' Union would put up independent Democrats as candidates in order to secure the Democratic vote. When a reporter asked Richard Croker whether Tammany would endorse such a candidate, especially to target Mazet and the Nineteenth District, Croker replied, "I wouldn't be surprised if we did." When further asked whether Tammany would agree to consult with the Citizens' Union over nominations, Croker replied, "Certainly." "Croker Flirts with Citizens' Union," the *Tribune* declared. Croker got ready to do in 1899 what Platt had refused to do in 1897.

Of all the Republican leaders, none was in a better position to act as a bridge between the two factions in New York City than Governor Roosevelt. As governor, he of course had regular contact with Platt and the machine. Yet he also relied heavily upon independent Republicans in the legislature, such as Gherardi Davis, assemblyman of the Twenty-Seventh District, and State Senator Nathaniel A. Elsberg. Knowing this might make them targets for the machine in the 1899 elections, Roosevelt began working to protect them as early as June. In a meeting with Platt and Odell on June 6, Roosevelt secured a promise that the machine would not "take sides either way in the 27th Assembly district." Roosevelt did not seek to secure machine support for Davis, but, he said, "I do emphatically ask that nothing shall be done against [him] and let the district settle for itself." Davis and Elsberg he characterized as part of the "body of men upon whom I especially relied in the Legislature from New York City." Roosevelt included Mazet in that body of men, too. With his contacts among advocates of good government and housing reform, and in charitable institutions and the Union League, Governor Roosevelt was in a unique position to mediate between the machine and independent Republicans—and to try to save Mazet and other urban reformers.

Meanwhile, the governor busied himself with celebrations to welcome home Admiral George Dewey, the hero of Manila Bay during the Spanish-American War. This included Roosevelt's attending a White House dinner in Dewey's honor on September 27. At the dinner, President McKinley asked Roosevelt to take the stump for Republicans in Ohio, where Mark Hanna was standing for US senator. Roosevelt agreed, but balked at requests for further campaign trips as far away as Iowa and Nebraska. His pessimism concerning the coming elections in New York was evident. To American diplomat Henry White, Roosevelt said, "I should not be surprised at a disaster," using the same word he had often repeated after the 1897 elections. The machine's efforts to form fusion tickets to save Republican seats in the Assembly had failed miserably. As a sign of Platt's failure in this area, Quigg visited Roosevelt in Albany to solicit the governor's aid in the city elections. Namely, the machine wanted the governor to speak and work for the combined machine-reform Republican tickets throughout the city. Quigg had been working to form such combination tickets since the summer. With no success, the machine now openly turned to the governor. Platt and Quigg saw Roosevelt as the only Republican leader who could draw in reformers. This was an extraordinary acknowledgment of Roosevelt's strength among city Republicans.

On October 19, Roosevelt spoke in New York in favor of a united party to a large Republican rally of 10,000. Roosevelt's popularity was on display as he entered: the entire crowd stood to clap, shout, and wave for a full minute. The governor spoke on behalf of Mazet and other reforming Republicans, such as Gherardi Davis and Edward H. Fallows. He lauded the work of the Mazet Committee, and he tore into Tammany Hall. "I denounce in Tammany Hall what I will not permit in my own party!" shouted Roosevelt to thunderous applause. Significantly, Roosevelt concluded with a warning to vote Republican rather than for an independent candidate, and thereby allow a Tammany legislature. "Men who are supporting Tammany Hall, or any of these little outside candidates, whose only effect is to help Tammany Hall," Roosevelt chided, "are warring for the forces of evil, and showing that in this crisis of the city's need they stand against her interests." This was classic Roosevelt. He was not only belittling the shortsighted actions of the Citizens' Union, but also labeling them "evil." "I appeal to you all," the governor concluded, "to vote with us from the top of the ticket to the bottom."

Almost immediately, Roosevelt departed for his promised campaign tour through Ohio, all the while suffering a heavy cold. The day after the Republican rally in New York City, Roosevelt wrote to Lodge from Cincinnati: "I had a good meeting and hit straight at Tammany." This was developing into Roosevelt's strategy for 1899, and it was similar to his strategy of demonizing Tammany and boss Croker during his gubernatorial campaign the previous year. To prevent another Republican disaster at the hands of Tammany and the Citizens' Union, Roosevelt attempted to strike at Tammany and convince reforming Republicans to stick with the party. A vote for the Citizens' Union, according to Roosevelt, was really a vote for Tammany Hall.

In Ohio, Roosevelt followed hard on the heels of William Jennings Bryan as the former Democratic presidential candidate denounced the American annexation of the Philippines earlier that year. Roosevelt compared such anti-imperialists to the Copperheads of the Civil War, going so far as to label one American congressman a traitor. From Ohio, Roosevelt traveled to Maryland and West Virginia. Meanwhile, New York Democrats attempted to turn the governor's vocal support of Mazet into a liability. At a massive Tammany Hall rally on October 26, Democrats took aim at the governor himself. "Let him clean his own skirts and those of the Republican administration in Albany," the chairman of the meeting, Randolph Guggenheimer, declared, "before he and his henchmen come to this enlightened city and attempt to vilify . . . men whose characters are above and beyond reproach!" Another speaker questioned Roosevelt's independence from boss Platt. "I challenge him to mention a single order . . . given him by Platt since the first of January that he has disobeyed," proclaimed John W. Keller, the president of the Department of Public Charities. "The Rough Rider of the last campaign is a very little tin soldier, indeed, in this one." The *Tribune* called the Tammany rally "lifeless," while noting that Roosevelt was welcomed in Maryland with "utmost enthusiasm."

Election Day brought mixed results. The Tammany–Citizens' Union alliance behind Democrat Perez Stewart had made Mazet's defeat almost inevitable, and he lost his seat in the Nineteenth District by about four hundred votes. The city almost witnessed a repeat of the 1897 elections, when both the Republicans and the Citizens' Union each won two seats. In 1899, of New York City's thirty-five Assembly seats, Republicans won only four, down from eight the year before. The Citizens' Union won no seat outright, as Perez Stewart's victory was seen as a plus for the Democrats. Statewide, the composition of the Assembly remained almost unchanged, as Republicans actually increased their majority by a single seat. However, while Mazet suffered defeat despite Roosevelt's support, others whom the governor had supported kept their seats. Gherardi Davis won reelection in the Twenty-Seventh District, in one of those four Republican victories in the city that year. Without Roosevelt's intervention, the Republican machine would have likely challenged Davis from the outset.

Still, Roosevelt could not claim complete victory in the city. The governor had supported the New York State Assembly candidacy of Homer Folks, the associate editor of *Charities Review* and a member of the Municipal Assembly of the City of New York. Folks had been nominated by the Citizens' Union and nominally endorsed by the Republican Party in the Twenty-Ninth District. Platt and the machine, however, did not support Folks, and he lost by a mere 150 votes. The machine also turned on Samuel Slater of the Thirty-First District, whom Roosevelt referred to as "one of our best Republican members." He lost his bid for reelection by fewer than 100 votes out of more than 11,000 cast. Across the board, Republicans and Citizens' Union supporters had agreed on fusion behind a total of eight candidates. Four of them lost, including Folks and Slater, and four of them won, including Gherardi Davis. In the Fifth District, the fusion candidate Nelson Henry won reelection by the slimmest margin of all: 40 votes out of more than 6,000 cast. At the October 20 Republican rally, Roosevelt had singled out by name Mazet, Davis, and Edward Fallows of his old Twenty-First District for reelection. Fallows won reelection handily.

Roosevelt's attitude toward the election results reflected their mixed nature. On the one hand, as he had in 1897, he expressed unhappiness with both the machine and independent Republicans. After all, there were good men, such as Mazet, who had not won reelection. On the other hand, he did not see the loss of these men as significantly weakening his position as governor. Quite the contrary, by preventing a repeat of the 1897 disaster and successfully intervening to save men such as

Davis and Fallows, Roosevelt viewed his position in the city, state, and party as very strong. In a November 10 letter to a Maryland reformer, Roosevelt explained the absurdities of the New York election. "The Citizens' Union actually turned in with Tammany to beat Mazet," Roosevelt wrote with his typical tone of disbelief. "This was not only bad in itself, but it irritated the machine republicans to turning in and beating Homer Folks, the Citizens' Union man whom the republicans endorsed," he added, also noting Slater's loss for the same reason. "As for me personally I have my hands full in keeping the machine up to the proper level," Roosevelt wrote, lamenting that he had not had the full support of the independents, as he "would have the right to expect." Roosevelt reserved special exasperation and scorn for independents such as E. L. Godkin of *The Nation* and *Evening Post*, who had backed the Citizens' Union's efforts to defeat reform Republicans such as Mazet. Godkin, Roosevelt declared, was just as bad "as Croker and his crowd." Only a few days after the election, the governor seemed to have much about which to be unhappy.

Within a week, though, Roosevelt was back in old form, cultivating the press and politely asserting his independence from Quigg, Platt, and the machine. On November 13, he pressed *Harper's Weekly* editor John Huston Finley to visit Albany in order to write an article on New York state government. Roosevelt was confident that Finley would like what he saw: "I can say with absolute conscientiousness," Roosevelt asserted, "that during the eighteen years I have been in public life, there has been no such high average standard of legislative and executive fidelity to the public weal as we have succeeded in ensuring for the past year." On November 27, he wrote separate letters to Quigg and Platt questioning the "jamming through" of a bill centralizing the police forces of the state's six biggest cities under a single commissioner in Albany and bringing them under the state civil service law. Roosevelt prevailed, although the state constabulary bill would have enhanced Platt's power as boss and removed the New York City Police Department from Tammany's control. Already Roosevelt was flexing his new, postelections muscle.

The intervention by a New York governor in city elections was almost unprecedented. That the machine itself had asked Roosevelt to intervene was a sign of his strength among city Republicans. Roosevelt had become what he had promised: governor of the entire party, working with and drawing strength from both the machine and independents. Not every New York governor could have done this, not even one as popular as Grover Cleveland had been. It helped that Roosevelt had been born in New York City, something that, surprisingly, few New York governors could claim. Of the score of men who held the office following the Civil War, only Roosevelt had been born in the city. The powerful Republican Levi Morton, for whom New York City's Republican headquarters, Morton Hall, was named, had been born in Vermont, and Roosevelt's predecessor, Frank Black, had been born in Maine. After Roosevelt, it would not be until Al Smith became governor in 1919 that the city would send another native son to Albany. And Roosevelt could claim New York for more than just his place of birth. By the time he became governor, he had been a New York City Republican for nearly twenty years. Platt, born in the small village of Oswego, New York, occupied Republican headquarters at the Fifth Avenue Hotel, but much of his power lay upstate. Roosevelt was the rare Republican who could draw strength from both north and south of the Harlem River.

During the summer of 1899, while Vice President Hobart lay ill, Roosevelt attended the Rough Riders reunion in Las Vegas. There was a brief boom for Roosevelt to become McKinley's new running mate for 1900, a fact he discussed in letters with Lodge all summer. The boom had died by the time of the early November 1899 elections that had left Roosevelt in such a strong position as governor. Hobart's death on November 21 immediately revived speculation among the public and Roosevelt's associates—including the Republican machine in New York—that Roosevelt might be placed on the ticket with McKinley.

By early 1900, Roosevelt had given another Annual Message as governor. He had also replaced Platt's man Lou Payn as superintendent of insurance. The notorious Payn had defended corrupt business practices in the Empire State, lining his pockets with payoffs from insurance companies. He had also opposed nominating Roosevelt for governor. Historians have concluded that Platt was simply seeking to remove Roosevelt as governor by placing him in the vice presidency—and they have cited Payn's dismissal and the Annual Message as being important to Platt's decision. Yet, in late November 1899, only a week after Hobart's death, Platt's lieutenant Quigg was already sounding the governor out on the topic. This was some weeks *before* both Lou Payn's dismissal and the Annual Message. To Quigg, Roosevelt demurred. And from his talks with Platt, the governor believed that the Easy Boss favored his renomination for governor in 1900. But by now, Roosevelt should have known better. As he wrote to his sister Anna in mid-December, "too much faith must not be put in princes, even of the democratic type." Platt's lack of forthrightness baffled Roosevelt. Although he knew by late December that Platt was openly discussing him for the vice presidency, the senator, as Roosevelt said, "gave me no hint of this, taking exactly the opposite view." "I do not understand what was up, or for the matter of that what is up now," he told Lodge. Platt would remain coy with the governor until the Republican National Convention that would give Roosevelt the vice presidential nomination in June 1900.

HISTORIANS ARE ALMOST unanimous in accepting that "independence" and "reform" played key roles in Roosevelt's departure from the Empire State. Roosevelt himself is partly responsible for this emphasis on reform. In his *Autobiography*, he discussed this period at length, particularly his relationship with Platt and the machine and Platt's concern that Roosevelt was becoming too "altruistic." Roosevelt cited an exchange of letters in which Platt noted that Roosevelt's actions had "caused the business community of New York to wonder how far the notions of Populism . . . have taken hold upon the Republican party of the State of New York." Roosevelt concluded that Platt wanted him out of New York because of opposition by big business. Students of Roosevelt's career have simply taken Roosevelt at his word and echoed this version of events.

That Roosevelt had become something of a radical and even a dangerous reformer by late 1899 is a notion that exists more in the minds of recent biographers, such as Edmund Morris and Nathan Miller—and of Roosevelt—than it did among contemporary observers. Certainly Platt himself did not agree with Roosevelt's characterization, stating instead in his own 1910 *Autobiography* that Roosevelt had been kicked upstairs in order to strengthen the national ticket. At the time, the press did not see Roosevelt's agenda for New York State as radical at all, or as significantly threatening business interests. The day after the governor's 1900 Annual Message, the *Times* observed that Roosevelt was essentially advocating "Letting Well Enough Alone." The message, the paper observed, was "almost barren of positive recommendations" and actually warned the legislature against passing "needless legislation." Concerning the burning issue of municipal ownership of public utilities—to better regulate the industry, as some argued, and keep rates low—Roosevelt declared it "undesirable that the Government should do anything that private individuals could do with better results to the community." "Everything that tends to deaden individual initiative is to be avoided," Roosevelt said, sounding as conservative as Platt himself.

Such conservatism on the eve of seeking renomination made sense. De Alva S. Alexander, a Republican congressman from New York at the time, commented that Roosevelt's many "deferential acts" to Platt indicated that he wanted the nomination again. Alexander also noted that replacing Lou Payn with Francis Hendricks, a close friend of Platt's, was at the time actually seen as a machine victory. Moreover, Alexander echoed the *Times* in seeing the Annual Message as devoid of "decisive opinion," and as lacking mention of many of the causes for which Roosevelt had fought, such as biennial sessions of the legislature and an employees' liability law. Indeed, Roosevelt now accepted making state transfer-tax appraiserships political appointments. The state transfer-tax appraisers were responsible for collecting the state tax on real-estate transfers. Roosevelt's acceptance of something that was viewed as part of the political patronage system was criticized by his fellow civil service reformers. By early 1900, it seems, Roosevelt was seeking to secure renomination by cozying up to Platt and the machine.

So why did Platt want Roosevelt out of New York? Platt worried that the locus of power in state politics was shifting from his headquarters in the Fifth Avenue Hotel in New York City to the governor's mansion in Albany. This was not because Roosevelt was acting independently, as the previous Republican governor, Frank Black, had. By the end of 1899, Roosevelt had actually displayed his ability to challenge Platt for the leadership of the state party. He had reached this position not by building a machine of his own and becoming a faction leader, but by bridging the gulf between the independent and machine Republicans of New York. He had served as mediator despite his great distaste for both groups. In September 1898, he had even declined the independent nomination for governor. As he asserted at the time, he did not want to represent a single faction of the Republican Party, either reform or machine. Instead, he desired to be "Governor of the entire party."

If any Republican was canny enough to note Roosevelt's strength in the state, it was Thomas Platt. By backing Roosevelt for the vice presidency, Platt arguably accomplished two important goals that strengthened his own hand in New York. First, he removed the threat to his leadership that Roosevelt posed. Second, by placing a favorite-son candidate and war hero on the national ticket, he ensured a Republican victory in the fall and a high Republican turnout in New York. Platt himself noted this reasoning in his *Autobiography*. "The wisdom of my insistence that Roosevelt should be McKinley's running mate was vindicated at the polls," he concluded. "The McKinley-Roosevelt team simply ran away from Bryan and his mate, and New York State was kept in the Republican column." Keeping New York State "in the Republican column" meant more power for Platt, as evidenced as recently as the 1896 Republican landslide. Platt understood as well as anyone the relationship between New York politics and national politics. New York had consistently given the margin of victory to presidential candidates, and because of the state's electoral importance, New Yorkers often appeared on the national tickets of both parties. The success of the national ticket translated into local success. In other words, Platt knew that a McKinley victory in 1900 would mean greater power for the state Republican machine, and for Platt personally, both at the national and state levels.

Indeed, the 1900 election results for New York State represented a boon for the boss. Platt successfully replaced Roosevelt as governor with his own lieutenant, Benjamin Odell, who secured a 110,000-vote plurality, much larger than Roosevelt's plurality only two years earlier. In Congress, New York Republicans gained four seats. In the New York State Legislature, Republicans secured massive majorities: 35 seats in the Senate (out of 50 seats) and 105 in the Assembly (out of 150 seats). All in all, the McKinley-Roosevelt victory of 1900 was one shared by Thomas Platt.

THE THEODORE ROOSEVELT governorship was marked by a number of progressive reforms. Roosevelt backed housing reform in New York City to make working-class tenements safer, healthier places to live. He supported a tax on public utilities. He improved labor laws and advanced forestry programs. He strengthened laws governing banking and insurance companies. Roosevelt did all this in only two years as governor while at the same time engaging in a political balancing act more difficult than a circus tightrope performance. He continuously had to maneuver between independent and machine Republicans; between the dual loci of state power in Albany and in New York City; and between men like Godkin and men like Platt. Herein lay his greatest success on the eve of becoming vice president of the United States. Roosevelt did not have a radical reform agenda; nor did he work independently of Platt and the machine. In fact, among the governor's contemporaries, this was his legacy: that, in the end, Roosevelt disappointed reformers in his conservatism and in his subordination to Platt. Reformers and Mugwumps such as Godkin labeled him a "coward." At the time, Roosevelt displayed great sensitivity to such criticism, and he would spend the opening months of his vice presidency addressing it.

ELEVEN

"The Direct Antithesis of McKinley"
The New York President

THE MARCH 1901 INAUGURATION of William McKinley for a second term boded well for the Old Guard of the Republican Party. McKinley had overseen not only a successful war, but also an economic turnaround since the slump of the 1890s. With Ohio businessman Mark Hanna still his most important adviser, McKinley remained dedicated to the principles of competition in the marketplace and unregulated industry. Such ideas were already being challenged by the reform wing of the party—a wing that included the new vice president–elect, Theodore Roosevelt of New York. As vice president, Roosevelt would have little opportunity to shape the administration's agenda over the next four years. Instead, he would have to wait his chance for the White House in 1904. Until then, barring some unforeseen tragedy befalling McKinley, Roosevelt's progressive impulses would have to remain firmly in check. This was the grim situation facing Roosevelt as he prepared to leave New York.

On the streets of the nation's capital, brass bands announced the arrival of military and civilian organizations from all over the country. By March 2, 1901, thousands of visitors had flocked to Washington,

DC, to see President McKinley sworn in for a second time, and to watch the Rough Riding colonel from New York sworn in as vice president. Restaurant prices provided a clue to the large number of out-of-towners: the cost of a dinner advanced overnight from thirty to fifty cents. Windows along the route of the inauguration parade went for as much as twenty-five dollars. Seven thousand seats were set aside for spectators at the east front end of the Capitol building. Four thousand of these were placed at the disposal of members of Congress, whose offices were inundated with 12,000 requests for tickets. To deal with so many visitors who were unfamiliar with the city, the Committee on Public Comfort dispatched an army of volunteers sporting red badges to meet arriving trains at the Baltimore and Ohio and Pennsylvania stations. Those arriving with no reservations for accommodation were sent by committee members to offices where rooms could be engaged. When told that room and board at a certain boardinghouse would cost $1.50, one man replied, "That's not what I want, I only want a place to sleep." The clerk suggested the cheapest place on his list, which would cost the man fifty cents for only a bed. "Is 50 cents a night the cheapest?" the man asked. "That's about the cheapest on the list," replied the clerk. The man expressed some surprise that beds were not available for twenty-five cents, but in the end he took the fifty-cent room. Still, he grumbled that twenty-five cents was enough for a man to pay for a bed in a big city.

While the capital was doing a fine job welcoming strangers to the city, one prominent visitor arrived unnoticed. Theodore Roosevelt was due to arrive at the Pennsylvania Depot at 4:10 p.m. The reception committee planned to present the vice president–elect with a medal to commemorate the inauguration. The medal bore a portrait of McKinley and the words "Second Inauguration of William McKinley" on one side, and on the reverse an image of the Capitol with both Roosevelt and McKinley's names. There was no picture of Roosevelt, and no special medal made for the vice president. The same medal had already been presented to McKinley at the White House. But when the train from New York arrived on time at 4:10, Roosevelt was not on it. The committee left the station disappointed. About an hour later, Roosevelt arrived accompanied by Edith and their children. No one at the station recognized him, and the next vice president made his way to the home of his brother-in-law, Captain William Sheffield Cowles. The reception committee learned of this and brought the medal to Cowles's house, where it was presented to Roosevelt. With thanks all around, the short ceremony ended and the visitors quickly departed. Roosevelt settled down for dinner with his family, denying reporters' requests for interviews. Here, perhaps, was a foretaste of the next four years. The next vice president had been met by no reception committee and went unrecognized at the train station. No medal had been struck for the inauguration of the vice president, and Roosevelt was forced to receive—almost curtly—a medal bearing only the face of the president. The strange events probably confirmed for Roosevelt the absolute uselessness of his next political office.

As HE HAD IN PAST presidential campaigns, Roosevelt did good work for the party in 1900 by campaigning hard for the ticket. Born only eighteen months before William Jennings Bryan, Roosevelt was an excellent foil to the Boy Orator of the Platte. Roosevelt followed Bryan's meandering election campaign throughout the country, often speaking to crowds shortly after the Democratic nominee's departure. Given the recent conclusion of the Spanish-American War and annexation of the Philippines under the Treaty of Paris, American imperialism was a hot campaign topic. Here, too, Roosevelt was a good choice for the Republican ticket. Bryan opposed American annexation of the Philippines during the campaign, although he had urged the Senate to ratify the 1899 peace treaty that had authorized the annexation. For Bryan, an anti-imperialist, it was an awkward position to occupy. After all, annexation had already occurred. Did Bryan seriously urge Americans to depart and leave the Philippines for Japan or for European nations to colonize? Bryan had joined a militia regiment during the war, but had never seen combat, as Santiago had surrendered a week before Bryan's Nebraska Third even reached Florida. Roosevelt, in contrast, had played a key role in the war, both as the assistant secretary of the navy, who gave Commodore Dewey his orders to move on the Philippines in case of war, and as the hero of Cuba. Indeed, Roosevelt often appeared at campaign stops flanked

by uniformed members of the Rough Riders. The 1900 electoral results were even more lopsided than those of 1896. Bryan lost even his
home state of Nebraska.

The elections of 1896 had handed the Easy Boss a sweeping victory
in New York, but the end of 1900 found Thomas Platt more powerful
than ever. Theodore Roosevelt, a possible rival to his power in the state,
was preparing to move to Washington, DC, and in his place, Platt had
gotten his man Benjamin Odell elected as governor. Odell had been
chairman of the Republican state committee, and Platt replaced him
there with the devoted George Dunn. Senator Platt even had three more
years in his term before he had to worry about reelection. He must also
have enjoyed the discomfort of New York reformers as they watched
one of their allies depart the state. Such discomfort manifested itself
in the grumbling over Platt's success in "shelving" Roosevelt. This was
a word frequently used at the time and one Roosevelt himself wrote to
Lodge. Platt himself always denied he had been motivated by the desire
to shelve Roosevelt, though. Instead, Platt liked to say that he "kicked
Roosevelt upstairs" to the vice presidency. One of Platt's allies in the
New York press made the case in the upstate *Lyons Republican*. Those
who thought Roosevelt had been "shelved," wrote Charles Betts, were
"actuated more by Mugwump malice than by reason." Moreover, they
did not understand how the campaign just past had elevated Roosevelt
to prominence as a national Republican figure. This, Betts said, Platt
had understood, and the election proved the Easy Boss's genius. "Time
has proven this," Betts concluded, "and it has also vindicated Senator
Platt's judgment and made his critics and enemies, who impugned his
motives, look mean and small indeed." By the end of 1900, Platt had
many reasons to be satisfied.

The vice president–elect felt stung by statements that he had been
railroaded into the job against his will. Editorials and articles claiming this appeared in the *New York Commercial Advertiser* and *Harper's
Weekly*. Roosevelt pointed out time and again that at the Philadelphia
convention he had swung a majority of the New York delegation
against his nomination for the vice presidency, "beating both Platt and
Odell combined." Instead, his nomination had been brought about by
the sheer enthusiasm of the western delegates. Replying to the *Harper's*

Weekly editorial, Roosevelt said that New York did not vote for a Roosevelt vice presidency until just about every other state had cast its vote for Roosevelt. "In other words," he concluded, "I got the New York delegation shut as tight as a bear trap." Roosevelt evidently felt the matter was important enough to correct the journal writer at length. New York and its Republican boss were shadowing Roosevelt all the way to Washington.

By early 1901, however, Platt was learning a lesson in the law of unintended consequences. No sooner had Odell become governor than he asserted his independence from the Easy Boss. Unlike Roosevelt, he failed to consult Platt over state appointments. Odell then publicly disowned and threatened to veto the State Constabulary bill that would have vested power over the New York City Police Department in the state government. Platt sought to bring Odell back into line by calling a conference of state Republican leaders. Odell simply refused to attend. Roosevelt expressed his "hearty approval" of Odell in a letter to a New York congressman, but the Mugwump press also made clear its feelings. The *Evening Post* in particular delighted in Odell's independence and took the opportunity to take a swipe at the former governor. In praising Odell, the *Post* criticized Roosevelt as basically a coward. "It is the very irony of fate," the paper stated in an editorial, "that the revolt against the boss should come in 1901 from an Executive who had always been a machine man before his election, instead of in 1899 or 1900 from a Governor whose independence before his accession had led the people to expect a display of backbone." Even the *New York Press*, a reliably Republican organ, criticized Roosevelt, saying that Platt had him "in a harrowing fear from the day he went into the Executive Chamber." Roosevelt's critics knew exactly which words would cut deepest with the former governor. The Colonel may have charged up Kettle Hill in the face of Spanish sharpshooters, but the Mugwumps still labeled him a coward.

The Mugwump attacks on Roosevelt so early in his term as vice president must have had an impact. Such outsized praise of Odell and criticism of Roosevelt perhaps explained Roosevelt's later erroneous assertion in his memoirs that Platt had favored him as vice president because of his independence. Roosevelt's own actions as governor, and contemporary observers, certainly did not support this view. But making this claim twelve years later helped Roosevelt allay the force of Mugwump attacks that had dogged his career since 1884. Time and again Roosevelt had gotten on the bad side of these independent reformers, from backing Blaine for president to working with Boss Platt. Publishing an autobiography that stressed his dedication to reform and independence was clearly meant to answer such critics. But in the meantime, the Mugwump attacks seemed to underscore the very weakness of the office of vice president. Had Roosevelt risen from the governor's mansion directly to the White House, it is unlikely that the New York press would have made such a bold attack on him. But with the vice presidency viewed as a powerless position, and one from which it was unlikely Roosevelt would rise any further, New York critics risked little by targeting the former governor. Finally, the March 1901 accusations that Roosevelt "knuckled under" to Platt and the Republican organization made it more likely that, if Roosevelt ever had the chance, he would be sure to affirm his independence from Platt, even to the extent of making war on the Easy Boss.

Odell's success as governor also made Roosevelt look several years into the future to the 1904 election. Roosevelt was far from being the party's favorite to succeed McKinley, whereas Odell was making a national name for himself. With this in mind, Roosevelt began inquiring about taking up the law back in New York City. Yet, as early as August 1901, he also attempted to nail down support for his own bid for the presidency. On a trip to Minnesota, Roosevelt stopped in Chicago, after which he concluded, "The Illinois people are openly for me." After his return, Roosevelt planned to meet with both Platt and Colonel Dunn, who had replaced Odell as chairman of the state Republican committee. In correspondence with William Allen White, Republican editor of the *Emporia Gazette* in Kansas, Roosevelt noted that both Platt and Dunn had pledged their support to him for 1904. As always, though, Platt was an enigma. On the one hand, he and Roosevelt had worked together in New York, and the Easy Boss was not pleased with Odell. On the other hand, as Roosevelt observed, Platt was "growing very old and feeble." "Under these circumstances I cannot be certain of the course Platt will really follow," Roosevelt concluded. But, the vice president told White, he would meet with the New York party leaders soon and get a more concrete answer, probably at the end of September.

Dramatic and unforeseen events made such a meeting irrelevant. After his wife fell ill, President McKinley rescheduled a planned June trip to the Pan-American Exposition in Buffalo to September. On September 5, McKinley addressed a crowd of about 50,000 at the Exposition. The next day, the press reported, the president would visit Niagara Falls, returning to the Exposition's Temple of Music to greet the public. Leon Czolgosz, inspired by anarchist Emma Goldman, approached the president in the Temple with a handkerchief covering the revolver in his hand. He fired twice, hitting the president once in the abdomen. The attending doctor on the grounds of the Exposition closed the wound with the bullet still inside. Roosevelt received word of the attempted assassination while camping in the Adirondacks. He immediately rushed to Buffalo. McKinley seemed to be recovering "splendidly," wrote Roosevelt, and the vice president was so unconcerned about the president's health that he made plans to see his sister Anna at the end of the month. He would then make October campaign trips to Iowa and Ohio—or so he thought. Within a week, McKinley was dead.

Theodore Roosevelt became (and remains, as of this writing) the only president ever born in New York City. Although Chester Arthur, another New York vice president who rose to the presidency after an assassination, made his career in the city, he was actually born in Vermont. With New York the most important state electorally, both parties had long placed New York politicians on their national tickets. Samuel Tilden, Grover Cleveland, Arthur, and Roosevelt all hailed from the Empire State. Only Roosevelt, however, was born and raised in the city, and always referred to himself as a New Yorker. No president had ever been so closely identified with America's largest city. Oddly, Roosevelt's New York City origins received virtually no attention in the city press after Roosevelt became president. New York papers noted his birth and career in the city, the eight previous generations of New York

Roosevelts, and his father's contributions to the city, but none speculated on what bearing Roosevelt's New York roots might have on the
new president.

WHEN THEODORE ROOSEVELT ascended to the presidency in
September 1901, the United States faced the same problems and challenges as New York City had in the previous forty years. At the time of
Roosevelt's birth, only one out of five Americans lived in urban areas.
By 1901 that ratio had doubled, with 40 percent of the population living in towns and cities. Roosevelt himself noted this fact shortly after
becoming president. "The growth of cities has gone beyond comparison faster than the growth of the country," Roosevelt observed. It was
true. By the early twentieth century, city populations were booming at
a rate faster than the population growth of the nation as a whole. What
had once been problems confined to a handful of big cities now tested
Americans and political leaders across the country.

Industrialization and urbanization had changed the American economic landscape. Syndicates and trusts controlled entire industries.
Working hours and conditions became increasingly intolerable for
American laborers, and labor unrest grew. Once only city dwellers had
reason to worry seriously about the condition and cleanliness of their
food in the face of the typhus threat. Now, with railroads, refrigeration
cars, and mass-produced canned food, all Americans faced the danger
of the unregulated food industry. As a massive wave of immigration
landed on American shores, urban populations exploded, requiring ex-
panded urban infrastructure and larger municipal governments. City
budgets skyrocketed. Along with these things came corrupt city management and the growth of the urban machines that both preyed on
and manipulated American citizens, especially the new immigrants
who were just arriving and most vulnerable to their schemes.

The situation demanded a response. At the dawn of the twentieth
century, the country needed leaders who were equipped to deal with a
variety of issues: economic concentration, such as trusts; labor crises,
such as strikes and unemployment; an increasingly diverse American
population; expanding government services and budgets; and political corruption and its apparent antidote, civil service reform. Such

challenges required strong executive power as well as sensitivity to eastern, urban problems, aided by a sense of duty instilled by wealth and privilege. But who was best equipped to provide that leadership? Interestingly enough, Theodore Roosevelt came to the presidency remarkably well-prepared to face head-on the problems of modern America.

Few presidents had had such intimate contact with labor before reaching the White House. From his first New York tenement visit with labor leader Samuel Gompers, to his signing of the eight-hour workday legislation as governor, Roosevelt had shown remarkable sympathy with workers and support for workers' rights. As police commissioner, he had even defended industrial workers' right to strike peacefully. When nearly a quarter of a million coal miners and related workers went on strike in the spring of 1902, they were met with the hostility of mine owners and managers. As the strike dragged on into a chilly fall, President Roosevelt acted to prevent a situation in which millions of Americans would suffer through the winter without adequate heating. In an unprecedented move, the president directly mediated between labor and management, threatening to send in the US Army to seize the mines and have soldiers mine the coal. Both sides agreed to abide by the decision of a five-man Coal Strike Commission, and miners went back to work by the end of October. In the end, the miners received higher wages and shorter hours. Labor claimed victory, and membership in unions soared nationwide.

Roosevelt had been born into the economic bust of the 1850s, and most recently, he had witnessed firsthand, on the streets of New York City, the effect of the depression of the 1890s. The grandson of New York merchant prince C. V. S. Roosevelt, he was also his father's son, having never worshipped at the altar of unfettered economic activity. Instead, he believed in, as he said in his first presidential Annual Message, "proper government supervision." During Roosevelt's presidency, his belief in government oversight of commerce resulted in the Elkins and Hepburn Acts, which regulated railroads. Roosevelt also created a new Department of Commerce and Labor to promote economic growth and collect economic data. Most famously, the president targeted trusts as dangerous concentrations of economic power that engaged in unfair business practices. In 1902, Roosevelt had his attorney general sue the massive railroad trust Northern Securities under the Sherman Antitrust Act. E. H. Harriman and J. P. Morgan had formed the holding company in order to join their railroad companies together and avoid the cutthroat competition that might ruin them. In 1904, the Supreme Court, in *US v. Northern Securities*, affirmed that the giant trust suppressed free competition. Roosevelt had won a stunning victory against the forces of unregulated capitalism. Northern Securities was dissolved.

Manhattan left its mark on the Roosevelt presidency. The city had taught Roosevelt the need for strong executive power, which President Roosevelt wielded, from the Panama Canal to the Preservation of Antiquities Act. In Panama, he aided a revolution against Colombia to secure a zone for the proposed isthmian canal. "I took the isthmus, started the canal, and then left Congress—not to debate the canal, but to debate me," Roosevelt later stated in one of the boldest affirmations of presidential executive power in American history. Likewise, the Preservation of Antiquities Act gave Roosevelt the power, without resort to Congress, to declare national monuments and historic sites. In 1906, he championed the Pure Food and Drug Act, allowing the federal government to inspect and regulate what Americans consumed. Understanding the needs of labor, calling for the regulation of the economy, ensuring Americans would not be poisoned by tainted food and drugs, with all measures backed by strong executive power—these were the hallmarks of Roosevelt's Square Deal. The Square Deal was not shaped on western farms and ranches, but on the streets of New York City.

IN FOREIGN POLICY, Roosevelt kept McKinley appointees John Hay and Elihu Root, both of whom were New Yorkers, in the top positions in the State and War Departments. Roosevelt's foreign policy reflected an assertion of American power in the Western Hemisphere, as reflected in the Roosevelt Corollary of the Monroe Doctrine, which asserted America's "police power" in the Caribbean. The worldly Roosevelt, who had traveled through the Middle East, lived in Germany, and claimed intimate friends in all of Europe's capitals, also understood the limits of American power and the need to work with other nations. Roosevelt made sure the United States had a presence at the Algeciras Conference of 1906, which solved the Tangier Crisis between France and Germany, when Germany objected to France's attempt to establish a protectorate over Morocco. The president personally convened the 1905 Portsmouth Conference to end the Russo-Japanese War, for which Roosevelt won the 1906 Nobel Peace Prize. Students of Theodore Roosevelt are apt to place the roots of Roosevelt's foreign policy in the West, claiming him as the first president to conduct "cowboy diplomacy." In reality, Roosevelt's foreign policy reflected the cosmopolitan, not the cowboy. Roosevelt had a broad understanding of the world that resulted from an urban upbringing, a Harvard education, extensive travel, and personal connections.

When Roosevelt became president, he became the leader of the Republican Party in name only. He was immediately hampered by two related Republican realities: Mark Hanna, and the party's Old Guard. How Roosevelt overcame both obstacles reflected his twenty years of experience in New York politics.

For half a decade, since the campaign of 1896, the kingmaker within the party had been Mark Hanna, since 1897 a US senator from Ohio. In New York, Roosevelt had used the governor's appointing power to challenge Thomas Platt. Now, he did the same thing with presidential appointment power, setting up a network of federal appointees loyal to himself. As he had promised as governor to consult Platt and the organization on appointments, he now made the same vow as president. But, he added, "it is an entirely different thing to say that I shall consult no one but the organization." By 1903, it was evident that Hanna would challenge Roosevelt for the presidential nomination the following year. Roosevelt acted quickly and cleverly to remove the threat early. In May 1903, well over a year before Republicans would select their candidate for 1904, the senior US senator in Ohio, Joseph Foraker, submitted a resolution to the state Republican convention endorsing Roosevelt for president. If it was passed by the convention, the resolution would block opposition to Roosevelt in Ohio and neutralize Hanna. Hanna was stuck. If he rejected the resolution, he would appear to be in opposition to the president and attempting to secure the nomination for himself. If he accepted it, he would lose power to Foraker as the leader of the Roosevelt forces, and he would have to accept another four years of Roosevelt. Hanna made the mistake of putting his feelings on paper, sending a telegram to the president indicating his opposition to the resolution. Roosevelt wrote a reply and, more importantly, released a copy of it to the press. Hanna immediately wired back his changed position: he would not oppose the resolution endorsing Roosevelt for a second term. It was a brilliant stroke by Roosevelt and his allies, effectively securing the nomination a year in advance while illustrating in a very public way that power within the party had been transferred from Hanna to Roosevelt.

Part of the Hanna-Roosevelt feud stemmed from Hanna's leadership of the Republican Old Guard, those pro-business and pro-tariff conservatives who looked with alarm upon Roosevelt's reform agenda. In Congress, Roosevelt secured support from a broad spectrum of allies opposing the Old Guard. In the House and Senate, these men reflected various ideological, geographical, and often personal interests: liberal progressives, such as Robert La Follette of Wisconsin; western senators, such as William Allison of Iowa and John Spooner of Wisconsin; and even Democrats such as Benjamin Tillman of South Carolina and Joseph Bailey of Texas. Roosevelt adroitly courted party leaders, followed proposed legislation through endless committee meetings and floor debates, and always attempted to influence events through careful use of the press and public opinion. The archetypical cowboy never backs down from fighting for what he knows is right. This was not Roosevelt, who at every moment of his presidential career carefully calculated what was practicable and attainable. The president also showed willingness to compromise. Roosevelt had at one time favored tariff revision, but he soon realized he could not achieve both that and his agenda to regulate railroads. When forced to choose, he sacrificed the tariff to the greater goal. By doing so he maintained party unity, showed to the public and press a united Republican front, and came to an understanding with the Old Guard. Here was Roosevelt the pragmatic politician, who had worked with boss Jake Hess in Morton Hall and attended countless "Sunday School" meetings with Boss Platt at the Fifth Avenue Hotel in Manhattan. Roosevelt's reform agenda, and his ability to achieve it, were born in the smoke-filled meeting rooms of New York.

And when Roosevelt became president in 1901, Platt was still there. Almost at once there came a test of Roosevelt's relationship with both Platt and reformers in New York. In the fall of 1901, the Citizens' Union once again nominated Seth Low for mayor. Only four years earlier, still in Washington, Assistant Secretary of the Navy Theodore Roosevelt had watched the Republican debacle in New York unfold: Platt had refused to endorse Low, and in the city the Republicans had suffered a terrible defeat at the hands of Tammany. President Roosevelt was not going to allow a repeat of 1897.

Less than two weeks after becoming president, Roosevelt summoned to the White House Colonel Dunn, chairman of the New York Republican Committee. By that time, city Republicans and the Citizens' Union had agreed on Low for a fusion, anti-Tammany candidate for mayor. But what would Platt's and the state apparatus's attitude be toward Low? In a long talk with Dunn, Roosevelt pressed the state Republican machine to back Low. About a week later, Platt himself visited the White House and heard the same thing from Roosevelt. Roosevelt followed that meeting by writing to Low, "Beyond the shadow of a doubt [Platt] and the Republican machine are doing everything in their power to elect you." Although President Roosevelt could take no active part in the campaign, behind the scenes his influence was enormous. Before Election Day, he pressed Governor Odell to work actively for Low, assuring the governor that Low would not challenge his renomination the following year. Indeed, Roosevelt continued his role as broker among the various New York factions. Speaking with Odell, Roosevelt said, "I mentioned to [Low] how important I felt it was that all of us should work heartily together, each trying to help the others up; and that of course I knew that he felt as I did—that you must be renominated next year." It was an interesting and unprecedented spectacle: the president of the United States taking an active role, albeit out of public view, in the New York City mayoralty contest. By doing so, Roosevelt simply continued playing the role he had played in New York City politics for two decades.

Low's 1901 election further marginalized Platt. Low immediately made trips to Albany to confer with Odell, and even to Washington to speak with the president on municipal affairs. When Low did not indicate that he would speak to Platt, Roosevelt had to step in. "I think Senator Platt is a little disappointed at not seeing you sooner to talk over matters before you make your appointments," the president wrote. "I wish you could see him. Often consultation may smooth down difficulties, even though the appointment made after consultation is the precise one that would have been made anyhow." This is a nice insight into Roosevelt's relationship with Platt while governor, one that included constant consultation with the Easy Boss to "smooth down difficulties." Low immediately sent an invitation to Platt to "confer with me on matters relating to the city"—at Low's headquarters, not Platt's at the Fifth Avenue Hotel. Even Governor Roosevelt had paid homage to Platt in consultations dubbed Platt's "Sunday School." There would be no Sunday School for Mayor Low.

Although Roosevelt was trying to build a bridge between Low and Platt, he almost simultaneously struck at a pillar of Platt's power in New York. It was one with which Roosevelt had been familiar since his college days: the New York Custom House. Only a month after becoming president, Roosevelt had used his new power to reach into New York City and remove, as head of the custom house, Collector George Bidwell, a stanch ally of Senator Platt's. As a machine Republican from the city, Bidwell had often opposed Roosevelt. Moreover, as Bidwell also served as a district leader in the style of Roosevelt's old nemesis Jake Hess, his position in the custom house violated the spirit of civil service reform. In an awkward move, Colonel Dunn strongly asserted an opposing view to reporters, saying it was the desire of the state Republican apparatus—in other words, Platt—to keep Bidwell. Platt and Dunn even dispatched Robert Morris, chairman of the Republican County Committee, to Washington to press this position on the new president. The move was to no avail, and Roosevelt removed Bidwell against Platt's express wishes. It was a very public humiliation for Platt, coming in the midst of Low's election and Odell's growing independence. Still, President Roosevelt made a gesture to Platt's waning authority by appointing in Bidwell's place another organization man, just as Governor Roosevelt had once replaced insurance superintendent Lou Payn with a friend of Platt's.

Roosevelt, however, continued to reach into New York City and State in an almost unprecedented way. In the spring of 1902, and once again against the wishes of Platt, the president removed both the commissioner of Ellis Island and the commissioner general of immigration. With nearly 60,000 immigrants arriving at Ellis Island in March 1902 alone, the president could not allow inefficient political appointees to remain in office. The *New York Tribune*, for one, saw this as another "setback" for Platt's leadership. Still, the president was not finished. Slowly and quietly, changes to the New York State civil service system were enacted. The competitive system was extended to cover more applicants, rules were changed, and in general the Civil Service Reform Law was made more effective. Never before had a president so successfully asserted his power in New York, both the city and the state. As Platt himself would later say, "in some methods of dealing with public problems," Roosevelt was "the direct antithesis of McKinley."

It took another couple of years for Odell to completely replace Platt as head of the state Republican machine. Odell was renominated for— and reelected as—governor in 1902 over Platt's initial opposition. Platt was reelected senator in early 1903. But the situation in New York had already changed immensely. In February 1903, Roosevelt appointed George Holt to the United States District Court in New York. Holt was an Odell ally, and Platt had instead favored one of his own men, M. Linn Bruce. Odell had actually removed Bruce as chairman of the New York Republican County Committee, a direct blow to Platt and a cause of the final split between the two men. Platt responded by writing a letter that journalist Joseph Bucklin Bishop later called "peevish." Platt told the president that if Roosevelt went through with the appointment of Holt over his strong protest, he would "view it with absolute disgust"; moreover, he would "experience a diminution of that interest in public affairs that has been for so long a vital element of my life." It was as if Platt were stomping his foot and threatening to no longer play the game if he did not get his way. Roosevelt replied that the sentiment "seems hardly worthy of you." Perhaps as recompense, Roosevelt agreed the following month to approve Platt's choice for assistant treasurer of New York, William Plimley. But when business leaders raised an outcry against the appointment of a political hack, Roosevelt withdrew Plimley's name. Finally, in March 1904, Odell replaced Dunn as head of the state committee, making himself chairman. Roosevelt immediately recognized Odell's new position. At the September 1904 state convention, Roosevelt and Odell agreed upon the new nominee for lieutenant governor, again steamrolling over Platt's choice. Platt's role as boss of Republican New York was at an end. For the fall elections of 1904, Odell, now both governor and state Republican committee chairman, took control of the Republican campaign, while Republicans swept to victory on Roosevelt's popularity. Platt played virtually no part, and newspapermen barely bothered to ask for his opinion. In the decades-long struggle with the Easy Boss, Roosevelt had scored a complete victory. Platt was finished. Sunday School was adjourned.

BY THE TIME OF HIS fiftieth birthday on October 27, 1908, President Roosevelt was looking ahead to—if not looking forward to—his retirement. His chosen successor, William Howard Taft, seemed primed to defeat Democrat William Jennings Bryan, who was running for president for the third time. With Platt's departure and friendly Republicans firmly in control of New York, Roosevelt had had little cause during his second term to involve himself with New York affairs. A Wall Street panic in October 1907 briefly drew his attention, but the situation quickly stabilized. Roosevelt spent his birthday quietly, riding alone in Rock Creek Park and dining with family in the White House. There was only one exception: Roosevelt welcomed a delegation of the Hungarian Republican Club of New York, of which the president was an honorary member.

The large number of Hungarians in New York—100,000 by some estimates—was one of the many changes witnessed by the city in the half-century since Roosevelt's birth. It had become a modern city that would be recognizable even to later generations. The city's population stood at an astonishing 4.5 million, an increase of more than 1 million in only the past decade. Electric lights had replaced gas along Broadway. The elevated line and subway had also been electrified. Along the city's rivers, steamers had replaced police rowboats. The triangular Flatiron Building had been built at the intersection of Broadway and Fifth. Macy's had moved uptown to Herald Square. The Staten Island Ferry began operating. Subways had been built connecting Manhattan to Brooklyn and the Bronx. The Plaza Hotel opened. The first metered taxi appeared. All horse-drawn trolleys had been replaced by gasoline-powered buses. New Yorkers even welcomed the New Year by watching the illuminated glass ball drop in Times Square.

For Roosevelt, however, these were only superficial changes in the city of his birth. He could take pride in his role in entrenching an impartial civil service in the city and the state. He had helped reform and professionalize the city police force. Roosevelt helped clean up both the notoriously corrupt city government and the notoriously filthy city itself. He had advocated health reform and building reform, and during a killer heat wave he had taken steps to alleviate the suffering of the city's poor. He had helped shift the locus of power in the city from the Board of Aldermen to the mayor, who now enjoyed a four-year term. Currently that mayor was George B. McClellan Jr., son of the Civil War general. Although McClellan, a Democrat, had been backed by Tammany Hall, the mayor had then turned on Tammany and its boss, Charles Murphy. McClellan rooted out waste and inefficiency in city government, began public works projects to improve transportation, and embarked on a $100 million construction program in the Catskills to increase the city's water supply. Although Roosevelt himself had never been elected mayor, he could take some credit for the greater power of that position—power that allowed McClellan to take on Tammany and usher in reform. Such strong executive power was essential to give future New York mayors the ability to address a myriad of problems in the twentieth-century city.

Throughout his political career, Roosevelt's New York roots manifested themselves in unexpected ways. In the city he had grown up loving nature and the glimpse of it that the nineteenth-century city still allowed a small boy to enjoy. This ultimately led to Governor and President Roosevelt establishing parks and reserves to preserve America's flora and fauna, from the Adirondacks to the Rockies. His father, a respected patron of charity and the arts, had instilled in

Roosevelt a sense of duty to community and obligation to care for the most vulnerable citizens. Such noblesse oblige underpinned Roosevelt's sense of government duty to address social ills, from handing out free ice during a heat wave to backing efforts at housing and labor reform. When war broke out with Spain in 1898, Roosevelt attracted to the Rough Riders New York's college and clubmen, who fought and died alongside the cowboys and Indians from the US Southwest. Roosevelt was able to implement a progressive agenda while he was president because of his ability to balance party factions, a skill honed during twenty years in public service. Ever the amateur historian, Roosevelt even penned a history of his city.

As he looked to the future on his fiftieth birthday, beyond upcoming trips he had already planned to Africa and Europe, Roosevelt sought ways to stay connected with New York, eventually becoming an associate editor at the journal *The Outlook* with its offices on Fourth Avenue. Fittingly, one of his first columns related his experience observing the cigar-makers in New York tenements, and his backing of the law to stop the "evil" practice. Brownstone-born, Roosevelt's life and career reflected an astounding evolution of thought about government responsibility. Roosevelt did not believe government could create equality, but he did believe it could foster equality of opportunity. From his first year in the Assembly to the last days of his presidency, Theodore Roosevelt pressed a view of government that reflected his father's notion of noblesse oblige. Government and its representatives *were* responsible for the health and "general welfare" of its poorest and most vulnerable citizens. Roosevelt did not come to this conclusion on horseback during a cattle roundup in Dakota. Theodore Roosevelt became the leading figure of the Progressive Era because he was born and raised in America's greatest city and followed a political career there before becoming president.

Epilogue
"Fall Has Come"

WHEN IN JUNE 1910 Theodore Roosevelt stepped onto Manhattan for the first time in over a year, arriving home from his African safari and subsequent tour of Europe, he also stepped into a changing political situation. For months he and his friend US Senator Henry Cabot Lodge had been exchanging letters about Roosevelt's successor as president, William Howard Taft. A former US solicitor-general and circuit court judge, Taft had many of the same progressive impulses as Roosevelt and a devotion to enforcing the law. As a result, in only one term, the Taft Justice Department had filed nearly twice as many antitrust suits as the Roosevelt administration had during two terms. But Taft was also a political naïf, having never run for office before his campaign for the presidency in 1908, and he made many moves that angered progressives. He named pro-business Republicans to his cabinet and to the Republican Party leadership. He campaigned with Republican politicians known to be pro-business, such as Joseph Foraker of Ohio. He signed into law the Payne-Aldrich Tariff Act, which kept rates high to protect American industry. Most famously, Taft fired the chief of the US Forest Service, Gifford Pinchot, who had been appointed to the post by Roosevelt. Pinchot had publicly criticized both Taft and the secretary of interior, Richard Ballinger, who had restored millions of acres of forest preserves to private use. To

Roosevelt and other progressive Republicans, Taft appeared to be undoing Roosevelt's reform legacy. The question facing Roosevelt by June 1910 was: What was he going to do about it?

Just as Roosevelt had always made sure to return home for New York's campaign season, now, in the summer and fall of 1910, he took an active part in the midterm elections. He toured the country giving speeches, heading as far west as Wyoming. Republican leaders urged Roosevelt to express his support of Taft as often as possible, while progressives looked to Roosevelt to endorse their positions on labor and popular rule. As the summer progressed, Roosevelt seemed to be moving from one camp into the other. In Colorado in late August, he told the state legislature that the United States Supreme Court favored big corporations as opposed to "popular rights." On August 31, he traveled to Osawatomie, Kansas, the site of the 1856 battle where radical abolitionist John Brown tried to defend the town against pro-slavery partisans. In what became known as his "New Nationalism" speech, Roosevelt called for putting the national need before personal advantage. This would require a long list of progressive reforms: federal regulation, protection of natural resources, income and inheritance taxes, workmen's compensation, child labor laws, workplace safety laws, and a judiciary that placed individual rights over property rights. It was a radical speech that included lines such as, "Labor is prior to, and independent of, capital. Capital is only the fruit of labor, and could never have existed if labor had not first existed. Labor is the superior of capital, and deserves much the higher consideration." Roosevelt observed in his speech that such remarks could lead to his being denounced as a Communist agitator. They were not original to Roosevelt, however. The words and the sentiment were Abraham Lincoln's.

By 1911, the pressure had mounted for Roosevelt to run for the Republican nomination for the presidency once again. The former president's speeches since arriving back in the country had only underscored progressive Republicans' dissatisfaction with Taft. Still, Robert La Follette of Wisconsin, not Roosevelt, had long been the standard-bearer among progressives and seemed the natural foil to Taft within the party. Moreover, the two-term tradition was deeply entrenched in American presidential politics, even though it would not be formally set into law for decades. If General George Washington deemed two terms sufficient for any American president, who was Colonel Theodore Roosevelt to say otherwise? Only a virtual break-down by La Follette in February 1912 during a speech to newspaper reporters made supporters question the Wisconsin senator's sanity and temperament. They looked to Roosevelt to pick up the progressive standard, and by early 1912, Roosevelt was in the race. In taking on the sitting president of his own party before state primaries became binding, Roosevelt was following a difficult course. The Colonel actually beat Taft in the president's home state of Ohio, but Taft and Republican leaders still controlled the party machinery—including the delegates to the party convention in Chicago. When Roosevelt delegates were unseated in favor of Taft supporters, the Roosevelt people walked out of the convention, marched to Orchestra Hall, and founded the Progressive Party, with Roosevelt at its head.

Why did Roosevelt do it? Why did a lifelong Republican who railed against independent bolters become a bolter himself? Why did he split the Republican vote in 1912, allowing a Democrat to win, a phenomenon he had despised in New York politics? Was it simply ego or hubris? Critics had long underscored "Teddy's" child-like impetuosity. Had Roosevelt just proven them correct?

By 1912, much had changed. For Roosevelt, the Republican Party was neither a necessary vehicle by which to accomplish things nor an avenue to higher office. Roosevelt actually saw the party—with Taft's apparent cozying up to the antireform Old Guard—as something that might destroy his presidential legacy. Most importantly, having the party unfairly deny his delegates and his primary victories only underscored his progressive agenda. In his New Nationalism speech, Roosevelt had railed against special interests and their control of American political parties. If one word defined the progressive agenda, it was "popular," as in "of the people." The judiciary should be more responsible to the people. More power should be placed in voters' hands through the recall and referendum. And primaries should take the nominating power out of the smoke-filled room and place it instead in the hands of voters. The primary season of 1912, leading to the Taft coup at Chicago, proved more than anything the need for a progressive challenge to the entire Republican Party.

Roosevelt made the most of what would become a losing effort. In Milwaukee on October 14, 1912, that effort almost cost him his life, as thirty-six-year-old John Schrank, convinced that Roosevelt was attempting to overthrow the Constitution, shot Roosevelt in the chest with a revolver. Like something out a bad movie, the steel eyeglasses case in Roosevelt's coat pocket stopped the bullet, a fragment of which embedded in his chest. Roosevelt lived, even as he understood he was heading for a loss on Election Day. In a four-way race, with Socialist Eugene Debs winning nearly a million votes, Roosevelt came in second and Taft third as they split the Republican vote, handing Woodrow Wilson a landslide electoral victory.

Since his youth, Roosevelt had reacted to loss, rejection, and grief through manic activity in wild places. After an interlude in 1913 that found him writing his memoirs, Roosevelt and his son Kermit undertook a South American expedition down a dangerous, uncharted tributary of the Amazon River. Within days of their start, one member of the expedition had died and several canoes had been lost. When Roosevelt jumped into the water to try to save an out-of-control pontoon, he cut his leg badly on a rock. Fever set in, and he became delirious. Soon malaria and dysentery added to the misery of his infected leg. Knowing that his illness placed the rest of the expedition in jeopardy, including the life of his son Kermit, Roosevelt contemplated suicide. Rough surgery without anesthetic drained the abscess on his leg, and his condition improved. By the end of the expedition, however, the once-robust Roosevelt had lost fifty-five pounds. Arriving back in New York in May 1914, Roosevelt seemed a shadow of his former self, a spent force who would never again seriously challenge either Republicans or Democrats. In fact, the Colonel had one last fight in him.

When the European powers went to war in August 1914, Roosevelt confined himself to writing about it in an essay in *The Outlook*. The essay came down firmly on the side of the Belgians, whose sovereignty and neutrality had been trampled by Germany. Roosevelt pointed out that Wilson had pledged such strict neutrality as to tie America's hands even to protest injustice. Roosevelt wanted to use his journal article to criticize the president for his "supine inaction," but *The Outlook*'s editor cut the line. While this opening shot against Wilson may have jammed in the breach, more salvos were to come. Roosevelt became one of Wilson's fiercest critics, first calling for increased military preparedness, then for America's entry into the war. When war finally came in April 1917, Roosevelt made sure all four of his sons served. The Colonel even offered his services to the War Department as a volunteer commander. The offer from the fifty-eight-year-old former Rough Rider was turned down. His sons' efforts more than made up for Roosevelt sitting out the war. Archie and Ted were both wounded. Quentin, the baby of the family and a pilot, was shot down in July 1918 and killed. Since his youth, Roosevelt had worked through moments of grief and loss by frenzied action: mad galloping through a moonless night, tramping through the Maine woods or Elkhorn Mountains, rowing across Long Island Sound—and back—in one day, and even, on one occasion when he was a young man, following a dispute with Edith Carow, shooting a neighbor's dog because it barked at him. By the time of Quentin's death, Roosevelt had lost such energy. There was only an old man, sick with grief and in constant pain from rheumatism. Talk of Roosevelt as a presidential nominee in 1920 appeared to be wishful thinking.

Roosevelt turned sixty on October 27, 1918, just days before the armistice. By then he was barely able to walk or even sit in a chair. By December, he was showing signs of a pulmonary embolism. He continued to dictate articles and editorials, but the effort sapped his strength. Suffering from pain-induced insomnia, Roosevelt was given a shot of morphine just before midnight on Sunday, January 5, 1919. His valet, John Amos, stayed in the room to monitor Roosevelt during the night. When his breathing seemed to start failing, Amos called the nurse. Edith woke and hurried into the room at 4 a.m. to find that her husband had passed away in his sleep.

If there was one part of the nation or the world that felt Theodore Roosevelt's loss most keenly, it was New York City. "City Grieves for Colonel," one headline proclaimed. On January 8, at a minute before 2 p.m.—the moment of his burial at an Oyster Bay cemetery just down the road from Sagamore Hill—the city stopped in its tracks. The New York Stock Exchange and the courts closed. Church bells pealed as businessmen downtown attended special services held in Roosevelt's honor at Trinity Church and St. Paul's Chapel. At a downtown restaurant, the orchestra played Chopin's "Funeral March" while the patrons stood and removed their hats. The Board of Superintendents announced that a new high school in the Bronx would be named after the Colonel. (To this day, the sports teams at Theodore Roosevelt High School are the Rough Riders, and the mascot is a teddy bear.) Truck drivers stuck American flags into their horses' harnesses and hung black streamers from their manes. On the electric elevated railroads, power was shut off for a minute. The trains coasted to a stop as the lights in the cars were lowered and passengers removed their hats.

For their stories that day, newspapers solicited comments from top New Yorkers. Some had known Roosevelt since his start in public life nearly forty years earlier. Labor leader Samuel Gompers, who had guided the young assemblyman through the Lower East Side tenements, spoke of Roosevelt's unceasing desire to serve the people. Dr. Charles Parkhurst, whose investigations into the New York City Police Department had paved the way for Roosevelt's appointment as police commissioner, called him strong-willed and big-hearted. Former ambassadors, governors, and cabinet secretaries all spoke of his enormous contribution to the country. Roosevelt allies in civil service reform spoke of his untiring dedication to the cause of reform in New York City, Albany, and Washington, DC. Eighty-five-year-old former US senator Chauncey Depew reached back in time the farthest when he recalled giving the principal speech at the dinner that launched Roosevelt's first Assembly bid, when Roosevelt was only twenty-two.

With the great man's passing, it was natural for memorial planning to begin almost immediately. The two decades that followed witnessed unveilings throughout the country, the most notable being the inclusion of Roosevelt on Mount Rushmore during the presidency of his cousin, Franklin, in the 1930s. In Brooklyn's Seaside Park in 1924, veterans of the Spanish-American War presented a memorial to Roosevelt made from the metal of the sunken battleship *Maine*. The caption reads, "Aggressive fighting for the right is the noblest sport the world affords." A replica of Roosevelt's childhood home in Gramercy Park opened to the public in 1923. In Washington, DC, Roosevelt has his own island, located in the Potomac River and accessible via a foot-bridge from Arlington, Virginia.

In New York City, the most conspicuous memorial to Roosevelt is the equestrian statue outside the American Museum of Natural History. Unveiled in 1940, it is a period piece that feels out of date in the early twenty-first century. Roosevelt sits on horseback, in western garb—including a six-shooter. He is flanked by an American Indian and an African American, two figures meant to represent Roosevelt's aid to oppressed peoples. But more than out of date, the statue seems out of place. The western-themed statue faces the bustling thorough-fare Central Park West, and the great park itself across the street. Roosevelt is miles from his childhood home, and a mile from his later home on 57th Street and the Republican headquarters at Morton Hall. Although the statue might fit well in North Dakota, nothing about it reminds the observer of his New York origins. Only his governorship and presidency are noted on the statue, a mere decade of Roosevelt's life in public service.

Both the city and Roosevelt deserve a memorial that commemo-rates the way each shaped the other. A picture taken from that June 1910 homecoming might be a place to start. Roosevelt is in action, hand reaching toward the camera. He is in top hat and tails, his typical New York dress. A Vanderbilt, the New York City mayor, and New York's Finest flank him. Fittingly, he is doing that simple thing he did most of his life, and that millions of Americans do every day. He is walking along a New York street.

Acknowledgments

I would like to thank the following for their assistance in bringing this project to fruition: Bilkent University president Ali Doğramacı for his support of my research and publishing endeavors; the Bilkent University administration for granting me a crucial one-year sabbatical; Anthony Crubaugh, the History Department chair at Illinois State University, for inviting me to be a visiting scholar for a year; my good friend Alan Lessoff for easing the way for our stay in Bloomington/Normal, and for all of our many conversations about this project over the years; the helpful and efficient staffs of the Library of Congress Manuscript Reading Room, New York Public Library, New York Municipal Archives, New York City Hall Library, Sterling Memorial Library (Yale), Houghton Library (Harvard), Bilkent University Library, and Milner Library (Illinois State); Wallace Dailey, the exceptionally knowledgeable and always helpful curator of the Theodore Roosevelt Collection, Harvard University, whose assistance with this project reaches back to the summer of 2004; my agent Michelle Tessler; the good people at Basic Books, especially editor Lara Heimert and publicist Cassie Nelson; and my wife, Pelin, children, Arda and Alara, and parents, Bette Jane and Robert, for all their love and support.

Bibliography

Archival and Manuscript Collections
Henry Cabot Lodge Papers, Massachusetts Historical Society
Henry Luce III Center for the Study of American Culture, New York Historical Society
Office of the Mayor, Subject Files, Mayor William Strong Administration, 1895–1897, New York Municipal Archives
Thomas Collier Platt Papers, Sterling Memorial Library, Yale University
Theodore Roosevelt Papers, Library of Congress
Theodore Roosevelt Collection, Houghton Library, Harvard University
Carl Schurz Papers, New York Public Library

Newspapers and Journals
Brooklyn Daily Eagle
Chicago Tribune
Harper's Weekly
The Nation
New York Commercial Advertiser
New York Evening Post
New York Herald
New York Journal
New York Sun
New York Times
New York Tribune
New York World
Washington Post

Books and Articles
General sources on Theodore Roosevelt, his life, family, friends, and acquaintances; New York life, history, and politics; the Gilded Age and Progressive Era
Ackerman, Kenneth D. *Dark Horse: The Surprise Election and Political Murder of President James A. Garfield*. New York: Carroll Graf, 2003.

Alexander, DeAlva Stanwood. *Four Famous New Yorkers: The Political Careers of Cleveland, Platt, Hill and Roosevelt.* New York: Henry Holt, 1923.

Allen, Oliver E. *New York, New York: A History of the World's Most Exhilarating and Challenging City.* New York: Atheneum, 1990.

———. *The Tiger: The Rise and Fall of Tammany Hall.* Reading, MA: Addison-Wesley, 1993.

Allswang, John M. *Bosses, Machines, and Urban Voters: An American Symbiosis.* Port Washington, NY: Kennikat Press, 1997.

Auchincloss, Louis. *Theodore Roosevelt.* New York: Henry Holt, 2002.

Barth, Gunther. *City People: The Rise of Modern City Culture in Nineteenth-Century America.* New York: Oxford University Press, 1980.

Bender, Thomas. *New York Intellect: A History of Intellectual Life in New York City, from 1750 to the Beginnings of Our Own Time.* Baltimore: Johns Hopkins University Press, 1987.

Bennett, John W. *Roosevelt and the Republic.* New York: Broadway, 1908.

Binder, Frederick M., and David M. Reimers. *All the Nations Under Heaven: An Ethnic and Racial History of New York City.* New York: Columbia University Press, 1995.

Bishop, Joseph Bucklin, ed. *Theodore Roosevelt's Letters to His Children.* New York: Charles Scribner's Sons, 1919.

———. *TR and His Times.* New York: Charles Scribner's Sons, 1920.

Black, Gilbert J., ed. *Theodore Roosevelt, 1858–1919: Chronology, Documents, Bibliographical Aids.* Dobbs Ferry, NY: Oceana Publications, 1969.

Blodgett, Geoffrey. "The Mugwump Reputation, 1870 to the Present." *Journal of American History* 66, no. 4 (1980).

Blum, John Morton. *The Republican Roosevelt.* Cambridge, MA: Harvard University Press, 1954.

Brands, H. W. *TR: The Last Romantic.* New York: Basic Books, 1997.

Brinkley, Douglas. *The Wilderness Warrior: Theodore Roosevelt and the Crusade for America.* New York: HarperCollins, 2009.

Brown, Everit, and Albert Strauss. *A Dictionary of American Politics.* New York: A. L. Burt, 1888.

Brown, Henry Collins. *New York in the Elegant Eighties.* Hasting-on-Hudson, NY: Valentine's Manual, 1926.

Burrows, Edwin G., and Mike Wallace. *Gotham: A History of New York City to 1898.* New York: Oxford University Press, 1999.

Burton, David H. *Theodore Roosevelt.* New York: Twayne, 1972.

Calhoun, Charles W., ed. *The Gilded Age: Perspectives on the Origins of Modern America*, 2nd ed. Lanham, MD: Rowman and Littlefield, 2007.

Campbell, Helen, Thomas W. Knox, and Thomas Byrnes. *Darkness and Daylight; or, Lights and Shadows of New York Life.* Hartford, CT: Hartford Publishing, 1896.

Cashman, Sean Dennis. *America in the Gilded Age: From the Death of Lincoln to the Rise of Theodore Roosevelt.* New York: New York University Press, 1984.

Cerillo, Augustus, Jr. "The Reform of Municipal Government in New York City." *New-York Historical Society Quarterly* 57, no. 1 (1973): 51–71.

———. *Theodore Roosevelt and the Politics of Power.* Boston: Little, Brown, 1969.

Chace, James. *1912: Wilson, Roosevelt, Taft & Debs: The Election That Changed the Country.* New York: Simon and Schuster, 2004.

Connable, Alfred, and Edward Silberfarb. *Tigers of Tammany Hall: Nine Men Who Ran New York.* New York: Holt, Rinehart and Winston, 1967.

Cooper, John Milton, Jr. *The Warrior and the Priest: Woodrow Wilson and Theodore Roosevelt.* Cambridge, MA: Harvard University Press, 1983.

Cowles, Anna Roosevelt. *Letters from Theodore Roosevelt to Anna Roosevelt Cowles, 1870–1918.* New York: Charles Scribner's Sons, 1924.

Curtis, Francis. *The Republican Party, 1854–1904.* New York: G. P. Putnam's Sons, 1904.

Czitrom, Daniel, "Underworlds and Underdogs: Big Tim Sullivan and Metropolitan Politics in New York, 1889–1913." *Journal of American History* 78, no. 2 (1991): 536–558.

Dalton, Kathleen. *Theodore Roosevelt: A Strenuous Life.* New York: Vintage Books, 2004.

DeForest, Robert, and Lawrence Veiller, eds. *The Tenement House Problem; Including the Report of the New York State Tenement House Commission of 1900, by Various Writers.* New York: Macmillan, 1903.

Dobson, John M. *Politics in the Gilded Age: A New Perspective on Reform.* New York: Praeger, 1972.

Donald, Aida. *Lion in the White House: A Life of Theodore Roosevelt.* New York: Basic Books, 2007.

Dyer, Thomas. *Theodore Roosevelt and the Idea of Race.* Baton Rouge: Louisiana State University Press, 1980.

Ellis, Edward Robb. *The Epic of New York City.* New York: Coward-McCann, 1966.

Erie, Stephen. *Rainbow's End: Irish-Americans and the Dilemmas of Urban Machine Politics, 1840–1985.* Berkeley: University of California Press, 1988.

Finegold, Kenneth. *Experts and Politicians: Reform Challenges to Machine Politics in New York, Cleveland, and Chicago.* Princeton, NJ: Princeton University Press, 1995.

Garraty, John A. *Henry Cabot Lodge: A Biography.* New York: Alfred A. Knopf, 1953.

Gosnell, Harold F. *Boss Platt and His New York Machine.* Chicago: University of Chicago Press, 1924.

Griffith, Ernest. *A History of American City Government: The Conspicuous Failure, 1870–1900.* New York: Praeger, 1974.

Grondahl, Paul. *I Rose Like a Rocket: The Political Education of Theodore Roosevelt.* New York: Free Press, 2004.

Hagedorn, Hermann. *The Roosevelt Family of Sagamore Hill.* New York: Macmillan, 1954.

———. *Roosevelt in the Bad Lands.* Boston: Houghton Mifflin, 1921.

Hammack, David C. *Power and Society: Greater New York at the Turn of the Century.* New York: Russell Sage Foundation, 1982.

Harbaugh, William Henry. *Power and Responsibility: The Life and Times of Theodore Roosevelt.* New York: Farrar, Straus and Cudahy, 1961.

Hawley, Joshua David. *Theodore Roosevelt: Preacher of Righteousness.* New Haven, CT: Yale University Press, 2008.

Hoffman, Charles. *The Depression of the Nineties: An Economic History.* Westport, CT: Greenwood, 1970.

Homberger, Eric. *The Historical Atlas of New York City: A Visual Celebration of Nearly 400 Years of New York City's History.* New York: Holt Paperbacks, 1998.

Hoogenboom, Ari. "The Pendleton Act and the Civil Service." *American Historical Review* 64, no. 2 (1959): 301–318.

———. *Rutherford B. Hayes: Warrior and President.* Lawrence: University Press of Kansas, 1995.

Hurwitz, Howard Lawrence. *Theodore Roosevelt and Labor in New York State, 1880–1900.* New York: Columbia University Press, 1943.

Jackson, Kenneth T. *The Encyclopedia of New York City.* New Haven, CT: Yale University Press, 1995.

Jackson, Kenneth T., and David S. Dunbar, eds. *Empire City: New York Through the Centuries.* New York: Columbia University Press, 2002.

Janvier, Thomas. *In Old New York: A Classic History of New York City.* New York: St. Martin's Press, 2000 [1894].

King, Moses, ed. *King's Handbook of New York City, 1892.* Boston: Moses King, 1892.

Kisseloff, Jeff. *You Must Remember This: An Oral History of Manhattan from the 1890s to World War II.* Baltimore: Johns Hopkins University Press, 1989.

Kluger, Richard. *The Paper: The Life and Death of the* New York Herald Tribune. New York: Alfred A. Knopf, 1986.

Kurland, Gerlad. *Seth Low: The Reformer in an Industrial Age.* New York: Twayne, 1971.

Lang, Louis J., ed. *The Autobiography of Thomas Collier Platt.* New York: B. W. Dodge, 1910.

Leech, Margaret. *In the Days of McKinley.* New York: Harper and Brothers, 1959.

Lodge, Henry Cabot, ed. *Selections from the Correspondence of Theodore Roosevelt and Henry Cabot Lodge, 1884–1918.* Vol. 1. New York: Charles Scribner's Sons, 1925.

Lubove, Roy. *The Progressives and the Slums: Tenement House Reform in New York City, 1890–1917.* Pittsburgh: University of Pittsburgh Press, 1962.

Matlin, James C. "Roosevelt and the Elections of 1884 and 1888." *Mississippi Valley Historical Review* 4, no. 1 (1927): 25–38.

Mayer, Grace M. *Once Upon a City: New York from 1890 to 1910.* New York: Macmillan, 1958.

McCabe, James D., Jr. *Lights and Shadows of New York Life; or, the Sights and Sensations of the Great City.* New York: Farrar, Straus and Giroux, 1970 [1872].

McCullough, David. *Mornings on Horseback: The Story of an Extraordinary Family, a Vanished Way of Life, and the Unique Child Who Became Theodore Roosevelt.* New York: Simon and Schuster, 1981.

McFarland, Gerald. *Mugwumps, Morals, and Politics, 1884–1920.* Amherst: University of Massachusetts Press, 1975.

McNickle, Chris. *To Be Mayor of New York: Ethnic Politics in the City.* New York: Columbia University Press, 1993.

Millard, Candace. *The River of Doubt: Theodore Roosevelt's Darkest Journey.* New York: Doubleday, 2005.

Miller, Nathan. *Theodore Roosevelt: A Life.* New York: Morrow, 1992.

Morison, Elting E., ed. *The Letters of Theodore Roosevelt.* Cambridge, MA: Harvard University Press, 1951.

Morris, Edmund. *Colonel Roosevelt.* New York: Random House, 2010.

———. *The Rise of Theodore Roosevelt.* New York: Coward, McCann and Geoghegan, 1979.

———. *Theodore Rex.* New York: Random House, 2001.

Mowry, George E. *Theodore Roosevelt and the Progressive Movement.* New York: Hill and Wang, 1946.

Myers, Gustavus. *The History of Tammany Hall.* New York: Dover, 1971.

Nevins, Allan, and Milton Halsey Thomas, eds. *The Diary of George Templeton Strong.* 3 vols. New York: Macmillan, 1952.

O'Toole, Patricia. *When Trumpets Call: Theodore Roosevelt After the White House.* New York: Simon and Schuster, 2005.

Parkhurst, Rev. Charles H. *Our Fight with Tammany.* New York: Charles Scribner's Sons, 1895.

Patton, Clifford W. *The Battle for Municipal Reform: Mobilization and Attack, 1875–1900.* College Park, MD: McGrath, 1969.

Peskin, Allan. "Who Were the Stalwarts? Who Were Their Rivals? Republican Factions in the Gilded Age." *Political Science Quarterly* 99, no. 4 (1984–1985): 703–716.

Pringle, Henry. *Theodore Roosevelt: A Biography.* New York: Harcourt Brace, 1984 [1931].

Putnam, Carleton. *Theodore Roosevelt.* Vol. 1, *The Formative Years, 1858–1886.* New York: Charles Scribner's Sons, 1958.

Reeves, Thomas C. *Gentleman Boss: The Life of Chester Alan Arthur.* New York: Alfred A. Knopf, 1975.

Riis, Jacob. *How the Other Half Lives: Studies Among the Tenements of New York.* New York: Penguin, 1997 [1890].

———. *Theodore Roosevelt: The Citizen.* New York: Outlook, 1904.

Robinson, Corinne Roosevelt. *My Brother Theodore Roosevelt.* New York: Charles Scribner's Sons, 1921.

Robinson, Solon. *Hot Corn: Life Scenes in New York.* New York: De Witt and Davenport, 1854.

Roosevelt, Theodore. *Theodore Roosevelt: An Autobiography.* New York: Da Capo
    Press, 1985 [1913].
————. *The Works of Theodore Roosevelt,* 20 vols. New York: Charles Scribner's
    Sons, 1926.
Rosenwaike, Ira. *Population History of New York City.* Syracuse, NY: Syracuse
    University Press, 1972.
Ryan, Mary P. *Civic Wars: Democracy and Public Life in the American City During
    the Nineteenth Century.* Berkeley: University of California Press, 1997.
Schiesl, Martin J. *The Politics of Efficiency: Municipal Administration and Reform in
    America, 1880–1920.* Berkeley: University of California Press, 1977.
Schriftgiesser, Karl. *The Gentleman from Massachusetts: Henry Cabot Lodge.* Boston:
    Little, Brown, 1944.
Smith, Carl. *Urban Disorder and the Shape of Belief: The Great Chicago Fire, the
    Haymarket Bomb, and the Model Town of Pullman.* Chicago: University of
    Chicago Press, 1995.
Socolofsky, Homer E., and Alan B. Spetter. *The Presidency of Benjamin Harrison.*
    Lawrence: University Press of Kansas, 1987.
Summers, Mark Wahlgren. *Rum, Romanism, and Rebellion: The Making of a
    President, 1884.* Chapel Hill: University of North Carolina Press, 2000.
Teaford, Jon C., "Finis for Tweed and Steffens: Rewriting the History of Urban
    Rule." *Reviews in American History* 10, no. 4 (1982): 133–149.
————. *The Unheralded Triumph: City Government in America, 1870–1900.*
    Baltimore: Johns Hopkins University Press, 1984.
Thelen, David. "Urban Politics: Beyond Bosses and Reformers." *Reviews in American
    History* 7, no. 3 (1979): 406–412.
Thomas, Evan. *The War Lovers: Roosevelt, Lodge, Hearst, and the Rush to Empire,
    1898.* New York: Little, Brown, 2010.
The Timeline History of New York City. New York: Palgrave Macmillan, 2003.
Wagenknecht, Theodore. *The Seven Worlds of Theodore Roosevelt.* New York:
    Longmans, Green, 1958.
Werner, M. R. *Tammany Hall.* New York: Doubleday, Doran, 1928.

Specific Sources by Chapter
Chapter 1: New York at Roosevelt's Birth
Boyer, M. Christine. *Manhattan Manners: Architecture and Style, 1850–1900.* New
    York: Rizzoli, 1985.
Garmey, Stephen. *Gramercy Park: An Illustrated History of a New York Neighborhood.*
    New York: Balsam Press, 1984.
Kohn, Edward P. "Pride and Prejudice: Theodore Roosevelt's Boyhood Contact
    with Europe." In Hans Krabbendam and John M. Thompson, eds., *America's
    Transatlantic Turn: Theodore Roosevelt and the "Discovery" of Europe.* New York:
    Palgrave Macmillan, 2012, 15–30.

Rixey, Lilian. *Bamie: Theodore Roosevelt's Remarkable Sister.* New York: David McKay, 1963.

Roosevelt, Theodore. *Theodore Roosevelt's Diaries of Boyhood and Youth.* New York: Charles Scribner's Sons, 1928.

Sanderson, Eric W. *Mannahatta: A Natural History of New York City.* New York: Abrams, 2009.

Chapter 2: Roosevelt at Harvard

Adams, Henry. *The Education of Henry Adams.* Boston: Houghton Mifflin, 1961 [1918].

Blodgett Geoffrey. "Yankee Leadership in a Divided City, 1860–1910." In Ronald P. Formisano and Constance K. Burns, eds., *Boston, 1700–1980: The Evolution of Urban Politics.* Westport, CT: Greenwood Press, 1984.

Eliot, Charles W. "Inaugural Address." In *Addresses at the Inauguration of Charles William Eliot as President of Harvard College.* October 19, 1869.

———. "Wise and Unwise Economy in Schools." *The Atlantic Monthly,* June 1875, 712–720.

Goodman, Paul. "Ethics and Enterprise: The Values of a Boston Elite, 1800–1860." *American Quarterly* 18, no. 3 (1966): 437–451.

King, Moses. *King's Hand-Book of Boston,* 7th ed. Cambridge, MA: Moses King, 1885.

Puelo, Stephen. *A City So Grand: The Rise of an American Metropolis, Boston 1850–1900.* Boston: Beacon Press, 2010.

Richardson, Charles Francis. "Cambridge on the Charles." *Harper's Magazine,* January 1876, 191–208.

Smith, Ronald A. "Harvard's Response to Excellence and Winning in College Athletics, 1869–1909." In Jack Tager and John W. Ifkovic, eds., *Massachusetts in the Gilded Age.* Amherst: University of Massachusetts Press, 1985, 164–190.

Wilhelm, Donald George. *Theodore Roosevelt as an Undergraduate.* Boston: J. W. Luce, 1910.

Chapter 3: 1881: A Year in New York

Cowles, Virginia. *The Astors: The Story of a Transatlantic Family.* London: Weidenfeld and Nicolson, 1979.

Karabell, Zachary. *Chester Allen Arthur.* New York: Henry Holt, 2004.

Kavaler, Lucy. *The Astors: A Family Chronicle of Pomp and Power.* New York: Dodd, Mead, 1966.

Millard, Candice. *Destiny of the Republic: A Tale of Madness, Medicine, and the Murder of the President.* New York: Doubleday, 2011.

Peskin, Allan. *Garfield.* Kent, OH: Kent State University Press, 1978.

Wilson, Derek. *The Astors, 1763–1992: Landscape with Millionaires.* New York: St. Martin's Press, 1993.

236   *Bibliography*

Chapter 4: Roosevelt's Work in the New York Assembly
Kohn, Edward P. "A Revolting State of Affairs: Theodore Roosevelt's Aldermanic Bill and the New York Assembly City Investigating Committee of 1884." *American Nineteenth Century History* 10, no. 1 (2009): 71–93.
New York State. *Report of the City Investigating Committee*, March 14, 1884.
———. *Special Committee Appointed to Investigate the Local Government of the City and County of New York, Hearings*, Vol. 1, 1884.

Chapter 5: Roosevelt's Trips West
Barsness, John A. "Theodore Roosevelt as Cowboy: The Virginian as Jacksonian Man." *American Quarterly* 21 (1969): 609–619.
Kohn, Edward. "Crossing the Rubicon: Theodore Roosevelt, Henry Cabot Lodge, and the 1884 Republican National Convention." *Journal of the Gilded Age and Progressive Era* 5, no. 1 (2006): 18–45.
Pomeroy, Earl. *In Search of the Golden West: The Tourist in Western America*. Lincoln: University of Nebraska Press, 1957.
White, G. Edward. *The Eastern Establishment and the Western Experience: The West of Frederic Remington, Theodore Roosevelt, and Owen Wister*. Austin: University of Texas Press, 1989 [1968].
Wood, Frederick S. *Roosevelt as We Knew Him: The Personal Recollections of One Hundred and Fifty of His Friends and Associates*. Philadelphia: John C. Winston, 1927.

Chapter 6: Roosevelt's 1886 Bid for Mayor
Condon, Thomas J. "Political Reform and the New York City Election of 1886." *New-York Historical Society Quarterly* 44, no. 4 (1960): 363–393.
Gardner, Robert Wallace. "A Frustrated Minority: The Negro and New York City Politics of the 1880s." *Negro History Bulletin* 29, no. 4 (1966): 83–84, 94.
George, Henry. *Progress and Poverty*. New York: Robert Schalkenbach Foundation, 1987 [1880].
Kohn, Edward P. "A Necessary Defeat: Theodore Roosevelt and the New York Mayoral Election of 1886." *New York History* 87, no. 2 (2006): 205–227.
Nevins, Allan. *Abram Hewitt: With Some Account of Peter Cooper*. New York: Harper and Brothers, 1935.
O'Donnell, Edward T. "Henry George and the 'New Political Forces': Ethnic Nationalism, Labor Radicalism, and Politics in Gilded Age New York City." PhD dissertation, Columbia University, 1995.
———. "'Though Not an Irishman': Henry George and American Irish." *American Journal of Economics and Sociology* 56, no. 4 (1997): 407–419.
Post, Louis F., and Fred C. Leubuscher. *Henry George's 1886 Campaign: An Account of the George-Hewitt Campaign in the New York Municipal Election of 1886*. Westport, CT: Hyperion Press, 1976 [1887].

Scobey, David. "Boycotting the Politics Factory: Labor Radicalism and the New York City Mayoral Election of 1886." *Radical History Review* 28–30 (1984): 280–325.

Stoddard, William Osborn. *The Volcano Under the City.* New York: Fords, Howard, and Hulbert, 1887.

Weir, Robert E. "A Fragile Alliance: Henry George and the Knights of Labor." *American Journal of Economics and Sociology* 56, no. 4 (1997): 421–439.

Chapter 7: Roosevelt as Civil Service Commissioner

White, Richard D., Jr. *Roosevelt the Reformer: Theodore Roosevelt as Civil Service Commissioner, 1889–1895.* Tuscaloosa: University of Alabama Press, 2003.

Chapter 8: Roosevelt as Police Commissioner

Berman, Jay Stuart. *Theodore Roosevelt as Police Commissioner of New York.* New York: Greenwood Press, 1987.

Costello, Augustine E. *Our Police Protectors: A History of the New York Police.* Patterson Smith Reprint Series in Criminology, Law Enforcement, and Social Problems, Publication No. 127. Montclair, NJ: Patterson Smith, 1972 [1885].

Gilje, Paul A. *The Road to Mobocracy: Popular Disorder in New York City, 1763–1843.* Chapel Hill: University of North Carolina Press, 1987.

Jeffers, H. Paul. *Commissioner Roosevelt: The Story of Theodore Roosevelt and the New York City Police, 1895–1897.* New York: John Wiley and Sons, 1994.

Johnson, Marilynn. *Street Justice: A History of Police Violence in New York City.* Boston: Beacon Press, 2003.

Kohn, Edward. *Hot Time in the Old Town: The Great Heat Wave of 1896 and the Making of Theodore Roosevelt.* New York: Basic Books, 2010.

Lexow, Clarence, and Jacob Aaron Cantor. *Report and Proceedings of the Senate Committee Appointed to Investigate the Police Department of New York City.* New York: J. B. Lyon, State Printer, 1895.

New York City Police Department. *Police Department Census of the City of New York Taken in April, 1895. By the Police Department and Compiled by the Health Department,* 1896.

———. *Report of the Police Department of the City of New York for the Year Ending December 31, 1896.*

Richardson, James F. *The New York Police: Colonial Times to 1901.* New York: Oxford University Press, 1970.

Rosenzweig, Roy. *Eight Hours for What We Will: Workers and Leisure in an Industrial City, 1870–1920.* Cambridge, UK: Cambridge University Press, 1985.

Walker, Samuel. *A Critical History of Police Reform: The Emergence of Professionalism.* Lexington, MA: Lexington Books, 1977.

Zacks, Richard. *Island of Vice: Theodore Roosevelt's Doomed Quest to Clean Up Sin-Loving New York.* New York: Doubleday, 2012.

Chapter 9: Assistant Secretary of the Navy, War in Cuba, and Roosevelt's Path to Albany

Burroughs, John. *Camping and Tramping with Roosevelt*. New York: Houghton Mifflin, 1907.

Hagedorn, Hermann. *Leonard Wood: A Biography*, Vol. 1. New York: Harper and Brothers, 1931.

Hitchman, James H. *Leonard Wood and Cuban Independence, 1898–1902*. The Hague: Martinus Nijhoff, 1971.

Jones, Virgil Carrington. *Roosevelt's Rough Riders*. Garden City, NY: Doubleday, 1971.

Kurland, Gerald. "Amateur in Politics: The Citizens' Union Greater New York Mayoral Campaign of 1897." *New York Historical Society Quarterly* 53 (1969): 352–384.

Lane, Hack C. *Armed Progressive: General Leonard Wood*. San Rafael, CA: Presidio Press, 1978.

Roosevelt, Theodore. *The Rough Riders*. New York: New American Library, 1961.

Sears, Joseph Hamblen. *The Career of Leonard Wood*. New York: D. Appleton, 1920.

Chapter 10: Roosevelt, Thomas Platt, and the New York Governorship

Chessman, G. Wallace. *Governor Theodore Roosevelt: The Albany Apprenticeship, 1898–1900*. Cambridge, MA: Harvard University Press, 1965.

———. "Theodore Roosevelt's Campaign Against the Vice-Presidency." *Historian* 14, no. 2 (1952): 173–190.

Corry, John A. *A Rough Ride to Albany: Teddy Runs for Governor*. New York: John A. Corry, 2000.

New York State. *Report of the Special Committee of the Assembly Appointed to Investigate the Public Offices and Departments of the City of New York and the Counties Therein Included*, 4 vols. Albany, NY: James B. Lyon, State Printer, 1900. Available online at Internet Archive, www.archive.org, accessed April 12, 2009.

Chapter 11: The New York President

Rauchway, Eric. *Murdering McKinley: The Making of Theodore Roosevelt's America*. New York: Hill and Wang, 2003.

Index

Note: *References to Theodore Roosevelt in both main headings and subheadings are shown with the initials TR. In subheadings, references to New York City are shown as NYC.*

239

Urbanization and industrialization,
208–209
US Civil Service Commission. *See* Civil
Service Commission, US
US Department of Commerce and Labor,
209
US Forest Service, 4, 219–220
US House of Representatives investigates
TR, 136–138
US Supreme Court, 7, 210, 220
US v. Northern Securities, 210

Van Wyck, Augustus, 187
Van Wyck, Robert A., 171
Vanderbilt, Cornelius, III, 2, 13, 16
Vice presidency of TR
McKinley-TR team wins election
(1900), 195–196, 203–204
TR's progressive impulses restricted, 201
The Virginian (Wister), 89–90

Wadsworth, Craig, 174–175, 176, 179
Wallace, William, 135–136
Wannamaker, John, 137
Waring, George, 148
Washington Post newspaper, 136–137
Water aqueduct bill, 60–61, 62
Wertheimer, Jacob, 77
The West
conquered by independent English-
speaking peoples, 91–92
cowboy images vs. reality, 88–89
eastern travelers' lavish expeditions,
85–86
effects, influences, on TR, 87–88,
106–107

TR and Elliott's hunting trip (1880),
42–43
writings contribute to image of western
life, 89–91
See also Dakota ranches
Westbrook, Theodore, 69–70
Wharton, William, 128
White, Henry, 191
White, Horace, 94
White, William Allen, 206–207
Whitney, Elizabeth "Bessie," 42
The Wilderness Hunter (TR), 90,
128
Williams, Alexander "Clubber," 119–120
Wilson, James, 2
Wilson, Woodrow, 222–223
The Winning of the West (TR), 91, 128
The Winning of the West (TR), ix
Wister, Owen, 89–90
Wolcott, Edward, 167
Wood, Leonard, 175, 177, 178
Woodruff, Timothy, 2–3
Working poor
affected by TR's anti-saloon crusade,
152–156
aided by TR in heat wave of 1896,
158–159, 217
Governor TR's housing reforms, 199,
218
politics of, 48
tenement living conditions, 10, 71, 147
World War I, 222–223

Yellow fever, 178, 179
Yellowstone National Park, 89, 123
Youngwitz, Joseph, 5